CRIMES AND MERCIES

Also by James Bacque

FICTION
The Lonely Ones
Creation (with Kroetsch and Gravel)
A Man of Talent
The Queen Comes to Minnicog

BIOGRAPHY
Just Raoul

HISTORY
Other Losses

DRAMA
Judgement Day

CRIMES AND MERCIES

The Fate of German Civilians
Under Allied Occupation
1944–1950

JAMES BACQUE

LITTLE, BROWN AND COMPANY

A Little, Brown Book

First published in Great Britain in 1997
by Little, Brown and Company

A CIP catalogue record for this book
is available from the British Library.

Typeset in Goudy by M Rules
Printed and bound in Great Britain
by Creative Print and Design (Wales), Ebbw Vale

Little, Brown & Company (UK)
Brettenham House
Lancaster Place
London WC2E 7EN

To Herbert Hoover
and
Reverend John F. Davidson

CONTENTS

LIST OF ILLUSTRATIONS

p. xxviii
Map showing the division and control of Germany immediately after the Second World War. Source: *The Oder–Neisse Problem* by Friedrich von Wilpert (Bonn, Atlantic-Forum, 1962).

p. xxix
Map showing the expulsion of Germans from their eastern homelands. Source: *The Oder–Neisse Problem* by Friedrich von Wilpert (Bonn, Atlantic-Forum, 1962).

p. 42–3
German local governments were ordered by the US Army to warn citizens that feeding prisoners was a crime punishable by death. This order was found in the 1980s in the archives of the village of Langenlonsheim by Jakob Zacher.

p. 98–9
Printed notice for Germans to be expelled from Kraslice, in the Sudetenland, Czechoslovakia. Source: Sudetendeutsches Bild-archiv, Munich.

p. 127
This memorandum by Robert Murphy, Chief Political adviser to US Military Governor of Germany from 1945, was kept secret until the 1990s. Murphy predicts an excess of deaths over births of at least 2,000,000. Source: Hoover Institution, Stanford.

Plate section

1. Henry Morgenthau, US Secretary of the Treasury. His Morgenthau Plan for the destruction of German industry led to the deaths of millions of Germans years after the war's end. (US Army)
2. The Potsdam Conference in the summer of 1945, where the transfers of millions of Germans from Poland, Czechoslovakia and Hungary were approved. Truman is in the foreground, with his back to camera; Stalin is seated further to the right and Churchill is across the table on the left. (US Army)
3. US President Harry Truman (left) greets Herbert Hoover on 28 May 1945, before a 45-minute meeting during which they discussed world food relief. (Acme International/Bettman Archive)
4. In September 1945, US Secretary of War Robert Patterson and President Harry Truman controlled the most powerful military machine in human history. They soon used it for a huge food-relief campaign. (US Library of Congress)
5. Norman Robertson, Under-Secretary of External Affairs for Canada, led the Canadian food aid programme from 1945. Later he became Ambassador to the United States. (Herb Nott/Ontario Archive)
6. William Lyon Mackenzie King, Prime Minister of Canada.

He worked with Norman Robertson and Herbert Hoover to bring Canadian wheat to starving people around the world. (Gilbert Milne/Ontario Archive)

7. Painting by prisoner Kurt Spillman of the French camp at Thorée-les-Pins, near La Flèche, in early spring 1945. 'We arrived about 6 A.M. in a snowstorm. The dead lying on the right are comrades who suffocated during the journey. US soldiers look on as we are beaten by the French support troops.' (Kurt Spillman)

8. US Army camp at Sinzig, on the Rhine near Remagen, spring 1945. Millions of Axis prisoners were herded into open fields and kept for months without sufficient food, water or shelter. (US Army)

9. Aerial view of the infamous Russian camp at Vorkuta, two thousand miles north-east of Moscow, between the Barents Sea and the northern peaks of the Urals. (Hoover Institution)

10. On these tiny pages (shown actual size) the names of dead Austrian prisoners were written. Rudolf Haberfellner (now of Toronto) risked his life to smuggle this notebook out of his camp at Novo Troitsk, USSR. (Rudolf Haberfellner)

11. The Allies deprived Germany of chemical fertilizers, so this farmer near Bamburg uses liquid manure. The cows drawing the wooden tanks also provided milk and, when too old to work, meat for the hungry. (US Army)

12. April 1946: German engineers are forced to dismantle a power-plant at Gendorf for shipment to Russia as reparations. (US Army)

13. January 1946: civilians in Kiel clean up rubble in front of the Empire Building used by the British for their Army Welfare Service. (Gerhard Garms)

14. Demonstration in Kiel against the excessive Allied regulations, which helped cause food shortages in 1947. Signs

read: 'We demand control over food distribution'; 'Severe punishment for black marketeers'; 'We demand sufficient food for all'; and 'End dismantling. We want to work'. (Gerhard Garms)

15. Hamburg, 1946: a barefoot German boy scavenges for food. (Gollancz Archive, University of Warwick)

16. The British philanthropist and publisher Victor Gollancz denounced Allied crimes in passionate prose. He is seen here during his 1946 visit to Düsseldorf, in the British zone. (Gollancz Archive, University of Warwick)

17. A British nurse in Berlin helps three German refugee children expelled from an orphanage in Danzig, Poland. The boy on the left, aged nine, weighs 40lbs and is too weak to stand. The boy in the centre, aged twelve, weighs just 46lbs, and his eight-year-old sister, right, weighs 37lbs. This picture was first published in *Time* magazine on 12 November 1945. (Black Star/*Time* magazine)

18. Seven starving babies in the Catholic children's hospital in Berlin, October 1947. The infant on the right is near death. (US Army)

19. Canadian poster asking for contributions to help save the lives of children in Germany, undated but probably from 1947. (National Archives of Canada)

20. In 1946 Mrs Hugh Champion de Crespigny, centre, wife of the British Regional Commissioner of Schleswig-Holstein, helps with the Christmas celebrations of refugee children in the convalescent home established in a wing of their official residence in Kiel. (Gerhard Garms)

21. Children emerge from ruins. Many families in wrecked German cities lived in damp, unheated basements for years after the war. (Alfred de Zayas)

22. Expellees from the east, who left home with few supplies and little or no transport, pass US Army vehicles. (International News)

FOREWORD

Injustice has been with us since time immemorial, and will persist for as long as mankind exists. Two thousand years ago the Romans noted a thought that even then was a platitude: *homo homini lupus*. Man is indeed a wolf to other men.

The seventeenth century experienced the 'Thirty Years' War' (1618–48) with its incredible massacres of the civilian population. In Germany alone, one-third of the population perished in the name of religion. But Europe had seen many other genocides, fratricidal wars and natural disasters. We remember the Albigensian Crusade of the thirteenth century, launched by Pope Innocent III in 1209 against the Manichaean heretics of southern France, during which entire cities were exterminated in the name of the 'true faith' (over 20,000 men, women and children were slaughtered in Beziers alone), accompanied by the establishment of the Inquisition, the widespread practice of torture to obtain confessions and/or recantations, and culminating in innumerable butcheries of recalcitrant heretics and the '*Bûcher de Montségur*' in 1248, where more than 200 leaders of the Cathar hierarchy were burned at the stake.

War, famine and pestilence have also punished the twentieth

century. Indeed, the two so-called World Wars of the first half of the century could very well be called our 'thirty years' war', beginning in 1914 with the murder of the Austrian heir to the throne in Sarajevo and ending with the atomic bombs over Hiroshima and Nagasaki in 1945.

James Bacque gives us an account of crimes and mercies in the twentieth century. How have we lived up to our democratic principles, to our Judeo-Christian values of love, solidarity and forgiveness? Bacque shows us that, in war as in peace, suffering is *personal*, not collective. He shows us the dreadful statistics of the calamities inflicted by the victors on the Germans after the Second World War, but he asks us to personalize that pain, to see that behind statistics there is flesh and blood, lest we too become as indifferent as statistics.

The facts are so horrifying that they are hard to comprehend. The work I have done myself in *The German Expellees* and *Nemesis at Potsdam* revealed the horrifying statistics behind the mass expulsions of fifteen million Germans from the Eastern Provinces and the Sudetenland into the Occupied Zones in 1945–50. At least 2.1 million are known to have died. Chancellor Adenauer himself wrote in his memoirs that six million of them died. And the (West) German government under Adenauer in 1950 determined that 1.4 million prisoners of war had never returned to their homes.[1] They are missing to this day. Bacque revealed what had happened to them in his book *Other Losses* (1989). And now he uncovers evidence that as many as five million Germans may have starved to death while under Allied government after the war. These figures are so shocking that he has sent the whole manuscript to a world-famous epidemiologist, whom I met when he was working in Geneva as a special consultant to the World Health Organization. He is Dr Anthony B. Miller, Head of the Department of Preventive Medicine and Biostatistics at the University of Toronto. Miller has read the whole work, including the documents, and checked the statistics, which, he says, 'confirm the validity of [Bacque's] calculations and show that slightly more than five million deaths of German civilians occurred in Germany as a whole during the post-war period through to the census of 1950, over and above the reported deaths. These deaths appear to have resulted, directly or indirectly, from the semi-starvation food rations that were all that were available to the majority of the German population during this time period.'

After the fall of the communists, Bacque visited the KGB archives in Moscow where he found further evidence of the startling death figures in *Other Losses*. Those archives contain documents revealing some of the worst crimes of the twentieth century, committed by the Soviets. It is remarkable that such evidence was not immediately destroyed, but carefully preserved instead. As the Russian historian Dmitri Volkogonov has written in his book, *Lenin*: 'Lenin was not moved to halt the crime against men and women aged between fourteen and seventeen, and merely wrote "For the archives" on the document, thus establishing the tradition that no matter how callous, cruel and immoral an act of the regime might be, it would be recorded and stored in the archives for a history that would never be written as long as that regime lasted.'[2] Now Bacque has used those documents, along with others newly declassified in the Hoover Institute Archives in Stanford and the Library of Congress, to determine the fate of the majority of German civilians who were neither expellees nor prisoners of war. The most important of these papers belonged to a man I knew and admired, Robert Murphy, a sound, decent, warm-hearted American who was the diplomatic representative of the US government attached to the American military government in Germany from 1945 onwards. Ambassador Murphy witnessed and deplored the vengeance inflicted on Germany under JCS 1067, the chief American directive on occupation policy pursuant to the purportedly abandoned Morgenthau

Plan. In this section of the papers, which, so far as Bacque can determine, is published here for the first time, Murphy wrote in 1947 that 'owing to the present high death rate in Germany', the population would shrink by two million in the next two or three years. The evidence of that population shrinkage is clearly revealed in the two censusses of 1946 and 1950.

This fate is a reminder not only of the vengeance that awaits the crimes of the totalitarians, but of the way the totalitarian view can, like a virus, infect the body politic even in a democracy. Much of what Bacque tells us is new or very little known in the English-speaking world. Even the reasonably well-informed will be amazed to read about such disturbing facts as the deliberate continuation of the food blockade against Germany and Austria for eight months after the signing of the armistice of 11 November 1918, a blockade that cost an estimated one million lives needlessly. They will wonder whether in 1945 it was necessary and justifiable, in the light of the principle of self-determination of peoples, to deny fifteen million Germans the right to live in their homelands and to subject them to a form of 'ethnic cleansing', first forcing them to flee, then expelling them in a way that caused millions more deaths after the end of hostilities – deaths that were in the name of 'peace'.

Professional historians will probably demur and insist that of course they know all about these events. The reader, however, is allowed to ask why, if they do know, have they not written about it? Why have they failed to inform the public? Why have they not attempted to place these events in perspective, compare them to other wars and massacres?

In its core, Bacque's book poses fundamental human-rights questions that must be answered. He writes about the sufferings of German, Austrian, Japanese and other victims – and why not? Indeed, human-rights principles are tested not on the 'consensus' victims or on 'politically correct' victims, but rather on unpopular individuals and peoples. It is frequently the controversial cases, where hardly anyone wants to recognize the persons in question as victims, that allow us to vindicate the universal imperative of respect for human dignity, the *dignitas humana*. At this juncture it is important to stress that Bacque is just as keenly aware of, and sensitive to, the sufferings of victims of German and Japanese aggression. They deserve our respect and compassion. Yet Bacque is persuaded that there are other 'unsung victims' who must not be forgotten.

Readers may react with a sense of discomfort at Bacque's revelations, for a variety of reasons. First, because these grotesque crimes were committed in the name of the virtuous democracies, the United Kingdom, the United States, France and Canada. Secondly, because we hardly know about these crimes. Thirdly, because the victims have been consistently ignored and have received neither compassion nor compensation. Fourthly, because the intellectual establishment, the universities and the press have failed to come to grips with the implications of these events.

Of course the defeated Central Powers in the Great War and the Axis powers in the Second World War committed many horrendous crimes. Some of these crimes were the subject of prosecution, at the Leipzig Trials of 1921–22, at the Nuremberg Trials of 1945–46 (and twelve additional Nuremberg Trials under Control Council Law No. 10), and at the Tokyo Trial of 1946–48. Tens of thousands of war criminals have been convicted, and several thousand have been executed. Justice, however, demands respect for the presumption of innocence of the accused, and for rigorous observance of due-process guarantees in determining individual guilt. No one should be subjected to arbitrary or discriminatory treatment on the basis of guilt by association. Individual responsibility must always be established on the basis of credible evidence; and individual actions must be judged in the proper historical and political context – not in the light of subsequent events and/or knowledge which cannot be attributed or imputed to the accused. The concept of collective guilt is repugnant to human dignity and unworthy of any system of justice.

Still, it is this concept of collective guilt that has hitherto characterized and pervaded the approach of historians and journalists to the issues raised by Bacque. Because the Germans are perceived as collectively guilty, they somehow have no rights. Only a few voices have been raised to acknowledge the injustices perpetrated by us and our allies over so many decades. Only a few courageous individuals like Herbert Hoover, George Bell and Victor Gollancz have dared to remind us of the moral dilemma. Indeed, how could we go to war in the name of democracy and self-determination and then betray our own principles in the peace settlement? More concretely, how could we go to war against Hitler's methods only to apply similar methods during and after the war?

Bacque's chapter on the flight and expulsion of the Germans at the end of the war gives us much food for reflection. In this context it is worth recalling what the British publisher and philanthropist Victor Gollancz concluded in his book *Our Threatened Values*: 'If the conscience of men ever again becomes sensitive, these expulsions will be remembered to the undying shame of all who committed or connived at them . . . The Germans were expelled, not just with an absence of over-nice consideration, but with the very maximum of brutality.'[3]

Surely the inhuman treatment of Germans by ostensibly compassionate Americans and Britons constitutes one of the many anomalies of the twentieth century. And yet very few persons outside Germany are aware of such discriminatory, undemocratic, infrahuman treatment. Ask anyone whether he has ever heard of the ethnic cleansing of fifteen million eastern Germans. Besides the enormous cultural and economic consequences of this demographic revolution in the very heart of Europe, the phenomenon of compulsory population transfers raises many questions that go beyond the purely German experience, since the right to live in one's homeland, the right to remain in one's home, and the right of refugees to return to their homes, is one of the most fundamental human rights that require affirmation and vindication.

On 26 August 1994, the United Nations Sub-Commission on Prevention of Discrimination and Protection of Minorities adopted resolution 24/1994, which reaffirms this right to remain and right to return. It is not difficult for the reader of this book to apply this resolution to some of the events described here by Bacque.

Let us hope that many more Canadian, American, British and other historians and journalists will take these matters seriously and devote to them the attention they deserve. Especially now with the opening of the archives of the former Soviet Union and of the former communist states of Eastern Europe, it is to be expected that important new revelations will come to light. Bacque has already taken advantage of the new opportunity and conducted research in the Moscow archives. Let us also hope that Russian, Polish and Czech historians will take this opportunity to come to grips with aspects of their own history that hitherto could not be researched.

We owe James Bacque our recognition for his courage to raise new and uncomfortable questions. We thank him for the answers he proposes. Let the debate begin.

ALFRED DE ZAYAS

Member of the New York Bar
Visiting Professor of International Law, Chicago
J. D. Harvard Law School
Dr Phil. (History) University of Göttingen, Germany
Geneva, November 1994

INTRODUCTION

This book is my attempt to understand how we in the West in the twentieth century ignored peaceful wisdom in pursuit of victorious folly; how we often idolised the worldly worst among us while we ignored the kindly best; how in beating the devil, we imitated his behaviour; and how despite all this, there were those among us who steadfastly spoke from conscience and ever acted from mercy to save our victims, and thus to save ourselves.

The Allied Armies that landed in Europe in 1944 were the first armies in history that were organized for mercy as well as victory. They were ordered to defeat the enemy, liberate the oppressed and feed the hungry. Within two years of victory, 800 million people around the world had been saved from famine, chiefly by Americans and Canadians, but helped by Argentinians, Britons and Australians.

This was a mercy that came too late for many millions of Germans. As the Allies brought freedom to Hitler's slaves, they witnessed in the concentration camps scenes of horror such as Europeans and North Americans had scarcely seen before. The sight of these pitiful victims meant that the Germans were denied a share in the relief that was already on its way to the rest of the world. Thus, for several years, the Allies wreaked a vengeance on the Germans such as the world had never seen. A whole nation was converted to a starvation prison. At least 7 million civilians died after the war, plus about 1.5 million prisoners of war.

Here was the outline of a moral struggle so vast it defied definition. This seemed to me to be the same struggle between good and evil that had gone on in the mind of Jesus Christ, as he stood on a hillside in the desert and was tempted by the devil; it was the struggle between the devil and Faust for Faust's soul.

The struggle is without end, of course, but there are discernible stages in its development in the twentieth century. The first begins with the criminal folly of the First World War from 1914 to 1918, ending with the failure of the Treaty of Trianon (Versailles). Through all this time, many humanitarians, led by Herbert Hoover, saved many hundreds of millions of lives. After Versailles, many leaders of the Western democracies did their best to mitigate some of the horrors of war with disarmament conferences, reparations forgiveness, naval agreements, humanitarian treaties and capitulations, to the point of timidly appeasing the tyrant Hitler. Neither Hitler nor his ally Stalin was mollified, and the war that followed was the worst ever known. Not until years after the Second World War did the vast generosity and wise forbearance of the Western democracies begin to overtake the criminality to which they had been dragged by the tyrants. Under Hoover, Harry Truman, Mackenzie King, George Marshall and Clement Attlee, the Western democracies brought peace, prosperity and order to a despairing world. Simultaneous with the thousand crimes committed in the democracies' name since 1945, there has been a steady brightening of their civilizing genius. In freeing colonies, forgiving enemies, in arms control, the voluntary limiting of client-wars, in world health measures, food production, international law, human rights and hundreds of other ways, the Western democracies have shown this genius. The same spirit was clear in heroes like Sakharov, Solzhenitsyn and Pasternak in the Soviet Union, who led the effort to empty the Gulag and eventually freed the Russian people with very little bloodshed.

The struggle has been presented to us as a struggle between 'their' evil and 'our' good. But as Solzhenitsyn wrote: 'The line dividing good and evil cuts through the heart of every human being.' The struggle between the criminals and the merciful is so enormous and lengthy that I have only touched on a few of the outstanding events, mostly in the West. These seemed to me interesting because concealed, and instructive because unforeseen. In these Western democracies the ideals of self-determination, mercy towards the vanquished and freedom of speech, were thought to be highly regarded and strongly protected. These ideals have often been betrayed, a process which is going on to this day.

Another astonishment for me was to discover the disparity between our warm approval of ourselves, and the evidence. This is not because the actions which manifest our collective virtue are absent; it is rather that we attribute virtues to those who do not possess them. We have followed heroic leaders into disastrous wars while we have largely ignored the people who acted from kindness or wrote the truth. Having made false gods, we have made a god of falsity. If the truth will set us free, we must first set free the truth.

I owe my warm thanks first to Elisabeth Bacque, who has read and translated German, French and Italian for this book, as well as my own hieroglyphics, always with a cool eye to the major point: the fundamental decency of the men and women who made up our armies, and armies of mercy, in Europe after

1945. To Alfred de Zayas, a good friend, brilliant historian and scholar, the book owes more than I can say. He has contributed knowledge, balance, caution and lots of original material, as well as his persuasive Foreword. To Paul Boytinck, friend, guide and expert researcher, I owe wonderful research material of every kind, plus manifold leads to obscure journals and books in four languages. And the same is true of Colonel Dr Ernest Fisher, who has never stinted in his help or good advice. To Martin Reesink, I owe many thanks for the expert research he did and helped me to do in the archives of the Red Army and KGB, plus some wonderful dinners and hilarious rambles and drives around Moscow in 1992 and 1993. Andrei Kashirin and Alexander Bystritsky prepared the thoroughgoing *Spravka* for me, covering all the essential points of the treatment and statistics of prisoners of war in the USSR. Captain V. P. Galitski of Moscow gave generously of his time and knowledge on the same subjects. For supporting me through a lot of thick and some thin, thanks to John Fraser, a gutsy friend, fine editor and so-so baseline player. And thanks also to that dogged researcher, E. B. Walker of Birmingham.

Once again, my friend Dr Anthony Miller took much time from a busy schedule to read, appraise, criticize, and re-read the manuscript, giving each statistical section the benefit of his broad epidemiological knowledge. Thanks to John Bemrose, for warm friendship, good counsel and good editorial advice. To Professor Angelo Codevilla of Stanford University, many thanks for tough advice and great hospitality in the visiting scholar's condominium at Stanford. I have profited greatly once again from discussions with Peter Hoffman, and from the guidance of Jack Granatstein, Josef Skvorecky and Pierre van den Berghe. Their sharp editing kept me from many an error. I was moved to tears by the kindly, deeply-felt letter of appraisal from Professor Otto Kimminich of Regensburg. Thanks as well to Professor Desmond Morton for supporting me to the Canada

Council, and to the Canada Council itself for a timely grant which helped me go to Moscow and Stanford. Paul Tuerr and Paul Weigel of Kitchener have both helped me, especially with the organization of a conference at Massey College in Toronto to which many scholars came in spring 1996, to give papers on various aspects of the Allied occupation of Germany in 1945–50. Along with them, Karen Manion, Siegfried Fischer and Chris Klein helped to carry that burden.

To Ute and Wolfgang Spietz, *vielen Dank*. To Professor Hartmut Froeschle, Peter Dyck, Dr Gabriele Stüber and to Professor Richard Müller, thanks for advice and help. And to dear Annette Roser, who has taken up the cause and made it her own, as well as to Dr Ter-Nedden of Bonn, to Annaliese Barbara Baum, and especially Lotte Börgmann, friend and guide, whom I feel I know well though I have met her but once – *besten Dank*.

Alan Samson, my editor at Little, Brown in London, took the courageous decision to publish this book despite the harsh opposition it is bound to arouse. And then he and Andrew Gordon gave very effective advice on improving the manuscript.

Toronto, April 1997

The quality of mercy is not strain'd,
It droppeth as the gentle rain from heaven
Upon the place beneath: it is twice bless'd;
It blesseth him that gives and him that takes.
'Tis mightiest in the mightiest; it becomes
The throned monarch better than his crown;
His sceptre shows the force of temporal power,
The attribute to awe and majesty,
Wherein doth sit the dread and fear of kings;
But mercy is above this sceptred sway,
It is enthroned in the hearts of kings,
It is an attribute to God himself;
And earthly power doth then show likest God's
When mercy seasons justice.

WILLIAM SHAKESPEARE
The Merchant of Venice, IV. i. 179–192

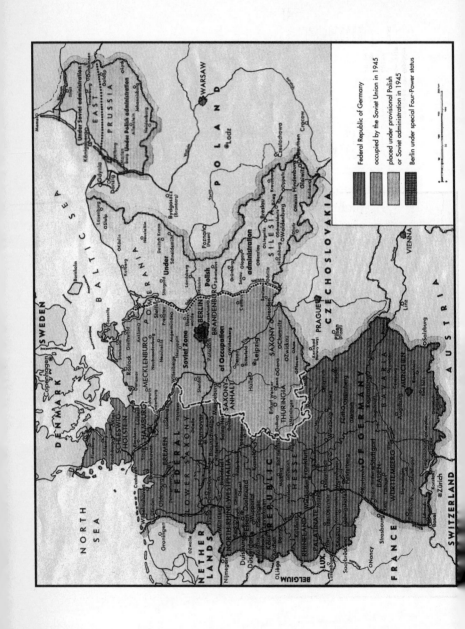

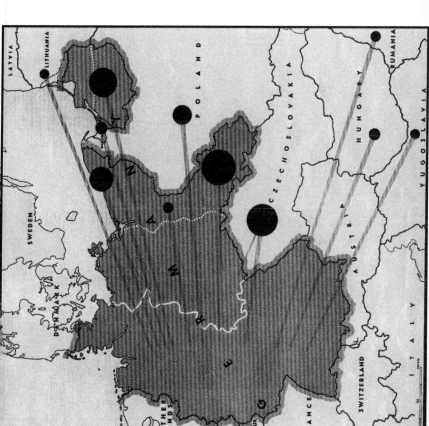

Before the Expulsion

German Population in the areas of expulsion in 1939   9,575,000

Eastern Areas of German Reich	2,473,000
of which East Prussia	1,084,000
East Pomerania	642,000
East Brandenburg	
Silesia	4,577,000
Danzig	380,000
Baltic States and Memel	250,000
Czechoslovakia	3,477,000
Poland	1,371,000
Hungary	623,000
Rumania	786,000
Yugoslavia	537,000

Surplus of Births 1939—1945   total(*)   16,999,000
                                              +   659,000

War Losses 1939—1945   17,658,0
                                                  — 1,100,0

German population in the areas of expulsion at war's end   16,558,0

*) plus 1.5—2 million in U.S.S.R.

After the Expulsion

Expellees   11,730,000

from the Eastern areas of the German Reich	6,944,000
from Czechoslovakia	2,921,000
from other lands	1,865,000

Remaining at home (as of 1950)   2,645,000

in the Eastern areas of the German Reich	1,101,000
in Czechoslovakia	250,000
in other lands	1,294,000

Avowedly still living prisoners (1950)   72,000   14,447,0(

Losses among Expellees   2,111,00

in the Eastern areas of the German Reich	1,225,000
in Czechoslovakia	267,000
in other lands	619,000

War losses   1,100,000   16,558,00
Expellee losses   2,111,000
Total loss: 3,211,000 persons, that is 18.9 % of the German population
                  living in the areas of expulsion in 19.

I

A PIRATICAL STATE

'The growing good of the world is partly dependent on unhistoric acts; and that things are not so ill with you and me as they might have been, is half owing to the number who lived faithfully a hidden life and rest in unvisited tombs.'

GEORGE ELIOT, MIDDLEMARCH

During the century before 1914, the Western democracies began a series of reforms such as the world had never witnessed. All of them abolished cruel institutions – duelling, slavery, religious discrimination and child labour. In Ontario, the first universal, free, mandatory, long-term education system in the history of the world was begun and perfected within forty years. In the US and UK, cures for diseases were discovered, electricity made useful, aeroplanes invented and hunger abolished among millions of people. All the democracies began the process of electoral reform that brought the polling booths to everyone by 1925.[1] In agriculture, industry and science, advances were made that produced prosperity for the great majority of their citizens, something that had never happened before. The democracies did these things under no threat from enemies, nor to surpass other societies. These things occurred because there was a civilizing genius among the people based on their ancient beliefs.

The rapid improvement of life that seemed inevitable in

1900 was slowed to a walk by the catastrophes of the twentieth century. These were prefigured largely in the century before. Darwin, Marx and Freud had all invented new beliefs for mankind, which had in common the idea that people must forever struggle against each other. In society, class must fight class; in the natural world, individual must compete against individual; and within the individual mind ego must war with libido, or instinct with learned behaviour.

These ideas ignored the fact that the very definition of society is people co-operating to a greater good. Co-operation and trust alone enabled societies to survive, but ideas such as permanent class warfare, the Oedipus complex and survival of the fittest created conflict and mistrust in personal relations, political revolutions, wars between nations and eugenics programs which were a major part of the social catastrophes of this century.

The nineteenth-century spirit of generous reform in England, Canada, France and the US continued into the twentieth century. But now the powers of the state were being vastly extended by the reformers themselves in order to implement their generous ideals. Under the fascists and communists, the reforming passions were taken over by the state. They animated the state and were controlled by it. In the brilliant phrase of the philosopher Michael Polanyi, 'The generous passions of our age could now covertly explode inside the engines of a pitiless machinery of violence.'[2]

What saved the democracies from the fate of the others were, largely, traditions deriving from the Protestant Reformation that previously had expressed and limited the faith of people in a central power, whether church, feudal monarchy or modern state. The people had already freed their individual consciences from the priests, aristocrats and bureaucrats who had controlled them through a vast machinery of patronizing moral condescension, the class system, hypocritical imputations of basic guilt, reciprocal loyalties and violence.

Totalitarianism was far stronger in Italy, Spain and Russia, where the Protestant revolution had not occurred, or where it had been curtailed by the older authoritarian traditions, as in Germany. Among the particular traditions that protected the democracies were freedom of conscience, expressed as freedom of speech; mass literacy; *habeas corpus*; the extended franchise; and the various other constitutional protections of individual rights all proceeding largely from the Reformation and the Enlightenment. That these traditions did not always guide the foreign policies of the democracies was clear to see in Ireland and in the American west. But by far the most spectacular failures were in Europe, after the German wars.

Two men struggled for the soul of the West in London during the First World War. They were Winston Leonard Spencer Churchill, First Lord of the Admiralty, the very model of the arrogant, conservative power of the British Empire, and Herbert Hoover. Churchill was then prosecuting a sea blockade, intended to strangle the German war effort but also starving millions of Belgian children. This deeply offended Hoover, an obscure mining engineer from Iowa, then living in London. He was typical of the reforming, generous, independent spirit of many Americans opposed to Empire and big government, with a naïve faith in the goodness of the United States.

Hoover began trying to get permission from the British government to ship food from Canada and the US through the blockade to Belgium. Churchill refused. The Germans, having occupied Belgium and northern France, were responsible for feeding the people, he said. Any food imported into Belgium would relieve some of the pressure that the blockade was exerting on the Germans.

Hoover's bullying moralizing soon got him into serious

trouble with Herbert Asquith, Prime Minister of Great Britain in 1915. Hoover had asked Asquith to release to his control 20,000 tons of Canadian flour stockpiled in England. He wanted this for seven million people 'surrounded by a ring of steel and utterly unable by any conceivable effort to save themselves'. As Hoover himself admitted, it was with 'some abruptness' that he told Asquith that the Belgians were starving because of the British blockade, yet the British claimed to be fighting to save Belgium. He said that he was not begging for the Canadian flour, but asking permission to buy it. If he were to leave the meeting without the flour, he would be forced to make this public, and the American public, sympathetic to Great Britain, would be disgusted. Asquith remarked that it was not customary for him to be addressed in such a tone. Hoover immediately apologized, saying that he was moved by the anticipation of emotions that must come from a negative reply on Asquith's part.[3]

In January 1915, Hoover persuaded several more of the highest leaders of Britain to consider his proposals. After Asquith he met Lord Grey, Foreign Secretary, and Lloyd George, Chancellor of the Exchequer. Receiving encouragement, he went to Berlin to see to the German side of the arrangement, where he dealt with people he found 'automatic and inhuman'.[4] But they agreed to co-operate, so he went back to London to find Churchill in alliance with Lord Kitchener, organizing opposition to all relief regardless of the widespread starvation in Belgium, now spreading to occupied France.

Churchill was so annoyed at Hoover's enterprise that he actually went to the Foreign Office to file charges of corruption against Hoover, alleging that he was spying for the Germans. Grey referred the charges to a Judge of King's bench; Hoover was not only exonerated but eulogized by the judge.[5]

For years Hoover struggled against Churchill, until finally, with Churchill discredited and out of office after the bloody

failure at Gallipoli, Hoover was granted the extraordinary privilege of addressing the British War Cabinet to explain a
proposal for which he alone was responsible – breaking the
blockade.[6]

That Hoover should have been invited to address a British
War Cabinet meeting was in itself astounding. The war was at
a critical stage, the Allies were losing, and what Hoover was
proposing could not decide the war. But the Allies had been
saying that they were fighting the war for the very ideals
Hoover was defending. The Germans were largely indifferent to
the fate of the Belgians whose country they had invaded and
were now occupying, but that did not justify the Allies in
neglecting Belgium's starving civilians. Mutinous French troops
were being urged to keep battling against a barbarous enemy
who was now said to burn libraries and make sport of spearing
Belgian babies on their bayonets. With Hoover, the British
ministers were arguing about the whole point of the war as it
had been advertised to their troops.

According to David Lloyd George, the Prime Minister who
succeeded Asquith and who was a most eloquent man himself,
Hoover's talk was 'virtually the clearest exposition he had ever
heard on any subject'. Hoover stood before the Cabinet table
on 18 April 1917, one hand in his pocket, the other gesturing
slightly as 'he spoke flawlessly, with not a word too few or too
many'.[7] He said that the Allies were in the war to preserve the
rights of small democracies such as Belgium. Victory would be
empty if many Belgians starved to death because of the Allied
blockade. He begged the ministers to show a magnanimity that
'would outlast all the bitterness of this war'. Two years before,
Lloyd George had agreed with Hoover following a meeting
with senior British officials, exclaiming, 'I am convinced. You
have my permission.'[8] Now in Cabinet in 1917, he declared
himself persuaded again.

The reasons that Hoover advanced for saving the Belgians

were known in those days as 'sentimental', because they were thought to originate in trivial emotions found mainly in the 'weaker sex'. For many aggressive empire-builders like Churchill, to act on them was 'ill-advised'. Hoover observed that Churchill believed that the 'incidental starvation of women and children was justified if it contributed to the earlier ending of the war by victory'.[9] The whole Belgian relief program was 'indeed full of sentiment', as Hoover said.[10] But the Cabinet turned the sentiment to cash for Hoover, pledging not only passage for the ships, but also the substantial sum of one million pounds per month in donations to the 'Hoover Fund'.[11] Secretly, the French government also put up money for Hoover's relief ships.[12]

The triumph belonged not to Hoover alone: he had dozens of devoted helpers, who obeyed his instructions to the letter and cheerfully nicknamed him 'Chief'. The Commission for Relief in Belgium was 'a piratical state organized for benevolence' according to one British official. The Commission had its own flag, a fleet of ships, and its own communications system; it negotiated agreements like treaties with European states, it raised and spent huge sums of money, it sent emissaries across battle-lines with what amounted to a passport, and when the members thought they might be spied upon, they communicated in their own private language or code: American slang.[13]

Without realizing it, Hoover had more or less invented the idea of universal 'human rights'. This idea, so familiar to us, was unknown round that Cabinet table,[14] although an act *ex gratia* to save lives was not rejected unless it was tinged with bolshevism or impinged on some imperial interest.

That was one stage in the birth of a great saviour. Hoover was a wealthy man with a fascinating career when war broke out. But the Quaker faith of his Canadian mother and American father made him immediately sympathetic to the North Americans stranded in Europe by the outbreak of war in 1914. Hoover abandoned his profitable business to pour his money and organizing skills into arranging transportation, loans, visas, permits, communications and lodging for the many Americans – still then at peace – who wanted to get out of Europe. In those few weeks of 1914, a passion was born in Hoover that never failed him, or the starving millions who later turned to him when everyone else had failed.

Next came the Poles. They asked him for help to bring in food after the invasion by Germany in 1914. Hoover set up a committee of generous Americans, including many expert on the Polish situation. They collected money and goods, made arrangements for foreign credits and for foreign governments to permit the supplies to travel, and then they sent them.

Hoover proved himself so reliable, energetic, honest, discreet, well-organized, imaginative, common-sensible and well-intentioned during this and the Belgian relief campaigns, that by 1918 the President of the United States, Woodrow Wilson, was relying on him not only to organize food and relief but also for advice on the political consequences of relief. For instance, after the end of the First World War, millions of Russian prisoners were still in prison camps in Germany. Until the Treaty of Brest-Litovsk ended the Russo-German war in 1918, the Russians had also held many German prisoners. Both sides treated the prisoners relatively well so long as this hostage system was in effect, but with the return of the German prisoners under the Treaty of Brest-Litovsk, the system collapsed, and the Russians still imprisoned in Germany began to starve. After the Armistice ended the fighting in the west in November 1918, the Allies kept up their sea blockade which deprived the Germans both of food imported by sea and of the means to earn cash by overseas trade to buy food. Now German

women and children began to starve, which was the purpose of
the Western Allies, who wanted to keep up the pressure on the
Germans to sign a peace treaty. It mattered not at all to the
Western Allies that the Germans had signed the Armistice on
the basis of Wilson's '14 Points' proposal, which included ces-
sation of the blockade. The '14 Points' were supposed to be the
framework of the eventual peace treaty, so the Paris Peace
Conference, which Hoover attended along with Wilson, should
have merely worked out details which had already been agreed
in principle with the Germans. But the blockade went on.

This was why the Russian prisoners began to starve, while
the Allies wondered what to do about them. If they fed them,
they were taking the pressure off the Germans. If the prisoners
were allowed to return to Russia, they might be induced or
pressed into the Red Army, which terrified the Western Allies.
If the Allies did nothing, the men would die, long after the
fighting had ended.

Hoover wrote to President Wilson in February 1919 to sug-
gest a plan that might get round a legal restriction on American
aid to the Russian prisoners, who were by then starving to
death 'wholesale, by neglect', as Hoover said.[15] Because his
relief funds were restricted by American law to charity, and
because the subject of aid to the prisoners was already assigned
to the Red Cross and the holding power (the nation imprison-
ing the soldiers) under international convention, it was not
strictly legal for Hoover to send American aid. But Hoover
pointed out to the President that the object of taking care of
the prisoners 'is to prevent them going back to Russia in the
middle of the winter and joining in the Bolshevik army, and
therefore is solely a military purpose'. He wondered if it might
be the duty of the American army to furnish supplies to save
them from both starvation and bolshevism – in Hoover's mind,
the two were synonymous. The army had plenty of supplies, its
communications were essential to their distribution, and no

questions would be asked if the decision were taken. The food went and the lives were saved. This was the first in a long series of American mercies extended to the Soviets, despite their avowed purpose to overthrow American capitalism by violence.

Hoover did not help communists because he approved of their politics, but because it was wise. He was certain that communism was so stupid that it would 'fall of its own weight'. In the meantime, he could demonstrate the vast superiority of capitalist democracy while preserving the lives of those who would soon see the light. Soon after the war he travelled around the USA raising money at lightning speed. He raised over one million dollars (about $15–20 million in 1997) in one evening from some of America's richest men, who paid $1,000 per plate to hear him speak while they stared at the dinner of rice and potatoes that was all the children of Poland could expect for that whole day. He was mainly responsible for persuading the government to give Poland over $159,000,000 in grants and loans, which equals around two and a half to three billion dollars today. In 1920, the American Relief Administration (ARA), staffed largely by volunteers working for little or no pay, was feeding over one million Polish children every day at 7,650 stations. Hoover managed this with a minimum of government help, and great popular support. As he told US Secretary of War Robert Patterson in 1946, there was such popular approval for his measures in 1919 that there was no need to threaten the American people with the spectre of German food riots. In 1919 and in 1946, the popular reaction was the same: feed the starving. And Hoover was prepared to satisfy their desire.

When Hoover visited Poland in 1919, some 30,000 children paraded across a grassy sports field in Warsaw to cheer him. 'They came with the very tin cups and pannikins from which they had had their special meal of the day . . . thanks to the charity of America organized and directed by Hoover, and they carried their little paper napkins, stamped with the flag of the United States, which they could wave over their heads . . . These thousands of restored children marched in happy never-ending files past the grandstand where sat the man who had saved them . . . They marched and marched and cheered and cheered . . . until suddenly an astonished rabbit leaped out of the grass and started down the track. And then five thousand of those children broke the ranks and dashed madly after him shouting and laughing . . .'[16]

Watching beside Hoover stood the head of the French Mission, General Henrys, a tough soldier who had survived the First World War, 'with tears coursing down his face until finally, overcome, he left the stand. He said to Hoover in parting, "*Il n'y a eu une revue d'honneur des soldats en toute histoire que je voudrais avoir plus que cette qu'est vous donnée aujourd'hui*" ["There has never been a review of honour in all history which I would prefer for myself to that which has been given you today."]' Hoover himself wept for joy before that young crowd.[17]

In the work Hoover attacked so vigorously, and with such huge success, we see foreshadowed many of the problems that have beset us to this day. The vengeful Versailles peace terms, which he wished to make more reasonable, led directly to the collapse of the Weimar Republic and the rise of Hitler; the racial conflicts among Serbians, Bosnians and Croats that precipitated the First World War continue in 1997; the cruelties and failures of Soviet Russia are only just ending; and the communism that triumphed in China in 1949 continues to blight millions of lives. Furthermore, the allegations of anti-Semitism in Eastern Europe foreshadowed Hitler and the fate of the European Jews, right down to reports of 'a holocaust . . . in which six million human beings [Jews] are being whirled towards the grave by a cruel and relentless fate'.[18] When he heard these reports of attacks on Jews in 1919, Hoover advised President Wilson to appoint a committee of investigation. Among the members recommended by Hoover was Henry C. Morgenthau, son of a US diplomat and philanthropist, and later Secretary of the Treasury, who helped prepare the report to Wilson 'exposing falsity and creating a generally more wholesome atmosphere'.[19]

Hoover dealt with all these problems, foresaw the consequences and accurately predicted the outcomes. On the prime threat to Europe, bolshevism, he was particularly acute. In March 1919 he told the President, '. . . the Bolshevik has resorted to terror, bloodshed and murder to a degree long since abandoned even amongst reactionary tyrants. He has even to a greater degree relied upon criminal instinct to support his doctrines than even autocracy did. By enveloping into his doctrine the cry of the helpless and downtrodden, he has embraced a large degree of emotionalism and has thereby given an impulse to his propaganda comparable only to the impulse of large spiritual movements . . . I have no fear of their propaganda in the United States.'

Bolshevist propaganda did not move him because he knew that the system had inherent defects which would destroy it without any outside pressure. He told Wilson that, 'Sooner or later the Bolshevik government will fall of its own weight or it will have swung sufficiently [to the] right to be absorbed in a properly representative government.'[20] Hoover advocated 'large financial and moral support of the Allied governments' to help 'establish a new government'.[21] In every detail of his analysis of the Bolshevik problem and of its future, Hoover was absolutely correct; his prediction has come true to the letter. Only Stalinist cruelties such as the world had never imagined, the failure of Christian Russians to resist and the mistakes of the Europeans and North Americans kept the regime in power decades longer than Hoover anticipated.

He saw the world's hope in his own country. He told Wilson

that 'It grows upon me daily that the United States is the one great moral reserve in the world today and that we cannot maintain that independence of action through which this reserve is to be maintained if we allow ourselves to be dragged into detailed European entanglements over a period of years. In my view, if the Allies can not be brought to adopt peace on the basis of the 14 Points, we should retire from Europe lock, stock and barrel, and we should lend to the whole world our economic and moral strength, or the world will swim in a sea of misery and disaster worse than the dark ages . . .'[22]

On Germany he was darkly prescient: 'The blockade should be taken off . . . these people should be allowed to return to production not only to save themselves from starvation and misery but that there should be awakened in them some resolution for continued National life . . . the people are simply in a state of moral collapse . . . We have for the last month held that it is now too late to save the situation.'[23]

In the midst of terrific pressure to bring food to the starving, when another man might have acted unilaterally to save time, Hoover scrupulously observed the limits of the rather vague mandate given him by Woodrow Wilson. Whenever he thought he was nearing the fringes of his power, he warned Wilson that he could not cope with the problem he had been given without further powers. He then pointed out the consequences of inaction and advised as to the solution. Very often President Wilson took his advice without checking it with anyone else. He often wrote on the bottom of Hoover's letters 'Approved, Woodrow Wilson'.[24] According to Henry L. Stimson, who had a brilliant career in American government in the 1930s and '40s, 'Hoover has the greatest capacity for assimilating and organizing material of any man I ever knew.'[25]

In all this, Hoover was personally disinterested; in all this he always saw clearly the interests of the unfortunate and downtrodden. In all this he was first a humanitarian, without ever ceasing to be gladly American; in fact, his feeling for the United States was founded partly on the ability of the United States to rise above its own preoccupations to succour the world.

Because of his supranational goals, he saved millions of people while other leaders – especially those at the Paris Peace Conference – had no idea what to do after the crash except to glue the wings back on. They believed they were practical, realistic men, but according to one brilliant British observer at the conference, A. J. Balfour, the chief Allied leaders were 'three all-powerful, all-ignorant men sitting there and partitioning continents with only a child to take notes'.[26] The 'system' they devised was as crude as a stone axe, truce pinned in place by the threat of slaughter. It lasted only as long as fear was stronger than resentment. Hoover saw the consequences of their decisions, he described them clearly, and he acted successfully on his views, within his own mandate. He could do so because he saw before anyone else that in those days, it was *in* the national interest to rise *above* national interest.

In 1923, Hoover received the thanks of three of the highest officials in Soviet Russia for his relief work. In a letter from the Kremlin dated 10 July 1923, L. Kamenev, Acting President of the Council of People's Commissars, and N. Gorbunov and L. Fotieva, also members, wrote:

> Unselfishly, the ARA [American Relief Administration] came to the aid of the people and organized on a broad scale the supply and distribution of food products and other articles of prime necessity.
>
> Due to the enormous and entirely disinterested efforts of the ARA, millions of people of all ages were saved from death, and entire districts and even cities were saved from the horrible catastrophe which threatened them.
>
> Now when the famine is over and the colossal work of the ARA comes to a close, the Soviet of People's

Commissars, in the name of the millions of people saved and in the name of all the working people of Soviet Russia and the Federated Republics, count it a duty to express before the whole world its deepest thanks to this organization, to its leader, Herbert Hoover, to its representative in Russia, Colonel Haskell, and to all its workers, and to declare that the people inhabiting the Union of Soviet Socialist Republics will never forget the help given them by the American people, through the ARA, seeing in it a pledge of the future friendship of the two nations.[27]

And indeed, that friendship continues today. Seventy years on, they are still in need of food, and we in the West have joined with the Americans in sending it to them. Now, in the late 1990s, we understand that Hoover in 1920 spoke the truth when others were dumb. In those days so long ago and so different from now, he was an accurate prophet. Yet he was simply carrying out one of the basic Christian precepts of Western society, to forgive your enemy, and do good to those who hurt you. One could say there was no prescience at all. The ideas of Hoover, as Gandhi said of his own ideas, are as old as the hills and so endure.

In 1919, Hoover was in Brussels to attend a conference to present to the Germans a formula he had devised for solving the blockade problem. A British Admiral, Sir Rosslyn Wemyss, was the head of the British delegation. He saw Hoover in the hotel lobby one day, and said brusquely, 'Young man, I don't see why you Americans want to feed these Germans.' To which Hoover immediately replied, 'Old man, I don't see why you British want to starve women and children after they are licked.'[28]

From Brussels Hoover went on to Paris, where he helped President Wilson negotiate the details of the German peace treaty. He was still struggling against his nemesis, Winston

Churchill, who energetically advocated continuation of the blockade in the House of Commons: 'Germany is very near starvation,' Hoover believed, '. . . [there is] the great danger of a collapse of the entire structure of German social and national life under the pressure of hunger and malnutrition. Now is therefore the time to settle.'[29] Churchill was opposed not only by Hoover and Wilson, but even by his former ally, Francesco Nitti, Prime Minister of Italy, who said, 'It will remain forever a terrible precedent in modern history that against all pledges, all precedents and all traditions, the representatives of Germany were never even heard; nothing was left to them but to sign a treaty at a moment when famine and exhaustion and threat of revolution made it impossible not to sign it . . .'[30]

Hoover protested to the British Prime Minister, Lloyd George, who immediately criticized Hoover for failing to send in the food. Hoover let him have it, in 'a torrent that he ought to remember even in his grave', slamming the British and French officials who were obstructing his relief work. He told Lloyd George that hundreds of thousands of tons of food were lying on the docks at Rotterdam waiting to go up-river to Germany, while Germans starved. He pointed out that the British navy was even preventing the German fishing boats from going out to catch fish.

To the Prime Minister's face, Hoover denounced the 'grasping attitude of your trickster minions'. As Hoover dryly noted after, Lloyd George was an over-worked but a reasonable man.[31] Lloyd George later quoted Hoover's words in a speech of his own, demanding that the French in particular cease their obstructionism, otherwise they 'would rank with Lenin and Trotsky among those who had spread bolshevism in Europe'.[32]

Somewhere between half a million and a million Germans starved to death after the war.

II

THE BEGINNING OF WISDOM?

For Britain, the most important aim of diplomacy in the 1930s had been to maintain in Europe a balance of power so that no nation would be strong enough to threaten her interests. In 1939, Britain hoped to achieve this partly by threatening Germany with war if Germany attacked Poland. Germany was seen as the only threat, and Poland was the place to end her aggressions. But, in fact, Poland was attacked in 1939 by two European aggressors, Germany and the USSR. Six years later, Poland was free of Germans, but the USSR was still in ugly possession of eastern Poland and other territories it had first taken with the help of Hitler. The British guarantee to Poland had not been fulfilled. And the Soviet threat to Europe in 1945 was great.

A decision was made in 1945 that shaped modern history. The last battle of the Second World War was not to be fought. As the Polish Minister Babinski in Ottawa said to the Prime Minister of Canada Mackenzie King in July 1945, 'Poland has lost the war she fought, and the Allies have lost the war . . . Russian communism has won the day.'[1] The weakness of the British *vis-à-vis* the Soviets is often assumed to be the cause, but the 'weak' British of 1939 had gone to war against Hitler; and in 1940, when they were even weaker, the British had continued to defy him. Now the victorious British of 1945 were meekly collaborating in the Soviet takeover of all eastern Europe. Why?

The answer begins with one of the dominant international facts of the twentieth century, the strength of Germany. The Axis alliance in 1941–42 seemed so strong that our leaders believed that it was imperative to ally ourselves wholeheartedly with the dictator Stalin against the dictator Hitler.

This was one of the more astonishing reversals in history, for the British, French, Canadians and Americans had all been deadly enemies of communism since the first days of the Russian revolution. They had failed to suppress communism in Russia, but their old enemy Germany had secretly begun to co-operate with Soviet Russia to re-arm in the 1920s. The Germans under the Weimar Republic had begun to rebuild their air force and army, which was illegal under the Treaty of Versailles. In Kazan, German tank units under General Heinz Guderian were secretly trained, and helped to train Red Army units; at Lipetsk airbase nearby, the Germans tested 'a whole new generation of German fighters and heavy bombers'.[2] And in August 1939, Germany and the Soviet Union agreed in a secret protocol to the Molotov–Ribbentrop pact, to conquer Poland together and then split the spoils. Assured of a speedy victory in Poland, Hitler courted the risk that Britain and France would declare war on Germany. Thus started the Second World War.

Hitler continued the war against the British and French with the help of the Soviets, who delivered oil, rubber, wheat and strategic metals in return for some machinery and for Hitler's compliance in their takeover of the Baltic states. Thus for almost two years, the UK and British Commonwealth – with a little help from France – fought against German armies fuelled and fed in part by the Soviets.

Desperate for help after the fall of France in 1940 and Hitler's attack on the USSR in June 1941, the British and Canadians began to revise public opinion about the tyrannical Soviet regime. It was clearly ludicrous to pretend that the Soviets were helping the democracies, but the Western Allies did it anyway, manufacturing public opinion through their control of press, film and radio. The major thrust of this propaganda was to demonize Germany and later Japan, while praising the Russians for their heroic struggle to defend their homeland. On the June day in 1941 that marked the beginning of Hitler's assault on Russia, Churchill said with a smile, 'If Hitler invaded Hell, I would at least make a favourable reference to the Devil in the House of Commons.'[3]

Pondering how to conduct the war from 1941 on, Western leaders did not choose the democratic way, to obey the public will. Instead, having determined their policy in secret, they deceived the public. They suppressed the brutal truth, that they believed the West was so weak that they had to support one criminal regime in order to beat another. So the Western leaders pretended that the greatest mass-murderer of all time, Joseph Stalin, was a wise and heroic leader resolutely defending Mother Russia against the fascist hordes. And it was the democracies' duty to help defend him.

Soon after Hitler declared war on the USA in December 1941, the American government, with the willing co-operation of the press, created a vast propaganda machine to dupe their people about the Soviets. This was necessary for several reasons, one being that the American public, even nine months after the Japanese sneak attack at Pearl Harbor, was still confused as to why they were in the war at all. According to a Gallup Poll in September 1942, almost 40 per cent of Americans had no idea 'what this war was all about'. The pollsters concluded that 'this large minority of the population has not been adequately sold on the war'.[4] There was such a widespread indifference or opposition to government policies that their report had to be marked confidential, and circulated only among the top echelons of the media, with recommendations on how to change public opinion to favour the war.

As the war progressed, the Allies gradually extended their military co-operation with the Soviets, championing their cause against all kinds of critics. The mass killer Stalin was pictured in the Western press with a benign smile over the caption 'Uncle Joe'. *Life* magazine stated unequivocally in 1943 that the Russians 'look like Americans, dress like Americans and think like Americans'. The *New York Times* took the long view, saying that 'Marxian thinking in Russia is out'.[5] No mention was ever made of the vast atrocities committed before and during the war by the Soviets.

Then Roosevelt and Churchill took the next step: they began to cover up Soviet war crimes against their allies, the Poles. And finally, after the war, they helped the Soviets commit new crimes, against the democratic leaders of Poland, and against former allies of the West. These were White Russians who had fought first with Western troops against the communists in the Russian Civil War, then later sided with Hitler against Stalin. Victory over Germany justified for some people in the West the totalitarian means that had gained the end, so these people were sent by force to Stalin, although they had never been Soviet citizens. Finally, the Western democracies co-operated in the bloody Soviet–Polish expulsions from eastern Germany, maintained camps where about one million German prisoners of war died of starvation, exposure or disease, and countenanced or contributed to the starvation of millions of German civilians from 1946 to 1950.

The influential American columnist Dorothy Thompson clearly saw and eloquently warned against the danger that Western democratic leaders would continue to adapt some totalitarian methods to their own use after the war. She was joined by Harvard President Conant and many others. Herbert Hoover condemned the whole process in 1948: 'I felt deeply that . . . we were aligning ourselves with wicked processes and that the old biblical injunction that "the wages of sin are death" was still working. We see the consequences today.'[6]

The democracies accommodated the Soviets in 1945 partly because they still feared and hated the Germans. The democracies were also indifferent to the Soviets' totalitarian cruelties. They were co-operating with the Soviets in hiding atrocities in the east, and in the murderous expulsions from the seized territories of Germany. But their refusal to fight the Soviets was more fundamental. A fascinating change had begun that is still going on in the English-speaking democracies: the peacemakers were beginning to win their struggle with the militarists.

In most crises in the Anglo-Saxon nations before 1945, the victors had usually been the militarists. And with good reason, for Anglo-Saxon military power was by far the most successful that the world has ever known. Neither England nor the United States had ever lost a war against non-Anglo-Saxons in over five centuries of struggles with the greatest military powers on every continent, in the air, on the sea, under the sea, on land, under every kind of regime.

After the United States, Britain in 1945 was probably the most powerful nation on the face of the devastated earth, with the biggest empire in the history of the world. The Soviets had to remember that in any confrontation with Britain, huge resources might be available to Britain from Canada and the USA, who were able to pour billions of dollars in food, munitions, and advanced equipment into her ports. The Royal Navy was the strongest on earth, after the American fleet; the Royal Air Force enormous and highly skilled; the armies numbering millions of men, well-equipped and flush with victory.

There was recent and powerful precedent for the British to resist Russian influence in Europe. Britain had actually sent troops and ships against Russia twice before in recent times, once against the Tsar in the Crimea, and once again during the Russian Civil War. To assist them in a land battle, the British could call on more than two million German captives in their possession in the summer of 1945. The warlike spirit was still strong in the land. Churchill in May 1945 was keeping many German prisoners ready for battle, in their original formations, with all their guns and other equipment intact.[7] For the British of yore, personified in Churchill, the commitment to Poland would have been a matter of Britain's national honour, and her ancient pride – a test of British mettle. To fulfil it by driving out Russia would have been a stern duty. But the Empire's power depended largely on the willingness of the Canadians and Americans to go on subsidizing the British. Billions of Canadian dollars had already been sent, billions more were on their way to shore up the British economy. How long would it last?

Mackenzie King, the grandson of William Lyon Mackenzie, who had been arrested and jailed for leading a Canadian rebellion against the British in 1837, was opposed to an Empire dominated by the British. On a visit to Downing Street in September 1945 to receive British petitions for food and money, he wrote: 'It is strange that Mackenzie [his grandfather] should have gone to Downing Street to try and get self-government, Canada's grievances remedied and that Downing Street today should be asking me to come to help Britain with her difficult problems.'[8] By King's decision, Canada would not send the troops Churchill had wanted to help the British reconquer south-east Asia. But his objections went deeper than that. 'I was thinking a day or two ago, that I had first my grandfather's work to carry on; then Mulock's work, Laurier's work, and now my own work. All on this one theme, seeking to have the organization of Empire such that it will hold together by its several supports rather than all fall asunder through the efforts of Tory imperialists to create a vaster Empire than has been, thereby sowing the seeds of another world war.'[9]

Bankrupt, short of food, weary of war, lacking warlike allies, the British made no threats against the Russians. Most of the imperial grandeur was swept overboard like cannon from the deck of a listing ship. The guarantee to Poland was ignored by all but the Poles.

The Americans had made no guarantee to Poland, but they felt strong sympathy for her people, and the politicians were keenly aware of the large Polish vote in the USA. Herbert Hoover had toured the US raising millions of dollars for relief to Poland in both the wars. By March 1945, even Roosevelt, invincibly credulous about Stalin, was beginning to wonder if the Soviets had any intention of accepting Anglo-Saxon ideas for sharing world power, or of making the United Nations work. By September 1945, when the Japanese war was over and the atomic cloud had spread around the world, no one could doubt that the Soviets were already breaking all their promises about Poland. The Western sympathizers in Poland were being arrested and murdered, the communist Lublin Poles controlled Poland in the interests of the Soviets.

The Americans now had a strong complaint against the Soviets, and a strong ally in Britain. They would gain much in other parts of the world by bringing the Soviets to heel. The Soviets threatened the growing American oil interests in the Middle East; they were helping Mao Tse-tung in China against the pro-American Chiang Kai-shek, and communist spies were caught stealing secrets from the highly advanced Canadian atomic development programme.

If the British and Americans had issued a joint ultimatum to the Soviets over Poland, one choice for Stalin would have been war against the most powerful nations in the world, whose aid was now essential to the Soviets just to keep the nation from starving. The USSR, strong compared to Germany, was feeble against the West. The USSR had huge armies in Europe, but much of their food came from Canada and the United States. Their soldiers marched into battle in fifteen million pairs of North American boots. Over 21,000 of their planes, half a million trucks, 12,000 tanks, and one-third of their merchant shipping fleet, were made in Great Britain, Canada or the United States.[10] Stalin said in 1943 that 'without this equipment, we would lose this war'.[11] Stalin's train arrived at Berlin for the Potsdam Conference on Canadian rails; much Russian bread was made from wheat grown in Canada and the USA.[12] Not only that, but there were revolts, insurrections and guerrilla movements in several places in the ramshackle Soviet confederation. There was guerrilla warfare in Poland and the Baltic countries; an uprising in the Ukraine; and low-grade protests in the army, in industry and in the Gulag, the Soviet administrative department responsible for maintaining prisons and labour camps. Not only did the allies know the full extent of the supplies the Soviets needed, they also had a statistical picture of the destruction that the country had suffered. In February 1945, the US State Department issued a confidential summary of the state of the Soviet economy, under the title 'Outline of Factors Determining Russia's Interest in American Credits'. The summary showed that the Allies judged that the Soviets had lost 25 per cent of their stock of fixed capital (i.e. buildings, dams, roads, equipment, bridges). The losses in inventory (stocks of food, clothing, etc.) would add approximately another 6 per cent to that. In all, the Soviets had lost close to one-third of inventory and equipment, plus millions of young men.[13]

In addition to the millions of men in their own world-wide forces, the British and Americans in the summer of 1945 held over six million German troops in their camps, while the Soviets had just over two million. The British and American armies nearly matched the Soviets in numbers, and they were far better supplied and more mobile. A lot of the Soviet transport was still drawn by horses, but the armies of the West were the first in the history of the world to be propelled entirely by engines. And the Westerners had the most powerful weapon ever known – the atomic bomb. Why, with the danger of the Soviets plain to see in every sphere, did these two victorious powers not stand firm while they were so superior? For the British, Poland was a matter of honour; for both British and Americans, Poland was a useful pretext to deliver an annihilating lesson to the Soviets. Why did they not do it?

First, there was the fear that Germany might rise from the wreckage and challenge the democracies again. This fear soon diminished as the Allies took over in Germany, then finally disappeared into the antagonism between communism and democracy. But even more important was the desire in the democracies to find a better way than war to settle the hostilities of the world. They had tried once before with the League of Nations, they would try once again with the UN. But the UN could not work without the USSR. To bring the Soviets into the world community of nations – to create that sense of community in the first place – the democracies sacrificed Eastern Europe, and Poland, East Germany, and placed their honour and their power in the balance.

Their policy was partly in Churchill's plan to share power with the Soviets in Europe,[14] partly a determination to crush Germany under an occupation so heavy that it could never again threaten the supremacy of the West. It was in the remnants of Wilson's 14 Points; it was partly in Mackenzie King's 'law of peace, work and health'; and it was partly in the determination of Roosevelt and other American leaders to 'get along with' the Soviets.

But there were people in the West who believed that the Second World War was only the crusade against Hitler. Victory was all, Poland scarcely mattered, the Soviet threat meant

24

little. After the war, these few powerful people kept the war going in the form of camouflaged vengeance. On the Western side, this vengeance was named the Morgenthau Plan after one of its progenitors, Roosevelt's friend Henry C. Morgenthau, who was also Secretary of the US Treasury. Morgenthau said it was necessary to reduce the military-industrial strength of Germans forever, so that never again could they threaten the peace.[15] To him and his friends, Poland and the security of Europe meant little or nothing. In fact, their plan was a serious threat to the safety of Europe because it distracted the Allies from the resistance they might have made to the Soviets. It caused quarrels among the Western Allies because they feared the communists would 'exploit' the misery the Morgenthau Plan would create in Germany. The reconstruction of Europe, which would avert that threat, was seriously delayed by the destruction of the German economy carried out under the Morgenthau Plan after May 1945. And the moral issues raised by the vengeance set people against each other throughout the West.

Western planning for vengeance against Germans and for the destruction of Germany began in England in August 1944, with its chief architects Morgenthau and Dwight D. Eisenhower.[16] The birth of the plan was witnessed by one of Morgenthau's aides, Fred Smith, who wrote:

On August 7, 1944 at approximately 12:35 P.M. in a tent in southern England, the Morgenthau Plan was born. Actually, it was General Dwight D. Eisenhower who launched the project . . . The subject first came up at lunch in General Eisenhower's mess tent. Secretary Morgenthau, Assistant to the Secretary Harry D. White and I were there. White spoke of Germany, which was now certain to be defeated . . . White said, 'What I think is that we should give the entire German economy an opportunity to settle down before we do anything about it.' Here Eisenhower became grim and made the statement that actually sparked the German hardship plan. [Smith notes here that 'This material is taken from notes made directly after the meeting.'] He said: 'I am not interested in the German economy and personally would not like to bolster it if that will make it any easier for the Germans.' He said he thought the Germans had punishment coming to them: 'The ringleaders and the SS troops should be given the death penalty without question, but punishment should not end there.'

He felt *the people* [emphasis in the original] were guilty of supporting the regime and that made them a party to the entire German project, and he personally would like to 'see things made good and hard for them for a while'. He pointed out that talk of letting Germany off easy after taking care of the top people came from those who feared Russia and wanted to strengthen Germany as a potential bulwark against any desires Russia might someday have . . .

The General declared he saw no purpose in treating a 'paranoid' gently, and the 'whole German population is a synthetic paranoid. All their life the people have been taught to be paranoid in their actions and thoughts, and they have to be snapped out of it. The only way to do that is to be good and hard on them. I certainly see no point in bolstering their economy or taking any other steps to help them.'

White remarked: 'We may want to quote you on the problem of handling the German people.'

Eisenhower replied that he could be quoted. He said: 'I will tell the President myself, if necessary.'[17]

Lord Keynes, the famous British economist, asked President Roosevelt in late November if he was planning 'a complete agrarian economy' for Germany. Although the American people had been told that the Morgenthau Plan had been abandoned, Roosevelt now told Keynes in secret that the plan would be implemented. The German economy would be reduced to a level 'not quite' completely agrarian, he said. The plan went 'pretty far' in de-industrializing the Ruhr and eliminating many of Germany's basic industries.[18]

The Morgenthau Plan has three remarkable aspects: that it was devised, that it was implemented after it had been cancelled, and that it has since been covered up so well. Now it has shrunk from sight in the West. The basic idea of the plan was to wreck or confiscate all important German industry, converting the country into a huge farm, while at the same time destroying the fertilizer plants on which German agriculture depended. It would also cut Germany into pieces, and allot a huge piece of territory to the Poles and Soviets.[19] Anthony Eden, the British Foreign Secretary, told Churchill at Quebec: 'You can't do this. After all, you and I have publicly said quite the opposite.' Churchill replied, 'Now I hope, Anthony, that you are not going to do anything about this with the War Cabinet if you see a chance . . .' Eden also said that he and Cordell Hull, the US Secretary of State, were both 'horrified' at the plan.[20]

Cordell Hull did not go with Roosevelt to Quebec, so it was odd that Roosevelt allowed Morgenthau to present a plan for the post-war treatment of Germany, a fantastically complicated subject for which Morgenthau had no training at all. His vengeful views were the opposite of Hull's views on Germany. It was a tragedy for the United States and all Europe that Hull had no influence at Quebec, or at the major summit conference at Yalta four months later.

Hull was never consulted about any of this vengeful business, which he hated. He said after Quebec that, 'This whole development at Quebec I believe angered me as much as anything that had happened during my career as Secretary of State.'[21] He knew and said, along with Secretary of War Henry L. Stimson, that the Morgenthau Plan would mean the deaths of some twenty million Germans by starvation and exposure. If the plan were leaked, it would give Hitler's propaganda minister, Joseph Goebbels, strong arguments for a bitter, futile resistance by the Germans. The plan was leaked, Goebbels soon obliged, and the Germans resisted to the bitter end. The Germans' fear of Allied vengeance was so powerful that William Donovan, Director of the OSS (Office of Strategic Services), wrote to the Joint Chiefs of Staff on 27 November 1944 that, 'The horrible prospects of exile to Siberia, eternal slavery, de-industrialization, break-up of Germany and even sterilization, have been carefully portrayed to the Germans by their Nazi leaders. It is considered that the German spirit of resistance has been bolstered greatly by fear of the consequence of unconditional surrender.'[22] The Germans fought even when their country had been cut in half, but the Japanese, who for years had defended their conquered possessions to the last man, gave up before they were invaded.

In shutting out Hull, who was supported by Secretary of War Henry L. Stimson, Roosevelt and the Morgenthau planners were also deliberately shutting out from government the opinions they represented. In the nation these were clearly in the majority. The majority of the press also opposed the Plan.[23] Hull was admired and respected throughout the United States and the world because he was free of the vengeful violence that infected the Morgenthau supporters. In 1945, he won the Nobel Peace Prize.

Churchill told Stalin a few weeks after Quebec that the public reaction to the Morgenthau Plan had displeased Roosevelt and him. They were 'not very happy about its reception'. But he added, 'Great Britain would not agree to mass execution of Germans, because one day British public opinion would cry out.'[24] Yet development of the Morgenthau Plan went ahead in secret.

Eisenhower began to carry it out on his own initiative in

1944. The first to suffer were the German prisoners. American prison camps under Eisenhower's command in France were kept far below the standards set by the Geneva Convention.[25] These camps were described by Lt. Col. Henry W. Allard, who was in charge of the US camps in France in 1945: 'The standards of PW [prisoner of war] camps in the ComZ [the US Army's rear zone] in Europe compare as only slightly better or even with the living conditions of the Japanese PW camps our men tell us about, and unfavourably with the Germans.'[26] To maintain such camps was a war crime punishable by death, according to the Americans after the war. They shot Japanese General Masaharu Homma in 1946 for maintaining camps in approximately the conditions described by Allard. After the German surrender on 8 May 1945, the American camps grew steadily worse.

The total occupation of Germany, and the destruction of Germany's armed forces, national government, political parties, coupled with the trials of the war criminals, was the beginning of the Allies' post-war policy. At the surrender in May 1945, schools and universities were closed, as well as radio stations, newspapers, the national Red Cross and mail service. Germany was also stripped of much coal, her eastern territories, industrial patents, lumber, gold reserves, and most of her labour force. Allied teams also looted and destroyed Germany's factories, offices, laboratories and workshops. So much food was confiscated that Max Huber of the International Red Cross complained about it in August 1945 in a letter to the US State department.[27] Starting on May 8, the date of the surrender in the West, German and Italian prisoners in Canada, Italy, the USA and the UK, who had been fed according to the Geneva Convention, were suddenly put on greatly reduced rations. In the US, some ex-prisoners allege, starvation set in.[28]

Gruesome expulsions of civilians from the eastern territories now began. These were described by some writers in the West as 'orderly and humane population transfers', while others reported the lethal conditions as they were. German industrial production in the winter of 1944–45, which even under the Allied bombings was 105 per cent of pre-war levels, was reduced under the Morgenthau Plan to 25 per cent of pre-war levels by autumn, 1945.[29]

The public was fooled time and again into believing that the Plan had been abandoned when it had not; that there was a fatal world food shortage, when world food supplies were down by only 2–10 per cent; that there was a shipping shortage, when scores of ships lay idle at wharves in North America and Europe.[30] Even so seasoned an observer as British historian Martin Gilbert has mistakenly written, after years of research on the war and its aftermath, that: 'In the event, it was the State Department which rejected it [the Morgenthau Plan].'[31] Morgenthau himself wrote, in the New York Post on 24 November 1947, after long study of Germany: 'Much has been said and written about the so-called Morgenthau Plan for Germany from its first beginnings until it ceased to be attributable to any one individual. Then it became part of the Potsdam Agreement, a solemn declaration of policy and undertaking for action . . . for the three greatest powers on earth.'

Morgenthau's friends were clearly more interested in vengeance than in reparations. As Senator William Langer of North Dakota stated in the United States Senate: 'History already records that a savage minority of bloody bitter-enders within this government forced the acceptance of the brutal Morgenthau Plan upon the present administration. I ask, Mr President, why in God's name did the administration accept it? . . . Recent developments have merely confirmed scores of earlier charges that this addlepated and vicious Morgenthau Plan had torn Europe in two and left half of Germany incorporated in the ever-expanding sphere of influence of an oriental totalitarian conspiracy. By continuing a policy which keeps

Germany divided against itself, we are dividing the world against itself and turning loose across the face of Europe a power and an enslaving and degrading cruelty surpassing that of Hitler's.'[32]

Senator Langer was not alone. His speech was warmly applauded. The Senate voted in approval of a resolution that stated in part, 'Whereas . . . reports reaching the United States indicate that . . . the policies of the victor powers are subjecting millions to mass starvation, and whereas the United States has been a party to the commitments and agreements reached among the victor powers which have led to these conditions; and whereas the Congress has been bypassed and the American people have been ignored in the formulation and implementation of these policies, and whereas it is essential that the Congress of the United States should obtain the necessary information to enact legislation and to request the President to take executive action designed to eliminate the starvation conditions resulting from the policies for which this Government is directly responsible, Therefore, be it resolved . . .' And the resolution went on to set up a group with a budget to study conditions in Germany and to report in detail.

This resolution was proposed by the influential Senator Kenneth Wherry, together with several others, including Capehart, Hawkes, La Follette, Hickenlooper, and Taft. In presenting the motion, Wherry said, 'Much has been said and little done relative to opening the mails to Germany and providing sufficient food to prevent mass starvation in Germany, Austria, Italy and other countries of Europe. Terrifying reports are filtering through the British, French and American occupied zones, and even more gruesome reports from the Russian occupied zone, revealing a horrifying picture of deliberate and wholesale starvation.' He criticized the Truman administration for doing nothing despite the 'rising chorus of pleas for intercession' to prevent a 'major tragedy' that was rapidly developing. He had questioned Governor Lehman, in charge of the United Nations Relief and Rehabilitation Administration (UNRRA), who admitted that the UN aid was not feeding any of the starving Germans. Yet President Truman had told Senator Wherry that UNRRA was feeding Germans. This was not true. UNRRA never fed Germans, who thus starved within reach of adequate food.

'Time and again,' the Senator continued, 'the administration has advanced the excuse that transportation facilities were lacking, but for months scores of ships have been lying idle in both eastern and European ports. So it is not a question of the lack of ships. Furthermore, hundreds of thousands of GIs in Europe are apparently sentenced to enforced idleness for want of something to do. Millions of dollars' worth of surplus trucks and jeeps are falling apart in their open-air garages in Europe.' Nor was food scarce, for there was plenty in the civilian and the military stores, Wherry said: 'The truth is that there are thousands upon thousands of tons of military rations in our surplus stock piles that have been spoiling right in the midst of starving populations.' The government's defence of the Morgenthau Plan was reduced to rubble by a couple of accurate criticisms, in which Senator Wherry was joined by Senator Richard B. Russell, Jr. The government had said that the policy had been established in agreement with the Allies not to feed ex-enemies, but Russell said that the Allies *were* feeding Italians, who had also been the enemy during the war, and he demanded to know why they received food while the Germans starved.[33]

What this actually meant to the mothers and children of Germany was a repetition on a larger scale of the Nazi-induced famine in the Netherlands during the winter of 1944–45.[34] Well over sixty million people were deliberately pushed to the edge of death by starvation. In Hamburg in 1946, in the British zone of occupation, one touring British writer said that about 100,000 people were in the last stages of starvation with hunger oedema.[35] In Düsseldorf and many other cities, people lived like rats in a few square feet of wet basement under a heap of rubble. The English philanthropist and publisher Victor Gollancz witnessed these conditions during his visit to Germany in 1946. He wrote:

I made a more extensive tour of Düsseldorf dwelling-places towards the end of the week. Down a long dark staircase and then along a black tunnel was a man of 79, alone in a hole which he had made habitable – according to the ruling standards – 'all by himself'. His wife was out on the search for bread. In another part of the same cellar was a mother with three children – [aged] 6, 10 and 14. All four of them slept in the only bed, two side by side in the ordinary way and the other two side by side at the foot of it. The mother came back while we were there: it was 10:30 and she had been queuing for bread since early morning and had returned empty-handed – 'bread nowhere'. One of the children was still in bed; none had yet had anything to eat, as the last bread had gone yesterday. The father was a prisoner of war in Russia. Two of the children had TB. There was a tiny stove, but no coal or gas, only a little wood, which they 'fetched'. For excretion they used a pail, which they emptied every morning into a hole they had dug in the courtyard above. They had twice been bombed out. On one wall was a small faded photograph of the mother and father at their wedding and on another some prince or king with the legend *'Lerne leiden ohne zu klagen'*: learn to suffer without complaining.[36]

Gollancz went round the city with members of the local Red Cross, who filled the starving Germans with 'gratitude and happiness'. One dwelling place he visited with them was 'down two long flights of stairs to an awful couple of rooms below'. There were no windows, no fresh air entering at all except by the door. This cellar had been flooded steadily for four weeks. In it were living two women and five children, from two different families. One of the women was pregnant; a child was covered with sores. The smell was so bad that Gollancz had to cover his nose and eat a lozenge on the way out. He visited cellar after cellar like this. A few were decorated with crucifixes, photographs. In some he found people were who nevertheless cheerful. 'All of them were grateful, terribly grateful, when they were given something.'[37] The deaths of children with TB was already nearly three times the pre-war rate in Düsseldorf; about one third of the children in Iserlohn had TB; in Hamburg, diabetics in the first stages of coma were trying to force their way into hospital because there was no insulin. The latest news was that in the British zone the starvation ration of a nominal 1,550 calories per day (cpd) would now be reduced to 1,000cpd for about six months. At the top level of the US Army, reaction to all this was expressed by General J. H. Hilldring, who said that the Germans were being treated too lavishly.[38]

These were some of the conditions that led Dr Amelunxen, Minister-President of North Rhine-Westphalia in the British zone, to predict that two to three million people in his province of eleven million would die in the next few years. (Deaths in two years at pre-war rates would be around 265,000.) The food ration did not improve in the following eighteen months, but grew slightly worse.[39]

A member of the (Quaker) Society of Friends in Germany, Hans Albrecht, also predicted a horrendous death rate. In September 1945 he said, 'No child born in Germany this year will survive the coming winter. Only half the children aged less than three years will survive.'[40] There was some evidence for this fear already in Berlin, where the infant mortality rate for several months had already been close to 100 per cent. In the summer of 1945 in Berlin, nearly every baby was born dead, or died within a few days. Albrecht was also predicting that among the estimated 2.5 to 2.7 million Germans aged three years and under, half would die. Among the infants alone, the toll would be well over one million, perhaps as high as a million and a half dead.[41]

Most children under ten and people over sixty[42] could not survive the coming winter, according to Probst Grüber, a man experienced in such matters because he had just been saved from one of Hitler's camps. Grüber wrote on 12 October 1945, 'In the forest around Berlin, countless dead are hanging from the trees. One becomes indifferent to death. Mothers see their children die and bury them by the wayside, apparently with none of that pain which usually tears a mother's heart apart . . . If this misery cannot be checked, it is no exaggeration to reckon on a figure of 20,000,000 dead this winter.'[43]

'The infant mortality rate in Berlin is sixteen times as high as it was in 1943,' reported the American journalist Edd Johnson. Johnson knew horror, for he had witnessed it in Hitler's concentration camps just weeks before. A German Red Cross official had predicted to him an infant mortality rate of 80–90 per cent for winter 1945–46, amid scenes of desolation hard to believe in modern times. 'Germans are going to die like flies this winter,' according to United States Public Health officers attached to the army. 'There is going to be a definite age group elimination of the German population.'[44]

In the French zone, things were even worse, perhaps because the French had suffered so much from German depredations and atrocities in France. A huge number of soldiers, bureaucrats and their families was imposed on the small zone. In 1946, the French billetted 18 persons per 10,000 Germans, whereas the British billetted ten and the Americans only three. The French took all their housing and most of their food from the locals, with the result that the local rations were always lower than the meagre rations decreed in the other zones. But the French did not feel that the enormous scale of their exactions and the suffering of the Germans were justified, for they camouflaged what they were doing, according to Price, Waterhouse and Company. The big American accounting firm reported that the 'defective nature of the accounts' kept by the French 'made it impossible to produce an accountant's report on the foreign trade of the zone'.[45] The Germans complained bitterly about these false accounts. No German accounting of the foreign exports was permitted by the French, who took the goods, at prices they set themselves, and paid not in the precious dollars received, but in marks, thus depriving the Germans of the one way they had to buy foreign food.[46]

For all these reasons, 'population losses were significant', according to the American writer F. Roy Willis. The death rate for the town of Landau in the Rheinland-Pfalz was 39.5%%* in 1946, which was more than triple the pre-war rate. In 1947, it was 27%%, more than double the pre-war rate.[47]

In the British zone, Field Marshal Bernard Montgomery feared that the loss of life in the winter of 1945–46 was going to be 'very heavy'.[48] The daily ration for an average adult then was 1,042 calories, which he said meant that 'we are going to let them starve: gradually'.[49] There were many voices at home and abroad raised in protest against the treatment of Germany. The Lord Bishop of Chichester, Lord Bertrand Russell and Victor Gollancz protested vigorously in England, and many as well in the US. The former Chief Rabbi of Berlin, Dr Baeck, was reported in an influential US magazine to have 'horrified the hate cult in this country by calling on his Jewish colleagues to join with him in demanding relief feeding for Germany . . .'[50]

All this protest had no serious effect at first on the US President, Harry S. Truman. Neglected, uninformed, like most of the members of Roosevelt's Cabinet, Truman was ignorant of many important matters when he arrived in office following

*Where %% means per thousand.

Franklin Delano Roosevelt's death in April 1945. The ailing Hull, like his successor Edward Stettinius, was ignored, and Henry Morgenthau, a great favourite of Roosevelt's, in effect became Secretary of State for the most important decision of all about Germany. Harry Hopkins, who had never been elected, carried out the most important missions for the President. In the spring of 1945, Truman was a minor figure whose great service had been to run on the FDR ticket in 1944. He was not well prepared to deal with the disasters now impending around the world.

He had sufficient wit to call on Herbert Hoover in May 1945 for advice on the world food problem, but not enough to accept the advice. Hoover warned Truman of the disasters that were about to occur, but Truman ignored him, to his cost. As the situation grew worse, with rumours of French mistreatment of prisoners emerging in the press and predictions of disaster emerging from authoritative people in Germany, Truman was cornered. He was caught between the consequences of the Morgenthau Plan and the widespread opposition in the administration to revising any part of American policy in Germany. Truman had never approved the Morgenthau Plan and only discovered that it was being implemented when he had to deal with its disastrous consequences.

Within a couple of months of taking office, Truman rid himself of Secretary Morgenthau. This was probably not because of the plan, but because he had found Morgenthau over-reaching himself in other ways. Soon after, Truman was sending missions to Europe to look into conditions in refugee camps. And then in the face of a famine that had already killed off hundreds of thousands of Germans in later 1945,[51] he called on Herbert Hoover for the second time.

The circumstances of that call are interesting. As the situation in Germany had grown worse and worse, various senators visiting the American zone discussed the situation with army officers.

They also received letters and reports from American civilians and officers on the scene. Soon they were informed, and disgusted.[52] Just after Christmas 1945, they met and discussed what to do. It was decided to call on the President himself. This they did on 8 January 1946. They made a personal appeal to him to take immediate steps to permit the American people to relieve the suffering directly. They particularly requested that the United States raise the ration allowed to Germans and restore mail and package services to the American zone. The sort of language Truman heard was also audible in the Senate a few days later, in the voice of Senator Wherry: 'The American people should know once and for all that as a result of this government's official policy they are being made the unwilling accomplices in the crime of mass starvation . . . Germany is the only nation where UNRRA is not permitted to feed its nationals. Germany is the only nation subjected to a deliberate starvation policy of 1,500 calories per day.'[53]

This was fresh in Truman's mind when he finally wrote to Hoover in January 1946 and asked him to do something about food relief in Europe and round the world, except for Germany. Once again, Hoover agreed.

While Hoover began to make his preparations for the 1946 world tour which would eventually save hundreds of millions of lives, the senators kept the pot boiling. Senator Wherry quoted at length from an editorial in the *Christian Century* to help him express his feelings. Calling it 'one of the most angry and inspired editorials on this whole tragic subject', he read the whole last paragraph for the Congressional Record of the Senate. 'There is not a day to be lost . . . With every day the opportunity grows less to make real to the people of Germany the Christian testimony to mercy and brotherhood. With every day that Christian love is thwarted by shortsighted and vengeful government policies, the prospect for a future catastrophe grows. It is time that a united demand went up from all

American churches and church organizations for an end to the armed barriers which now keep Christian charity from our late enemies. It is time to let Washington know that American Christians will no longer acquiesce in the Potsdam outrage.'[54]

A few weeks later, on 29 March 1946, Senator Langer had received new information which caused him to rise again in the Senate, to speak as follows:

> [We] are caught in what has now unfolded as a savage and fanatical plot to destroy the German people by visiting on them a punishment in kind for the atrocities of their leaders. Not only have the leaders of this plot permitted the whole world situation to get . . . out of hand . . . but their determination to destroy the German people and the German Nation, no matter what the consequences to our own moral principles, to our leadership in world affairs, to our Christian faith, to our allies, or to the whole future peace of the world, has become a world scandal . . . We have all seen the grim pictures of the piled-up bodies uncovered by the American and British armies, and our hearts have been wrung with pity at the sight of such emaciation – reducing adults and even little children to mere skeletons. Yet now, to our utter horror, we discover that our own policies have merely spread those same conditions even more widely . . . among our former enemies.[55]

The senators spoke with deep feeling, at great length. Side by side with the hatred of evil so vigorously expressed was a moving pity for the miserable victims. Clearly, without such compassion there could hardly be the hatred of the evil-doing, which brought hot shame to the cheeks of Langer, Gollancz and all the others. In this pity, of course, there is nothing new: it is as old as victims.

What seems to be new here is that it appeared at such a

moment among such victors. Neither the British nor the
Americans were known as gentle warriors. Nations and tribes
all over the world, from the Irish, French, Spanish and Scots to
the Sioux, Seminole, Filipinos, Zulus, Germans, Boers and
Indians, had felt the furious power of Anglo-Saxon militarism,
and the vengeance that sometimes followed it. What is new
here is that among these warlike peoples, victorious once again
in a world-wide war, compassion for the enemy was expressed
by senior figures as a matter of duty, honour and pity, in deep
opposition to the policy already being carried out.

Mackenzie King expressed this plainly on 1 September 1945,
during the ceremonies in Ottawa at the end of the Japanese
war: 'All the United Nations were now committed to further
the law of peace, work and health, and to wishing success at the
dawn of the new era. I stressed particularly the colossal loss of
life and what we owe to the men who had given their lives.
Blessed are the peacemakers.'[56] This speech got a terrific reception, perhaps the warmest that this mild, cautious man had
ever received. These words were not only rhetoric: they
expressed profound feelings among hundreds of millions of
English-speaking people in the world. Mackenzie King was not
only the Prime Minister of a country which had made a major
contribution to defeating Hitler, he was also a friend and con-
fidant of Roosevelt, John D. Rockefeller, Winston Churchill
and many other leaders. 'Peace, work and health' expressed
perfectly what 'common people' had always wanted. This policy
was chosen by the English-speaking nations that could easily
have continued a winning war. They were implementing it in
the face of a great danger from the Soviets. And they were carrying it out massively, internationally, with superb organization
at high speed and terrific cost, to the needy nations of earth
save only one.

Nothing like this had ever happened before.

III

'FROM THERE NO PRISONER RETURNED'

Never had so many people been put in prison. The size of the Allied captures was unprecedented in all history. The Soviets took prisoner some 3.5 million Europeans, the Americans about 6.1 million, the British about 2.4 million, the Canadians about 300,000 and the French around 200,000.[1] Uncounted millions of Japanese entered American captivity in 1945, plus about 640,000 entering Soviet captivity.[2]

As soon as Germany surrendered on 8 May 1945, the American Military Governor, General Eisenhower, sent out an 'urgent courier' throughout the huge area that he commanded, *making it a crime punishable by death for German civilians to feed prisoners.* It was even a death-penalty crime to gather food together in one place to take it to prisoners. This astounding order contradicted an earlier message from Eisenhower to the Joint Chiefs of Staff on 10 March, saying that he would make the German civilians feed the prisoners. The Joint Chiefs of Staff had approved this in late April.

The order was sent in German to the provincial governments, ordering them to distribute it immediately to local governments. Copies of the orders were discovered recently in

Abschrift

Der Regierungspräsident   Koblenz, den 9. Mai 1945

Durch Kurier!

An den
Herrn Landrat
in Bad Kreuznach

Betrifft: Lebensmittel für die Gefangenen.

Die Militärregierung hat mich ersucht, bekanntzugeben, dass
unter keinen Umständen unter der Bevölkerung Lebensmittel ge-
sammelt werden dürfen, um sie deutschen Kriegsgefangenen zuzu-
stellen. Wer dieses Gebot übertritt und gegebenenfalls unter Umge-
hung der Absperrung, den Gefangenen trotzdem etwas zukommen zu l
sen, setzt sich der Gefahr aus, erschossen zu werden.

In besonderen Einzelfällen - Zuwendungen an nahe Verwandte -
kann dies nur durch den Militärkommandanten vermittelt worden.

Ich ersuche, hiernach alles daran zu setzen, etwaige Samm-
lungen zu unterbinden und die Bevölkerung in geeigneter Weise
über diesen Tatbestand aufzuklären.

                      Im Auftrag
                      gez. Unterschrift

Der Landrat
des Kreises Kreuznach   Bad Kreuznach, den 15. Mai 1945
Kreishauptamt
o/92

           An
           den Herrn Amts - Bürgermeister

                in Langenlonsheim

Abschrift übersende ich zur genauesten Beachtung.
Die Bevölkerung ist in geeigneter Weise aufzuklären.

              gez. Sieben
              Beglaubigt:

              Angestellte

Copy

The President of the Government   Koblenz. 9, May 1945

By Courier!

To the Landrat [highest district official]
in Bad Kreuznach

Re: Food supplies for the Prisoners.

The military government has requested me to make it known,
that under no circumstances may food supplies be assembled among
the local inhabitants, in order to deliver them to the prisoners
of war. Those who violate this command and nevertheless try to
circumvent this blockade to allow something to come to the
prisoners place themselves in danger of being shot.

Special individual cases - contributions of near relatives-
will be negotiated through the military commander.

I request you accordingly to make every effort, to stop
possible collection and to explain to the local inhabitants in
suitable terms about the facts of the matter.

By order
signed
Signature

The Landrat of the
District of Kreuznach
Central office
c/c2

Bad Kreuznach, 15, May 1945

To the Burgermeister's [the Mayor's] Office

in   Langenlonsheim

I am sending on a copy for your close attention, so that
the local inhabitants may be suitably informed.

signed. Sieben

43

several villages near the Rhine, among them Langenlonsheim. The message, reproduced on page 42–3, reads in part: '. . . under no circumstances may food supplies be assembled among the local inhabitants in order to deliver them to the prisoners of war. Those who violate this command and nevertheless try to circumvent this blockade to allow something to come to the prisoners place themselves in danger of being shot . . .'[3]

Eisenhower's order was also posted in English, German and Polish on the bulletin board of Military Government Head-quarters in Bavaria, signed by the Chief of Staff of the Military Governor of Bavaria. Later it was posted in Polish in Straubing and Regensburg, where there were a lot of Polish guard companies at nearby camps. One US Army officer who read the posted order in May 1945 has written that it was 'the intention of Army command regarding the German POW camps in the US Zone from May 1945 through the end of 1947 to exterminate as many POWs as the traffic would bear without international scrutiny'.[4] Since this fatal order contravenes the order given by the Joint Chiefs of Staff to Eisenhower, and since it entailed the deaths of thousands of prisoners, it is important to German civilians, to the prisoners, and to Army records in general. But in the course of six months' research in the US archives, and also in the Truman and Eisenhower libraries, the author has been unable to locate the original of this order. Nor has he found any trace of an order from the Joint Chiefs of Staff to Eisenhower ordering him to reverse the feed-ing policy agreed on just two weeks before.

The army's policy was to starve prisoners, according to sev-eral American soldiers who were there. Martin Brech, retired professor of philosophy at Mercy College in New York, who was a guard at Andernach in 1945, has said that he was told by an officer that 'it is our policy that these men not be fed'.[5] The 50,000 to 60,000 men in Andernach were starving, living with no shelter in holes in the ground, trying to nourish themselves on grass. When Brech smuggled bread to them through the wire, he was ordered to stop by an officer. Later, Brech sneaked more food to them, was caught, and told by the same officer, 'If you do that again, you'll be shot.' Brech saw bodies go out of the camp 'by the truckload' but he was never told how many there were, where they were buried, or how.[5]

Former prisoners have led the way to putting names to prisoners and one civilian who were shot for the 'crime' of passing food through the barbed wire. Civilian women and teenage girls were shot, shot at, and imprisoned for trying to take food to the camps, although the Eisenhower order had purportedly given individual camp commanders a chance to exempt family members trying to feed relatives through the wire.[7] The prisoner Paul Schmitt was shot in the American camp at Bretzenheim after coming close to the wire to see his wife and young son who were bringing him a basket of food. The French followed suit: Agnes Spira was shot by French guards at Dietersheim in July 1945 for taking food to prisoners. The memorial to her in nearby Büdesheim, written by one of her children, reads: 'On the 31 of July 1945, my mother was suddenly and unexpectedly torn from me because of her good deed toward the imprisoned soldiers.' The entry in the Catholic church register says simply: 'A tragic demise, shot in Dietersheim on 31.07.1945. Buried on 03.08.1945.' Martin Brech watched in amazement as one officer at Andernach stood on a hillside firing shots towards German women running away from him in the valley below.

The most gruesome killing was witnessed by the prisoner Hanns Scharf, formerly of California, who was watching as a German woman with her two children came towards an American guard in the camp at Bad Kreuznach, carrying a wine bottle. She asked the guard to give the bottle to her husband, who was just inside the wire. The guard upended the bottle into his own mouth, and when it was empty, threw it on the ground and killed the prisoner with five shots. The other prisoners howled, which brought round US Army Lieutenant Holtsman of Seattle, who said, 'This is awful. I'll make sure there is a stiff court martial.'[8] In months of work in the Washington archives of the army, no court martial of this or similar incidents has ever turned up. Captain Lee Berwick, who was in command of the guard towers at Bretzenheim nearby, has said that he was never aware of any court martial for shootings at Bretzenheim or at Bad Kreuznach.[9]

The former prisoners leading the way in new research had been officially ignored for forty-four years, but they are now actively trying to uncover the truth behind the historical forgeries which have been accepted as real up to now. At Lambach in Austria early in 1996, during excavations for a new power plant, a mass grave was opened on an 80m square site near the river Traun. One theory is that these were the bodies of Jews who died during transport, but the evidence suggests strongly that these were German prisoners of the Americans. In 1945 there were three American-run POW camps in the region, one at Hofau, another at Grüberfeld a little farther to the east, and one for SS men at Kuhweide to the west. Horst Littmann, an expert recommended by the Austrian Ministry of the Interior, concluded that the bodies were the dead prisoners from these American camps, men between the ages of nineteen and twenty-two, judging from the good condition of their teeth, the shape of their heads and other evidence.

Such in-ground investigations could happen in Austria, and people could dig up mass graves of prisoners at former Soviet camps recently in eastern Germany, but west German farmer Otto Tullius was prevented by the police from digging his own land for evidence of prisoners on the site of a former American/French camp.[10]

The official US Army ration book, smuggled out by an ex-prisoner, for the huge camp at Bretzenheim, shows that these captives who nominally had prisoner-of-war status – supposedly the best-treated of all – got only 600–850 calories per day. The prisoners starved although 'food was piled up all round the camp fence', according to Captain Lee Berwick of the 424th Infantry Regiment, guardians of the camp.[11]

Martin Brech has confirmed that Eisenhower's terror policy was harshly enforced down to the lowest level of camp guard. At the time that Brech was ordered to stop feeding prisoners on pain of being shot himself, it scarcely seemed credible to him that the army intended these prisoners to die. Now, seeing the new evidence in 1995, Brech has said that, 'It is clear that in fact it was the policy to shoot any civilians trying to feed the prisoners.'

Of course, individual French and American soldiers like Brech were honorable exceptions to the orders from higher up. The French Captain Julien of the IIIeme Regiment de Tirailleurs Algérien, who took over at Dietersheim from the Americans in July 1945, forbade shooting at his camp. In fact, Julien was so appalled at the condition of the prisoners that he immediately organized food to come in from the village. But Julien got into serious trouble with the French Army for quarrelling with a fellow officer, Captain Rousseau, who shot at German women in Julien's presence, at about the time and in the same place as a French officer shot Frau Spira. Rousseau is remembered to this day in the village as a bad man. At Bad Kreuznach, William Sellner of Oakville, Ontario, one day saw civilians throw food over the wire while guards watched indifferently. And yet, at night, guards would shoot machine gun bullets at random into the camps, apparently for sport. In Bad Kreuznach, Ernst Richard Krische wrote in his diary on 4 May: 'Wild shooting in the night, absolute fireworks. It must be the supposed peace. Next morning forty dead as "victims of the fireworks", in our cage alone, many wounded.'[12]

One American who tried to help the prisoners was Dr John

Allensworth, now of Mineral Wells, Texas, who was an officer in the US Army Medical Corps. He was sent to Gummersbach, east of Bonn, just after the Ruhr pocket collapsed in March 1945. 'There was a huge mass of humanity in a field standing shoulder to shoulder in the mud, and I mean knee-deep. I would estimate that 75 per cent of them were wounded. The conditions were appalling.' He immediately set up a 150-bed hospital in a tent for the prisoners. He said, 'My headquarters leaned over backwards to do everything they could to help the prisoners,' so he was able to get all the supplies he required immediately.[13]

But the number of prisoners served by the tent hospitals was less than 1 per cent of the total on hand. And this was before the German collapse, so that millions of Allied prisoners were still being held hostage by the Germans. Thus the attitude of SHAEF (Supreme Headquarters Allied Expeditionary Force) was probably more conditioned by fear for the hostages than by the Geneva Convention, which was in fact about to be abrogated by the US State Department.[14]

Conditions in the camps deteriorated further after the hostage system collapsed. Despite the restrictions, other individual American guards tried to help the German prisoners long after the war ended, among them Captain Frederick Siegfriedt. He was detailed as prison officer in an undermanned Prisoner of War Overhead Detachment at a camp near Zimming in eastern France in December 1945, where there were about 17,000 prisoners, 'all presumably SS'. According to Siegfriedt, the previous prison officer had been relieved of his duties because of psychiatric problems. A lifelong friend of Siegfriedt was the medical officer for the detachment. 'Captain L. had been an extremely hardworking and conscientious person all his life. It was evident that he was under extreme stress, trying to cope with the conditions at CCE 27 and receiving no co-operation, no help, no understanding, without even someone to talk to. I was able to serve to fill the latter need. He explained to me that most of the men had dysentery and were suffering from malnutrition. Some men in the cages had as many as seventeen bloody stools per day, he said. He took me to one of the former French bar-racks that served as the hospital. It had eight hundred men lying all over, on the cold concrete floors as well as on beds . . . almost without exception the other [US] officers were alco-holics or had psychiatric problems . . .'

The rest of the men were kept in Nissen huts, made of chicken wire covered with tar paper. Water was supplied by a single tap inside the hut, which was usually frozen that winter. The prisoners slept on the muddy ground, about 180 to a hut. So crowded were they that it was impossible for them all to lie on their back at once. Sometimes at the roll calls in the morn-ing, men fell over dead.

'The operation of CCE 27 seemed typical of the entire system,' Siegfriedt has said. 'When an enclosure got a bunch of prisoners they didn't know what to do with, or could not oth-erwise handle, they were shipped unannounced to another enclosure . . . I have no idea how many died nor where they were buried. I am sure the Americans did not bury them and we had no such thing as a bulldozer. I can only assume that a detail of German PWs would bury them. I could look out the window of my office and tell if the body being carried by was alive or dead by whether or not there was a fifth man following with the man's personal possessions. The number could have been from five to twenty per day.

'The officers' mess was in a French two-storey house. It had a staff of forty-two [prisoners] with the *maître d'* of the German luxury liner *Europa* in charge. Although there were usually no more than six or eight officers dining at one time, there were always at least that many uniformed waiters. One could not get a cigarette from pocket to lips without a light waiting. The facility was completely redecorated, that is repainted with murals for each special occasion, i.e. Christmas, New Year's,

Valentine's Day, St Patrick's Day, etc. For lunch there was chamber music with four to six musicians and for dinner a choir of fifteen to twenty made up of the stars of the Munich and Berlin operas. In short, the staff was much more concerned with living the luxurious life than it was about the operation of the prison camps.'

Siegfriedt attempted to alleviate the conditions by bribing guards at excess vehicle camps with cigarettes so he could take their trucks to scrounge some hay in the neighbourhood 'to get the PWs off the ground. When the weather warmed up, the cages became ankle-deep in mud. I located a pierced-plank airfield* and, with a convoy of trucks, brought it back to get the men out of the mud. These, however, were band-aid measures for major problems that no one seemed to be in a position to deal with, nor did anyone seem to care.'

Captain Siegfriedt concluded: 'Obviously we, the US Army, were not prepared to deal with so many prisoners even when I arrived on the scene in December 1945.' This was close to the Vosges area of France that US Army Colonel Philip Lauben described as 'one big death camp'.

Prisoners who survived the camp at Bretzenheim have described arriving there on 9 May 1945. They saw three rows of corpses along the road in front of the camp. Seventy-five dead from Bretzenheim were acknowledged by the Americans to have been buried in Stromberg on 9 May and another sixty on 10 May.[15] Not all were killed by the usual disease, starvation and exposure.

The village of Bretzenheim has also been the locale of much new research into the fate of prisoners. Herr and Frau Wolfgang Spietz of Bretzenheim took up a challenge from the local Protestant pastor in 1985 to prepare a display about the local

*One composed of sectional wooden parts pierced to grip the earth and allow drainage.

camp which had been under American and later French control. With the official support of Bürgermeister Grünwald, this grew into the present documentation centre. A sensational find came in 1990 with the visit of Rudi Buchal of Grossenhain, in the east of Germany, who had been a prisoner in the American time. Buchal had served as a medical orderly-clerk in the so-called POW 'hospital' for prisoners, a tent with an earth floor inside the camp. It had no beds, no medical supplies, no blankets and starvation rations for the first month or more. Later, a few supplies were scrounged at random by American teams 'ferreting' the German towns nearby.

Another of the prisoners who have come forward recently to the Spietzes is Jakob M. Zacher, a former teacher and school principal of Bretzenheim. He was especially interested in the fate of the prisoners because he had been held in several camps, including Bretzenheim itself. In the 1980s, he decided to look in the archives for 1945 of the village at Langenlonsheim, which was so close to the Bretzenheim camp that prisoners could see the spires of its churches above the trees to the north. In the town hall under the spires, he found the document showing that the Americans had threatened to shoot anyone who tried to take food to the camps. Other copies of the order have been found since in other villages.[16]

Also in Bretzenheim in the Spietzes's house, four ex-prisoners met in 1991 to discuss their experiences. Max Müller of Bad Kreuznach laid on the Spietzes' dining-room table the water-stained original US Army ration book for Bretzenheim, a hard-cover German ledger book with the name of a clerk who had kept it still legible in pencil on the cover. This was Robert Hughson, of the 424th Regiment, 106th Infantry Division. Later in the USA, the Supply Officer of the 106th told this writer, 'Yes, I remember Hughson.' And Captain Lee Berwick said, 'We had supplies stacked all round the camp.' He could not explain why the prisoners got only about 600–850 calories per day, which was the ration according to Hughson's records.[17] And these prisoners nominally had Prisoner of War status.

Berwick's statement about food supplies is at odds not only with the official army ration book, but with the reports of ten prisoners and several civilians received by the author. Without exception, they describe starvation conditions prevailing through the seventy-odd days when the camp was under US control.[18] The prisoner Herbert Peters has reported similar conditions at the huge US camp at Rheinberg: 'Even when there was little for us to eat, the provisions enclosure was enormous. Piles of cartons like bungalows with intersecting streets throughout.'[19]

As the Americans prepared to leave Bretzenheim in July, Buchal was told by drivers of the 560th Ambulance Company, who had carried bodies and sick prisoner 'evacuees' away, that 18,100 persons had died in the six camps round Bretzenheim in the ten weeks of American control. The destination of the corpses was not revealed to Buchal. He also heard the figure of 18,100 dead from the Germans who were in charge of the hospital statistics, and from other American hospital personnel. The six camps were Bretzenheim, Biebelsheim, Bad Kreuznach, Dietersheim, Hechtsheim and Heidesheim. The reliability of Buchal has been attested by the US Army itself. When he was finally discharged, Buchal received a paper stating that in the opinion of the US Army officers who commanded him, 'During the above mentioned period [April–July 1945] he proved himself to be co-operative, capable, industrious and reliable.'[20]

Captain Berwick said on reading Buchal's report of 18,100 corpses in a draft of this chapter, 'That might be true.' The 18,100 figure is in general confirmed by reports from five prisoners who survived Bretzenheim. Several report deaths of over fifty per day for a long period in the camp alone, apart from the hospital.[21] One reported 120–180 bodies per day coming out of the camp, apart from the hospital.[22]

The death total of 18,100, taken with the known period of ten weeks and the known average population of the six camps, 217,000, means that the death rate was 43 per cent per year. This is much higher than the figure 35.6 per cent apparent from Table X in the Medical History of the European Theater of Operations, which was used to help determine the overall death rates in *Other Losses* in 1989. A high number of corpses on many days was also observed by several American guards at the camp.[23]

Captain Berwick was in charge of the German *Lager* captains who had to carry out the dead bodies every day. Berwick estimates that three to five bodies per day were taken from each of twenty cages within the larger enclosure, during the worst time, which lasted some sixteen days. This means that from the camp proper, excluding the hospital, some 960 to 1,600 bodies were taken away in only sixteen days from Bretzenheim alone. Berwick does not know where they were taken. Adding the probable hospital deaths computed from statistics for the hospitals at both Bretzenheim and Bad Kreuznach nearby, and from the overall medical records of the 106th Division, which guarded Bretzenheim and Bad Kreuznach, the overall death rate at Bretzenheim – in the open camp, in the hospital inside the camp, and among those evacuated to outside 'evacuation hospitals' – was above 40 per cent per year during those ten weeks. Berwick has also said that, because the guards made efforts to improve the camp, the death rate there dropped very significantly after the disasters of the early weeks. 'By July, the deaths were negligible,' he said.

My book *Other Losses* was criticized for making estimates of the deaths of prisoners far higher than the critics felt were justified by the evidence offered. Now, however, detailed evidence from the US Army 106th Division medical records and from the records of the 50th Field Hospital adds depth to the picture.

Assessing the deaths, the first thing to notice is that there were three areas where corpses accumulated. First was in the open air inside the camps themselves, where the living might die of malnutrition, disease, exposure, be buried alive when their earth-holes collapsed on them, or drown in the latrine ditches. Many of the bodies of those who died from starvation and disease were pulled out to the camp gate and driven away by truck.

The second death area was in the camp hospitals themselves, usually located inside the camp in a tent.

The third area was during the transportation to, or in the 'evacuation hospitals'. For several of the camp hospitals, we have detailed records.[24] These hospitals were part of a system of sixteen field 'hospital units',[25] each one set up usually in tents inside or very near to the camps. Their capacity was some 14,000 patients at peak. On average, in May, their capacity was around 9,500. Occupancy for two observed camp hospitals was around 90 per cent.[26]

About half the patients admitted to these hospital units in May–July 1945 were reported to have been evacuated further on, to 'evacuation hospitals' in Europe but far from the camp. Some of these 'evacuation hospitals' were purported to be located in former German civilian hospitals, which were supposed to be administered by a few Germans under American supervision. Others were staffed by Americans.

The records show that thousands of sick prisoners were taken from the camps and sent to these hospitals, and while there disappeared from the records. For instance, from 1 May to 10 July 1945, 44,646 prisoners were taken from the camps to hospital, including both camp hospitals and evacuation hospitals, but only 12,786 returned to the camps after treatment. The deaths recorded were 1,392. There is no record of the fate of the remaining 30,468. There is a strong clue however in the ambulance records of the medical department of the 106th Division. From 1 May to 10 July, the 106th Division ambulances carried 21,551 sick prisoners away from the camp hospitals to the evacuation hospitals. The page showing arrivals in the evacuation hospitals has a series of zeroes under ENEMY.[27]

This cannot be a statistical blip. First, the same pages of forms record with apparent coherence what happened to American personnel. And for them, there are regular arrivals at the evacuation hospitals, and departures from the same hospitals. Also, the 106th report is set up with columns and headings defining various categories of patients including Casuals and Enemy (Allied, Civilian), as well as US troops. All these categories are recorded on the same sheets of paper. *Only* the enemy prisoners depart for these places and fail to arrive. *Only* enemy prisoners do not turn up as returning 'to duty' – i.e., to the original prison camp. Nor does the report give breakdowns of enemy prisoners by communicable disease, for number of deaths, or for surgical cases, though these breakdowns are given in every case for sick Americans in their evacuation hospitals. The Germans become a series of zeroes.

At least one German doctor, Siegfried Enke of Wuppertal, who worked in American camp hospital units, has said that mortally ill patients were moved away to another building (probably called an evacuation hospital) and he never saw them again.[28] This was also the experience of Rudi Buchal at Bretzenheim. Many of the mortally sick evacuees were taken to Idstein, north of Wiesbaden. Buchal has recently stated: 'And I can remember that from there no prisoners returned.'

A vivid description of one such evacuation 'hospital' is given from the inside by a French doctor from Lorraine who volunteered to help the French and Americans to care for German prisoners in May 1945. Dr Joseph Kirsch writes: 'I volunteered to the Military Government of the 21st [French] Military region [near Metz] . . . I was assigned to the "French" Military hospital at the little seminary of Montigny . . . In May 1945, the Americans who occupied the hospital at Legouest brought

CRIMES AND MERCIES

us every night by ambulance, stretchers loaded with moribund prisoners in German uniforms . . . these ambulances arrived by the back door . . . we lined up the stretchers in the central hall. For treatment, we had nothing at our disposal. We could only perform elementary superficial examinations (auscultation). Only to find out the anticipated cause of death in the night . . . for in the morning, more ambulances arrived with coffins and quicklime . . . These prisoners were in such extremely bad condition that my role was reduced to comforting the dying. This drama has obsessed me since the war; I consider it as a horror.'[29] The reader may judge what opinion the Americans had of these 'hospitals' by the fact that beside the patients they loaded quicklime and coffins.[30]

The notion of hospitalizing sick Germans got a bizarre twist as the Americans advanced into Germany. The army actually removed sick Germans when they were captured lying in their hospital beds. These patients were forced, regardless of their condition, into the open-air camps.[31] Thus in the spring of 1945, the army reversed the meaning of the term 'hospital'. Sick prisoners were not sent there. The sick were evacuated *from* the hospitals, which then stood silent.[32]

The evidence that evacuations were nearly all hidden deaths grows even stronger with the arrival of the French in July. The French, who took over the whole Rhine area – including camps and hospitals – from the Americans in July, complained that the Americans had said that there were 192,000 men in the camps and hospitals, but the French actually found only 166,000.[33] US Army Colonel Philip S. Lauben admitted in a memorandum to General Paul of the US Army on 7 July that the prisoner total to be turned over was 'only in the neighborhood of 170,000'.[34] Since this was the area controlled by the 106th, Lauben's missing 22,000 prisoners are probably accounted for a second time, in this book. Not only could the French not find them, the US Army couldn't find them either.

56

Lauben had a broad view of the whole prisoner situation. As a member of the SHAEF HQ staff, he was in charge of returning prisoners from Norway, of the hand over to the French, and of other special missions, with overall responsibility for prisoners through the German Affairs Branch. Since both Lauben and the 106th Division surgeon admitted they were not there, and the French did not find them, is any other fate but death imaginable for these people?

The most impressive of the detailed evidence of deaths recorded by hospital units comes from the 106th Division. In the hospital units of the 106th, not including 'evacuation hospitals', 1,392 people died in seventy days among a patient load of 23,095. This means that for more than two months, by US Army medical records, the prisoner-of-war death rate *in hospital* was 2.6 per cent per month, or 31.2 per cent per annum.[35] This is exactly the same as the rate of 0.6 per cent per week used in *Other Losses* to compute deaths for prisoners of war in the same camps in the same period.

A subsidiary report from the 50th Field Hospital Detachment A at Bad Kreuznach confirms the overall picture. At Bad Kreuznach, a camp of some 56,000 in the 106th command, the deaths in hospital recorded by Major Jennings B. Marshall, commander, numbered 174 among 1,825 patients in twenty-four days, or 9.5 per cent.[36]

At Bretzenheim, just three miles away, Max Dellmann, the camp's Protestant pastor in 1946, was told by the German doctors of the 50th Field Hospital HQ Detachment in the camp, that between 3,000 and 4,000 men had died there while the Americans were in command.[37] The German doctors knew only of the deaths in the camp itself, which did not include the deaths in the 'evacuation hospitals'.[38] So to find the complete total for Bretzenheim, the Dellmann total must be added to the Bretzenheim share of the death totals in the hospital units reported by the 106th medical section (above).[39] On this basis, the overall death rate for Bretzenheim in April–July 1945 works out to between 45 and 57.5 per cent per year. It is important to remember that the total 'death production' for the camp during the period has three components: the dead in the camp itself, who were either buried there or trucked away; the dead in the camp hospital; and those who died in or en route to 'evacuation hospital' and euphemized as 'evacuated'. The totals are:

Camp, including the camp hospital: 3,000 to 6,240[40]
'Evacuated':   3,380 to 4,142[41]

The overall total for Bretzenheim is between 6,380 and 10,382. This works out to an annual death rate somewhere between 44.9 and 73 per cent.

The conclusion is simply inescapable that nearly all the men missing on handover to the French were actually dead.[42] When these missing are added to the known dead actually recorded in army figures for May 1 to July 10, the toll rises to between 26,000 and 33,557.[43] This means the overall death rate in the Adsec (Advance Section, US Army) camps during the ten weeks starting May 1 was between 27.6 per cent per year and 35.6 per cent per year.[44] The latter figure is exactly the same as the figure based on Tables IX and X in the Medical History of the ETO.[45] And it is close to the rate at which prisoners were dying according to the 'Other Losses' category reported in the weekly PW and DEF reports* of the Army in 1945 and confirmed by Colonel Lauben himself, before he was re-educated by a US Army official in 1990.[46]

It is clear from a scrutiny of the records that the army in 1945 was disposing of the news of their dead by falsifying statistics.

*Reports of prisoners of war and disarmed enemy force.

This extended to the highest levels. For instance, on 4 August 1945, 132,262 DEF prisoners were reported by the prisoner of war section of Eisenhower's command (hitherto SHAEF) to have been 'transferred' to Austria, where General Mark Clark was the political commissioner. Clark as political commissioner was responsible for immigrants and emigrants, including DEF prisoners arriving in Austria, so he reported that in the month of August a total of 17,953 DEF prisoners arrived in Austria. Clearly, no transfer of 132,262 ever took place. If the 114,309 missing prisoners were transferred away as 'Other Losses', but never arrived in Austria, what happened to them? There is only one way to leave a place and not to arrive anywhere else, and that is to die.

The prisoner-of-war death figures reluctantly given out by the Americans and French from the 1950s to the 1990s to cautiously inquiring Germans were so ridiculously low that they were under the civilian death rates for the time. This extraordinary news – that starved people ridden with lice, pneumonia, TB and typhoid fever, sleeping in mud, have a lower mortality than civilians eating every day in houses – did not strike the German observers as odd. They blithely ignored evidence that was howling at them.[47] For instance, the authority on whom the German writer Kurt W. Boehme depends for prisoner facts for France, General Louis Buisson, was not only the head of the Prisoner of War Service of the French Army and the author of the ridiculously low French death figures, he also did not include in his prisoner-of-war totals 166,000 men the French received in camps in Germany from the Americans. Yet a few pages further on in his manuscript, Buisson asserts that a number of these same POWs were 'relâché sur place', or released on the spot, in Germany. So 166,000 men disappear from view in Buisson's manuscript, those who were released are used to reduce the total of the remainder in French camps, and for forty-seven years no one notices this double-dealing.

These prisoners were supposedly being held in order to provide labour to help rebuild the damage caused in the war. The French had a strong claim to the labour of Germans, because Hitler had broken the truce agreement of June 1940 to return French prisoners to their homes. He kept one and a half million French soldiers and civilians slaving in Germany for years during the war. The French also wanted German labour to repair some of the damage done to their country during the campaigns. Having captured very few prisoners themselves, they asked the British and Americans for part of their bag. The Americans granted them around 800,000, the British some 55,000.[48]

Vengeance predominated in the French camps. As the months passed, so did the lives of hundreds of thousands of their Germans. After the French press began reporting mass deaths in the French camps in September–October 1945, senators in the United States began a vigorous protest against this aspect of US Army policy. In March 1946, when deaths in one part of the Buglose-Labouheyre camp system had peaked at 25 per cent for one month,[49] Senator Langer said in the Senate: 'On 12 October 1945, the United States Army officials stopped turning over German prisoners to the French after the International Red Cross charged the French with failing to provide sufficient food for German prisoners in French camps . . . General Louis Buisson, Director of the War Prisons, said that food rations were "just enough to allow a man to lie down, not move, and not die too quickly".'[50] The Senator went on: 'In spite of the certain fate awaiting German prisoners of war in French hands, this government continues to be a party to sentencing German prisoners of war to starvation in continued violation of the articles of war of the Geneva Convention.'[51]

He was right about the conditions the French camps, but he

had been deceived about the US Army's transfer policy. The army had pretended to stop delivering German slaves to the French, but in fact they continued. More than a hundred thousand were delivered after the ban was announced. Some Germans who had already been discharged by General Mark Clark in Austria were seized again and sent to France.[52]

The British also were using some 400,000 German prisoners as low-paid forced labour in the United Kingdom, and the Americans had some 600,000 Germans at work in the fields of the United States or in labour camps in Europe.[53] The prisoners in the US, having been well treated until May 1945, were then put on rations so low that some were in danger of death, though the records are not clear as to how many actually died. However, the death rate was probably quite low.[54]

President Truman decided in the spring of 1946 to keep at least 50,000 Germans imprisoned and working in the USA, while their families were starving, partly for lack of labour in Germany. During the discussion of what to do about the Germans in the US, Secretary of War Robert Patterson said that he wanted to return 'all prisoners of war as soon as possible'. He pointed out that the programme of return had been announced four months previously, and he added, 'It would not do to depend indefinitely on what amounted to slave labour while millions of our own people were unemployed . . . The Secretary of State supported me in this view.' Truman ordered as 'an emergency measure' that 50,000 prisoners be kept for at least three more months, while disclaiming any intention of keeping them longer. The last non-criminal Germans were not released from US captivity until 1947, still during Truman's presidency. It is hard to see what emergency the prisoners could have helped solve in the US, for there was unemployment in the US at the time, and the labour force was already over sixty-four million. The 50,000 slaves thus constituted 0.08 per cent of the labour force.[55]

In the many angry speeches made by US senators in 1946, not a word was uttered on the subject of the American prison camps in Europe, where more than 500,000 people died in 1945–46.[56] At first it seems very strange that not a word appears about these American camps. At that very time, General Mark Clark in Austria wrote a memo saying that he had ordered his men to clean up the 'deplorable' camp at Ebensee, even though he doubted he had the authority, which rested with Eisenhower.[57] Colonel Lauben was thinking that 'the Vosges was just one big death camp',[58] and General Allard was describing Eisenhower's camps as hardly better than the Japanese camps.[59] But the senators, for all their righteous wrath, said nothing. Why?

The senators were kept in ignorance. All these American army officers kept these secrets for forty years or more. Clark wrote his memo 'for files', where it stayed until disinterred in 1990 by the archivist Jane Yates in Charleston. General Allard made his criticism in secret in 1946, in a training manual that stayed in the archives at Fort Leavenworth until it was dug out by the researcher E. B. Walker of Alabama in 1991. The statement by Colonel Philip Lauben was not recorded until 1988, forty-three years after the event. And all the hundreds of English-speaking reporters who were in Europe at the time either failed to get the story, or knowingly suppressed it.

The secret of the camps was kept so well that not even the Chief Delegate in France of the International Committee of the Red Cross (ICRC) knew about them, though he was responsible for inspecting them under the Geneva Convention. Jean Pierre Pradervand, head of the French delegation of the ICRC, did not discover until he was told by the present writer in 1986 that the American army had prison camps in France in 1945.[60] The ICRC refused this writer permission to use its archive on prisoners of war. They told me this was because they never allow anyone to use their archives. However, at the same time, they permitted three other writers, one American, one Swiss and one Israeli, to investigate their archives for books on the German expellees, or for reports of ICRC actions in Hitler's concentration camps in the same period.

Much concerning these atrocities has been deliberately suppressed, some has been forgotten, some falsified, but perhaps the most poignant anecdote was given by an ex-prisoner, Johannes Heising, who in the 1990s published a book about his experiences in the US camp at Remagen.[61] After the book was published, Heising was talking in 1991 with another former Remagen prisoner, Franz-Josef Plemper, who reminded him of something Heising had not described in the book: one night, the Americans had bulldozed living men under the earth in their foxholes. Plemper described the scene to him: 'One night in April 1945, I was startled out of my stupor in the rain and the mud by piercing screams and loud groans. I jumped up and saw in the distance (about 30–50 meters) the searchlight of a bulldozer. Then I saw this bulldozer moving forwards through the crowd of prisoners who lay there. In the front it had a blade making a pathway. How many of the prisoners were buried alive in their earthholes I do not know. It was no longer possible to ascertain. I heard clearly cries of "you murderer".'

And then Heising remembered.

IV

A HOLIDAY IN HELL

East of the American and French camps, in a different world, similar atrocities were happening. One was described by a survivor: 'The old women are bolder than the rest. You couldn't turn them bad. They believe in God. And they would break off a piece of bread from their meagre loaf and throw it to us. And old camp hands – non-political offenders of course – weren't afraid either. All camp veterans knew the saying, "Whoever hasn't been here yet will get here, and whoever was here won't forget it." And look, they'd toss over a pack of cigarettes, hoping that someone might do the same for them during their next term. And the old woman's bread wouldn't carry quite far enough, what with her weak arm, and it would fall short, whereas the pack of cigarettes would arc through the air right into our midst, and the convoy guards would immediately work the bolts of their rifles, pointing them at the old woman, at kindness, at the bread: "Come on old woman, run along."' This description, mirrored to the gesture in the US camps, was actually written by Alexander Solzhenitsyn, writing about Stalin's Gulag.[1]

The Gulag (Glavnoye Upravleniye *Lagerei*) was terrifying in part because it was so hidden. Like Soviet Russia itself, the prison system run by the MVD/NKVD/KGB was virtually unknown, while at the same time being universally feared. It was the same with the parallel Gulag for the prisoners of war, also run by the MVD/NKVD/KGB.

This was a vast system of 6,000 camps spread across the USSR from Minsk in the west to Karaganda in the south-centre, Vorkuta in the north and Magadan in the north-east.[2] Magadan was especially horrible. Solzhenitsyn visited the remains of the camp on his way home to Moscow in 1994, to pay homage to the dead slaves who had lived and died alongside him. Vorkuta, a dismal collection of huts thousands of kilometres north-east of Moscow, was reached after a terrifying voyage in an open barge or scow, when the prisoners were in danger of freezing to death as they were sprayed with icy water.

In these camps they mined for coal, iron, copper or gold; they cut timber; they were sent out on work details to build roads, bridges and railway embankments. Some of them were detailed to build houses in Moscow, which stand to this day and are proudly displayed to tourists as 'the German houses'. Others were co-opted into re-education camps such as Krasnogorsk, west of Moscow, where they were indoctrinated in communism. A few with technical skills worked on high-technology installations such as the new telephone exchange north of Moscow.

The first European prisoners, Poles and Finns, were taken in 1939. To them were added Lithuanians, Latvians and Estonians in 1940, Germans, Italians, Romanians and so on after June 1941. The surviving Poles were released in the autumn of 1941 at Churchill's suggestion, to form battalions of freedom-fighters who would try to liberate Poland from the Nazis with the help of the USSR.

The camps for Germans and other Europeans were at their worst at the beginning of the war.[3] After the initial disorganization following the German defeat at Stalingrad in February

1943, the NKVD (People's Commissariat for Internal Affairs) worked very close to the front, taking over and recording prisoners. The death rate was very high at first among the Germans and Italians captured at Stalingrad, caused in part by the fact that the Axis soldiers were already dying when captured. Before surrender, the Germans were losing between 400 and 500 per day because of frostbite and disease.[4]

Between 10 January and 22 February 1943, the Red Army took prisoner 91,545 men. Conditions even after capture were appalling. Former POW G. Kurtz said later: 'I survived Stalingrad, the exhausting marches, I even survived the death camp of Beketovka, where in a couple of weeks, of my 55,000 comrades, 42,000 died from hunger and disease.'[5] Beketovka was so bad in comparison with other camps that an investigation was conducted between 22–25 March. The doctors reported that 29 per cent of the prisoners were well, but that 71 per cent were sick, infested with lice, and exhausted. Most had inadequate clothing; some were dressed in civilian clothes. Better accommodation and more food were supplied. The rations ordered for the prisoners were 600 grams of bread per day, plus 120 grams of fish, 600 grams of potatoes or vegetables, 20 grams of sugar, with matches, soap and other supplies. By the end of the war, the camp had its own vegetable gardens. By 1949 these were so productive they were selling 1,819,000 roubles' worth of produce per year.[6]

Among the one million German prisoners on hand in summer 1945, until the last prisoner went home in 1955, about 94,000 died (9.4 per cent).[7] Once the Soviets were organized, only a day or two elapsed usually between a soldier's capture and his entry into the NKVD camps and *into the record books of the NKVD, where his fate was accurately recorded*. These books were kept by NKVD officers, each of whom signed his name to the statistics it contained. He was responsible not only for the prisoners, but for their production and consumption. Junior officers were ordered to feed the prisoners a plentiful ration in October 1944.[8] The ration included 600 grams of black bread every day, spaghetti, meat, sugar, vegetables, rice, amounting in all to more than 1,400 grams or more than three pounds of food per person per day. The weak, the sick and the officers got more, the war criminals less.

Dozens of reports from returned prisoners show that this ration was not always given, because the officers and guards stole the prisoners' food for themselves. Several Germans have reported that once they began to receive food parcels from home, they shared the food with their guards.[9] In contrast with the American policy threatening death to civilians for feeding prisoners, the Soviet policy was to feed the prisoners adequately. And this policy emanated from the highest, most frightening authority in the Soviet Union, Stalin himself.[10]

The death rate was sharply reduced by 1945, mainly because the Soviets wanted to get useful work out of the prisoners. As Stalin told Harry Hopkins, an emissary of Presidents Roosevelt and Truman, in May 1945, he liked the German prisoners best because they worked the hardest. However, the actual production was by Soviet measure, slightly less than the cost to the state of keeping and guarding them. This is not surprising since the whole country has been grossly inefficient.

Russian work camps have always been like this. The fate of Tsarist prisoners was much studied in the nineteenth century by prison officials and by one famous writer, Anton Chekhov. When he was rich and famous, he risked his life and reputation to inquire into the fate of the lowly prisoners on Sakhalin Island. While serving their terms, Chekhov wrote, the convicts in the Due mine in 1889–90 produced coal at the rate of about 10.8 poods per day, which was 4.2 poods below the norm set by the camp administration. When freed, some of them stayed on the island and worked for wages in the mine. Now that they were paid by the pood (approximately 36 pounds, or 16 kilos), their output immediately rose by between 70 and 100 per cent.[11]

The sources of wealth and poverty are plain to see in Sakhalin. So long as totalitarian power was applied, it hurt society twice, by impoverishment and by the spread of human misery, in the prisoners themselves, and in the guards, because of their soul-destroying work. With the end of state power over the prisoners, everything got better. Wealth was born of freedom. This was the judgement of one of the world's great writers, in a book that resulted in considerable reforms to the legal and political system in Tsarist Russia.

The MVD/NKVD/KGB reproduced Sakhalin on a vast scale with their camps for prisoners of war. The worth of the output of the prisoner-slaves was measured by the MVD in 1946–49.[12] The slaves' output was never enough to pay for their meagre maintenance; the output came to around 80 per cent of the cost of maintaining the camps. Such was the effect of slavery on the people, mainly Japanese and German, who spring from nations renowned for the intelligence, organization and general efficiency of their working people. Alex Adourian, now of Toronto, experienced this paradox when he was a prisoner in a Soviet camp in 1945–53. The guards told them in 1949 that now they would be paid for their work. At the end of the first month, the administration calculated that the prisoners owed them money. They were forgiven the debt.[13]

In sub-camp 12 of the BAM-line (Baikal–Amur) railway construction camps east of Lake Baikal in 1946, the prisoners were led out one day in winter to a forest, where they were supposed to survey the trees to be cut to help build the BAM railway east from Baikal to the Amur river. A Soviet forestry expert came to mark off with paint the tall straight trees to be cut down. They were to be used for the construction of work camps on the railway and for railway ties. After a week or so of tree-marking by the Soviet expert, the prisoners were led out with axes. They were guarded by NKVD troops numbering about ten per hundred prisoners. The guards spread out in the forest a great distance from the prisoners, so they were not aware at first what was going on. The prisoners deliberately cut all the crooked, useless trees. Once they were down, the useless trees impeded all further work until moved. So the work was nearly all wasted, and the railway slowed down. The prisoners were not punished because they pretended it was a mistake. And they had actually cut their 'norma' or norm for the period, so it did not matter. Such things as these helped keep production so low that the Soviets would have been better off without the Gulag. NKVD statistics show that the output of the camps (lumber, housing, coal, gold, high-tech construction such as telephone exchanges) was, in 1946, around 75 per cent of the cost of the camps in guard wages, food, clothing and supplies. By 1948 this had improved to over 85 per cent, but in all the years of measuring the output never exceeded the cost. The prisoners were being subsidized to stay there. It was in effect free lodging, a holiday in hell.

Allied support for the Soviets had still not been entirely cut off as late as 1948, for returned prisoners of war have reported that they were still building the BAM line with steel rails marked 'Made in Canada'.

One or two of the camps, such as Krasnogorsk, west of Moscow, were re-education centres where likely candidates were sent during the war to be retrained into communist ideology. This was the brainwashing later made infamous in Korea. A famous German General 'graduate' from Krasnogorsk, Field Marshal Paulus, had fought hard for the Wehrmacht at Stalingrad. Another was a fighter pilot, Heinrich von Einsiedel, of a famous aristocratic German family. Men who later became leaders of East Germany were trained here. The camp was comfortable, well run, efficient, successful. Both Japanese and Germans were indoctrinated in communist ideology in these camps, then sent home to help bring about the communist revolution. (The British maintained similar camps in the UK after the war. Some primitive re-education was also done in Canada.)[14]

The labour of the prisoners not only cost the USSR a subsidy, the prisoners themselves endangered the USSR in the end, because they left the USSR with valuable information. Many Japanese and German prisoners were interviewed by officers of the United States Air Force, who were looking for information about the location, size, dispersal, importance and purpose of factories, bridges, airports, railways and so forth in the USSR. The prisoners in the end were converted into spies. Thousands of these reports, a monument to the Cold War, are stored to this day in American archives in Washington.

The full story of the Gulag for foreign prisoners has not yet been told, although Solzhenitsyn has told of the sufferings in the Gulag for Soviet citizens. The general impression in the Western mind is that life in the Gulag was one of unvaried suffering under a relentless cruelty, but that is not the full story. Let us add to our existing picture of the Gulag some stories of a kind we have not heard before.[15]

One of the happier Japanese prisoners rolling home to Japan in August 1945 was a young man named Makoto, native of a very old district of Tokyo, Eddoko. Makoto was drafted at the age of twenty in 1945, then sent with no military training at all to the Kwantung Army in Manchuria. Smart, cheerful, quiet, Makoto got on well, though he was absolutely bewildered by the soldier's life. He was taken prisoner by the Russians along with about 640,000 others, and soon put in a locked car in a train their guards said was headed back to the Pacific and home. Makoto had the upper bunk of an ancient Tsarist prison car called a Stolypin car. There was a tiny window. He called out to the others what he could see as the train rumbled through the Russian forest. When they got to the edge of the ocean, they were permitted to run down to the water. Some tasted it, and found it was sweet, fresh water. Lake Baikal, thousands of kilometres from the sea. The Russians laughed and laughed.

Makoto was then shipped towards Karaganda far to the west, where he was put in a labour camp along with many Europeans. Makoto worked in the camp office, where he noticed that one of the Russian officers in charge of the camp's books was illiterate. Makoto taught himself Russian and soon took over the officer's duties for him. He was invited to the officer's home for dinner. The officer told him he was having marital troubles and asked for advice. Makoto obliged. He said that life in that Russian camp was better than in his district of Tokyo during the war.

Makoto's experience parallels that of a German soldier, Fred Pichler, who was kept in a remarkably open prison in Moscow after the war. Pichler, now of Grafton, Ontario, was walking along the street in Moscow one day in 1946 with his Soviet guard and other prisoners, en route to build houses. He was accosted by a young Russian woman who asked him to come into her house nearby. He asked permission of the guard, who smiled and said yes.

Pichler went in and the woman showed him a framed photograph standing on a table of himself in Russian uniform. Astounded, he asked how she had gotten it. She said that it was her husband, who looked exactly like him. She asked him if he would visit her and her two-year-old son who constantly asked when Daddy was coming home. Pichler was to pretend to be the boy's father. (They were by now speaking English to each other – she was an English teacher, and he had learned English in Germany before joining up.)

Fred Pichler did visit her many times, with permission, playing Daddy. This went on for over a year, until he was released. Pichler was eighteen years old, and very innocent, so there was

71

no question of sex. Since leaving the USSR, he has made repeated efforts to find the young mother, without success. He has said, 'I love those people,' meaning the Russians. 'I keep them close in my heart.'

The KGB generated millions of pages of detailed records of these people, from captivity to release or death. The documents are all still stored in a tall gloomy building in Moscow called the Central State Special Archive, or CSSA. So secret that it was fronted by a different building, and accessible only to a very few scholars and apparatchiks, the CSSA contained millions and millions of documents recording everything significant that went on in the prisoner of war Gulag. After the Soviets fell, and the CSSA archives were opened under the new democratic regime, I visited them in 1992. I was allowed to walk up and down the gloomy aisles and to take down at random any box I liked, to read its contents through my Canadian interpreter, to photocopy the documents, which I did, and to take them to Canada, where I now have scores of them.

I found gifts to Stalin from the prisoners who were hoping to get home sooner by fawning on their tormentor. There were silk banners with flattering poems to the great anti-fascist hero embroidered in red and gold, intricately carved boxes of mahogany, paintings, beautiful inlaid boxes, books of drawings, scrolls. On one shelf, it was rumoured, the Soviets preserved Hitler's teeth. And there were fantastically detailed records of the prisoners' fate.

A personal dossier was kept for each prisoner, recording his unit, name, serial number, date of capture, medical and legal history. One dossier included an X-ray of a broken bone mended in hospital in 1946. The dossier of an Austrian prisoner, the famous biologist Konrad Lorenz, is particularly thick, including descriptions of some of the scientific work he was able to carry out in camp. The dossiers average around twenty pages per prisoner. Some are over 200 pages long.

Here also lies the proof of certain crimes committed by the Western powers beginning with their co-operation with Stalin in 1941. These are Western crimes which are being covered up even now, by the governments of France, the UK, the US and probably Canada, with the help of some TV producers, some academics, archivists, editors and writers.

Since a clear understanding of the Western leaders' duplicity depends in part on the accuracy of certain documents in the Soviet archives, it is essential to compare their version of important events with what is known or believed in the West. Immediately, the reaction of most Westerners will be, 'How can one trust Soviet records, knowing that the Soviet system normally depended on mass deception?' This is a main reason that the Soviet archives are dependable. Virtually all the Soviet lying went on *outside* the archive. Soviet archives could safely record the truth because they were top secret, available only to the top members of the regime.

As General Dmitri Volkogonov has written, Lenin began the practice, enforced rigidly for seventy years, of storing most important documents recording Soviet actions and policies, no matter how brutal.[16] Thus the paradox foreshadowed by George Orwell became reality: what the people knew was not true, what was true was not known. This dizzying paradox was not unknown in the West at the time of Watergate, of the bombing of Cambodia, of the French atrocities in Indo-China and Africa, of the UK police actions in Northern Ireland, the arms sales to Iraq in the 1980s, of Canadian war crimes in Somalia, and so on.

Many of the statistics of the Gulag kept in the CSSA support both the picture of terrible suffering and of a strange but endurable prison-society whose major fault was captivity, much like the common picture of a Western jail.

What objective tests can we apply to the accuracy of these statistics? The most impressive evidence of the accuracy of the NKVD records is the story of the documents recording the

Katyn massacre. In April 1940, the Red Army slaughtered many thousand Polish officers taken prisoner during the Soviet attack on Poland in 1939. This massacre was of course hidden from the local population, and from other units of the army and the NKVD. Records of the slaughter were routinely made and sent to Moscow.

After the Germans invaded Russia, the surviving Poles became the allies of their captors. Released from prison to help form a Polish army to fight the Germans, the Polish General Anders met Stalin in Moscow. Unaware of the fate of the missing officers, Anders asked Stalin face to face to return them. Stalin dissimulated. Anders pressed the point, sending one of his staff officers all over the USSR to search for the missing men.[17] They found nothing definite, but vague, disquieting rumours. At first the Poles thought that some 3,000 had been massacred; later they suspected it was more, perhaps as many as 15,000.

After the Germans took the Katyn region and discovered some of the mass graves, they held an investigation that showed that the Soviets were guilty. When the Polish refugee government in London asked the International Red Cross to investigate, the Soviets broke diplomatic relations with them. After the Red Army retook Katyn, the Soviets held their own commission which found the Soviets innocent and the Germans guilty. But the German evidence of Soviet guilt was so compelling that both Churchill and Roosevelt covered it up as a matter of policy. Churchill told Roosevelt that the massacre had been committed by the Russians, and advised him to keep this secret. An American friend of President Roosevelt, Ambassador Earle, showed the President proof that the Soviets were guilty, but following Churchill's advice, the President forbade him to publish it.[18] *And Katyn was a massacre of Poles, who were allies of the West. It was to defend these people that Britain and France had gone to war against Hitler.*

At the Nuremberg war crimes trials in 1945–46, the Soviets

presented a case against the Germans so absurd, based on fum-
bling witnesses who muffed their rehearsed lines and a clumsy
forgery of evidence, that the Americans and British were able
to persuade them to withdraw it. For fifty years Soviets from the
lowest to the highest positions lied, deceived, dissimulated,
hypocritically accused others, offended friends, made new enemies, murdered those who told the truth and lost face while the
world argued over, and suspected, who had killed the prisoners
of Katyn. And for fifty years, the NKVD document ordering the
death penalty for the Katyn prisoners lay on the shelves of the
archives in Moscow, along with letters and memos ordering
the subsequent cover-up.[19]

In the same archive were other papers showing that
Molotov, Kaganovich and Stalin had ordered the execution of
38,679 army officers, poets, writers and apparatchiks in 1937
and 1938.[20] Surely, if the Soviets were ever going to falsify documents, it would have been those ones. And they remained,
intact, accurate, damning.

A war crime in which the British collaborated with the
Soviets was hidden by both powers in 1945 and for long after. In
fact, the British government and one officer, Lord Aldington,
are still denying responsibility. In 1945, the British delivered
thousands of prisoners of Russian nationality, including women
and children, into Soviet hands in the full knowledge that the
Soviets would shoot the leaders and enslave the rest. These
people were ethnic White Russians who had fought the Soviets
as allies of the British during the Russian Civil War. They fled
Russia before the Soviets could catch them at the end of the
war, so they had never been *Soviet* citizens.

Stalin had no legal rights to many of these people, and no
moral right to any of them. But the British delivered them
anyway, in scenes of dreadful suffering and protest so grotesque
that very soon the British soldiers were rebellious and their officers feared they would not be able to deliver any more prisoners.[21]

All this was revealed a few years ago in several books and a pamphlet by the renowned British author Count Nikolai Tolstoy, to the amazement and fury of high officials of the British government. They immediately closed ranks against the author, who says that they committed or procured perjury and illegally sequestered documents in order to help Lord Aldington succeed in a libel action against Tolstoy.

Tolstoy, along with a few others in the West, was relieved when many of the Soviet archives were at last opened by first Mikhail Gorbachev and then Boris Yeltsin. With the opening of the Soviet Red Army archives, important elements proving his case were revealed. Tolstoy flew to Moscow and found there documents 'of central importance' to his case, proving that 5 Corps command, of which Lord Aldington (formerly Brigadier Toby Low) was Chief of Staff, entered into a secret agreement with the Soviets to hand over thousands of White Russian émigrés from Western Europe who had sought refuge in Austria. This action violated orders received from the Allied High Command, which under the terms of the Yalta Agreement restricted forced repatriation to Soviet nationals. The victims included a large number of women and children, and the operation was carried out in violation of the Geneva Convention.[22]

Records recently revealed in the Soviet archives

The Soviets captured on their European front 3,486,206 prisoners from seventeen countries, according to the vast Soviet archive. The authoritative book on the subject, edited by G. F. Krivosheyev, shows that the Soviets captured 2,389,560 German soldiers between 22 June 1941 and 9 September 1945. Of these, 450,600 died. Of these, 356,687 died in rear camps run by the NKVD, and a further 93,900 died en route from the front to the rear camps.[23] A further 271,672 civilians were rounded up and termed *internyrovannye*, of whom 66,481 died.[24]

The Soviet records are extremely precise. For instance, the 356,687 German rear-camp dead are tallied separately from the deaths of ethnic Germans (from, for example, other European countries such as Poland and Czechoslovakia) and also from Austrians. In these latter categories 21,603 dead were entered.

The Russian Army military historian Andrei Kashirin also concluded that these figures from the CSSA archive were generally correct. In his opinion, the deaths totalled 423,168.[25]

The total deaths among the European prisoners between 1941 and 1952 is 518,480. Of those transported to the Soviet Union, all the names were recorded, with biographical data, date and place of capture, plus labour and medical records and death certificates for the dead. The Russians of today have nothing to hide.

It is now possible for the first time since 1945 to fit these records together with the German records to determine the number of German prisoners who died in Western camps. Beginning in 1948, German civil authorities in the American and British zones began to survey the country to determine how many prisoners were still in captivity or missing, not accounted for. The work went on for several years until October 1951, when the new West German government under Chancellor Konrad Adenauer deposited in the UN a nominal roll of over 1,100,000 names of soldiers still missing, presumed to be captive, according to the survey. In addition to the soldiers, another 300,000 paramilitary personnel and civilians had been taken. Most of the civilians had been seized by the Russians as substitutes for prisoners who had escaped during transport. The survey was about 94 per cent complete in the three Western zones, but only about 30 per cent complete in the Soviet zone.* In effect it was saying that over 1.1 million German soldiers died in captivity, plus the missing 300,000 paramilitaries and civilians. No one before 1989 could account for more than 24,000 of these. *Close to one and a half million Germans are still officially missing in 1997.*

Subtracting the proven Soviet deaths of Germans from the West German survey of the missing, we see that somewhere between 750,000 and 1,000,000 must have died in other camps, Polish, Yugoslavian, American and French. By far the greater number were held in and died in American and French camps. Approximately 600,000 to 900,000 died in American and French captivity. Many other Axis prisoners died in Western camps.

Thus the Soviet figures completely support figures published in *Other Losses* in 1989, *before* the Soviet archives were opened to the West. The research in the West has proven, *independently of the Soviet figures*, the death total in the West. It is also true that the figures published in *Other Losses* in 1989 predicted what would be found in the Soviet archives if they should ever be opened. The prediction has proven true.

Both sides in the Cold War proved equally cynical in their lies about the prisoners. At first they simply covered up their own atrocities, but then they began to use the dead prisoners as medieval armies had once hurled corpses into besieged cities to spread plague. A typical exchange occurred during the first few years of the Cold War. Following American and British charges that the Soviets had abused their Japanese prisoners, the Soviets replied with accusations that the British and Americans had abused theirs. The Soviets upped the ante by throwing in charges against the Australians as well.[26]

---

*'Complete' means 100 per cent of the households in the area were surveyed. For more detail see Appendix 7.

The UK representative in the UN's Third Committee, dealing with prisoners of war, 'charged that the USSR had not only violated specific agreements but had also infringed on the general principle to which it had subscribed by signing the Geneva Convention . . .' Using very incorrect figures, the UK representative ended by saying that the Soviets still had almost two million German prisoners of war. (At that point, according to the NKVD records in the CSSA, the Soviets had well under one million.) A 'voluntary registration carried out by the Government of the Federal Republic of Germany ending in March 1950' showed that 1,154,029 West Germans were still missing from their homes. A further 8,972 had similarly been listed by a registration of the people of the Soviet Zone of Occupation. 'The last news of some 923,000 of that figure had come from the USSR or areas occupied by Soviet troops.'[27] Thus the British lodged in the public mind the conviction that the nefarious Soviets were responsible for deaths that had actually occurred in the camps of Britain's friends, France and America.

Among the signal facts left out by the UK representative was that far more than 1,154,029 prisoners were missing from their homes, because the German survey was incomplete. As the disproportionately low return from East Germany shows, the West German survey covered mainly West Germans missing, not those from other areas, such as the lost German territories to the east, Romania, Italy and other important German allies.[28]

Far worse was the omission of the central fact that the so-called 'last news' from the 'missing' Wehrmacht soldiers was mainly an anti-Soviet fiction generated by the Allies themselves. This is clear from the statements of one of the senior German researchers, Dr Margarethe Bitter, who said of the survey done by the *Ausschuß für Kriegsgefangenenfragen* that the estimates of the location of soldiers who had gone missing were 'more or less theoretical calculations'.[29] This same flaw was reported clearly in the book *Gesucht Wird* by Kurt W. Boehme, showing that over 62 per cent of the last postal addresses of missing Germans had been recorded in 1944, or even as long ago as 1943.[30] Given the panicky flight of Germans to the West at the very end of the war, which is apparent in the total capture figures of the Allies, these 'last addresses' are worthless. The Western Allies took in a total of about 8,000,000 German soldiers and civilians compared with about 2,600,000 Germans captured by the Soviets. Thus the Western Allies had taken around 73 per cent of the total prisoner catch, of whom they had so far recorded only around 24,000 dead. They were accusing the Soviets of 99 per cent of the purported deaths (or 'missing').

The defenders of Eisenhower and De Gaulle allege that the Adenauer government report showed that most of the missing prisoners were last seen on the Eastern Front and died in Soviet camps. This lie is being repeated even in the 1990s. For instance, the German historian Major Rüdiger Overmans said on page 159 of *Eisenhower and the German Prisoners of War* that, 'Three-quarters of the disappeared were registered in the USSR or eastern or south-eastern Europe.'

I interviewed Dr Margarethe Bitter of Munich, who founded the committee that began the work which culminated in the Adenauer government's report.[31] She told me that it was not true that the committee determined the location of the missing prisoners. She said, 'We did not know where the missing prisoners were.' Dr Bitter said this twice, once on the phone in French and then in person voluntarily into a tape-recorder in her apartment in Munich, in English and in front of a witness, in June 1991.[32] Furthermore, in concentrating as they did only on missing Germans, the Western apologists were ignoring millions of prisoners from Hungary, Italy, Austria, Romania and ten other European countries who fought alongside the Germans. Of these, hundreds of thousands never returned home.

Now that the KGB archives openly refute the lies of Western propagandists, Allied apologists cast doubt on the KGB's accuracy. They say that the Red Army did not record their captures at the front, but only in the rear camps. This they believe shows that the missing German prisoners, who they maintain went missing on the Eastern Front, were never acknowledged as captives by the Soviets. They say that nearly all of them escaped or died en route from the front to the rear camps.[33] As we have seen, this has been totally disproven by the historian G. F. Krivosheyev in his book *Without the Seal of Secrecy*, but once again, Western apologists prefer their 'estimates' to the hard evidence.

These same apologists also say that the Americans captured fewer prisoners than appear in American records. The effect of this is that the fewer the Americans took, the fewer could have died. Major Overmans, writing for the American professor Stephen E. Ambrose, who adores Eisenhower, claimed that the Americans took only 3.8 million German prisoners,[34] whereas in fact the Americans in north-west Europe alone took 5,224,310 prisoners of all nationalities, according to SHAEF documents which have already been published. The Americans also took hundreds of thousands more prisoners in North Africa and Italy. Of the total – approximately six million – about 85 per cent were German, making a German total of more than five million. In fact, one senior US Army historian has written that the holdings of Germans in US camps in the summer of 1945 was 7,005,732.[35]

The effect of understating the prisoner catch of course is to minimize the deaths for which the army could be held responsible.[36] Also, by limiting their defence of the army only to German prisoners, the defenders of Eisenhower and De Gaulle conveniently set aside the hundreds of thousands of Italians, Romanians, Hungarians and so on who also were held in lethal conditions for a long time. Many among these died as well.

Major Overmans, because of his high position in the historical service of the Bundeswehr, is an official spokesman for the German government on this subject, but it is clear that his undocumented assertions about American captures are contradicted by the prime source in American army documents.

It is equally clear from Soviet records that the Soviets, for an important part of the war, took into their rear (MVD) camps *more* prisoners than the Germans thought they had lost. This discovery destroys one of the prime sources used by Western propagandists during the Cold War, the series of books on war prisoners edited by Erich Maschke and published under the control of the German government as the final official statistical summary.[37]

Maschke says that the Soviets still held alive 559,142 Germans at the end of 1944. He further estimated that by the end of April 1945, some 549,000 had died among all the prisoners caught to date. Adding the two together, we see that according to Maschke it is not possible that the Germans captured by the end of 1944 exceeded 1,108,000, whereas the Soviets actually recorded 1,248,000 Germans captured.[38] And of course, not all the 549,000 who eventually died, according to Maschke, had died by the end of 1944. For our purposes, to illustrate the impossibility of Maschke's estimates, we will take an estimate of 300,000 dead for the end of 1944. On this basis, the true comparison for the end of 1944 should be about 859,000 Germans captured, according to Maschke, as against 1,248,000 actually taken according to the Soviets.

Much more important for history is to compare the figures for missing shown in the OKW war diary with the Soviet actual capture figures. The OKW recorded on 31 January 1945 that the missing on the Eastern front totalled 1,018,365, whereas we have seen that the Soviets recorded 1,248,000 captured a whole month previously.[39] Clearly, the Soviet figures are more dependable than even the OKW war diaries. For other periods of the war in the east, the results are similar. The Soviets consistently reported more prisoners taken than the OKW reported to be missing. In Soviet hands, there were no unreported prisoners, so there could have been no deaths of unreported prisoners.[40]

On the Western Front, the picture is far different. The Americans themselves, from Major General Milton A. Reckord to Colonel Philip Lauben, say that they failed to account for many scores of thousands of German prisoners both in transit and *even while they were held in fixed camps*. In one train transfer, over 20 per cent of the Germans were missing. In one takeover of camps by the French from the Americans, according to Lauben, it was possible that as many as 105,000 prisoners were missing out of 275,000 previously reported by the same Americans.[41]

The general truth of the Soviet capture records is confirmed in detail by the experience of Panzer commander Colonel Hans von Luck, a colleague and friend of Stephen E. Ambrose. Von Luck was captured by the Soviets in the winter of 1944–45, ordered by the Soviets to assume responsibility for disciplining his men and marched with them to the rear camp near Dresden. En route, some Germans escaped, but as Von Luck wrote, 'The guards threatened to shoot me if further prisoners were to escape. But what was worse, they fetched civilians at random from the nearby villages to make up the number . . . I did not know unfortunately that the number of prisoners to be delivered had been precisely determined . . .'[42]

The Red Army practice was to telephone the numbers from the army camp to the NKVD rear camp ahead of time, which Von Luck did not know. Captain Harry G. Braun of the German navy also observed the same practice. Braun was captured by the Soviets near Stettin in the summer of 1945. He escaped through the bush, afraid that the Soviet guards would 'come back with a search party, maybe even with bloodhounds. It wasn't until much later that we found out we had no cause to worry. It was common practice for the Russians to simply go to the next village, grab the first two warm bodies they came across and then arrive at their destination with the correct number of prisoners.'[43] This practice of the Soviets was also confirmed by Captain Galitski during a historical conference in May 1996, at Massey College in Toronto. That the Soviets lost hundreds of thousands of prisoners to death between capture and first documentation, thus accounting for most of the missing prisoners, is clearly a fantasy. Yet it is advanced to this day by historians of nominal repute who, when asked, admit they have no documentary sources whatsoever.[44]

Another proof of the KGB accuracy is the record of the fate of the German civilians who were taken away as reparations slaves to the Gulag in 1945. During the Cold War, the German government found itself unable to believe the reports of the Soviet government on the subject, so they laboriously surveyed the families and published the results of the civilian study in a massive book entitled *The Expulsion of the German Population from the Territories East of the Oder–Neisse Line*.[45] They concluded that the Soviets had deported some 218,000 civilians to the Gulag as slaves. Deaths were suspected by the Germans to be about 20,000. However, as we saw above, when the NKVD/MVD/KGB archives on prisoners of war were opened recently, the Soviet documents showed that 271,672 people in this category had been deported, of whom a huge number, 66,481, had died.[46] Here was another Soviet atrocity suspected in the West, and confirmed in the Soviet archives. The great significance of this is that we now know that the Germans and Soviets agree that the Soviet records are authentic *on the subject of German prisoners*.

The Red Cross and the names

The Russian Red Cross has over the last twenty years responded to 500,000 requests from German families inquiring about the fate of their men, who they supposed had been taken to the Soviet Union. Using the KGB records, the Russians were able to trace 50,000 prisoners and report their fate. The Japanese have been given similar data for 62,000 of their prisoners. German researchers have been at work in the CSSA archive since 1991, transcribing data for millions of prisoners from the original Russian into German.[47] No such information is available in American, French, Canadian, Swiss or British archives.

Documents about the fate of some 640,000 Japanese prisoners taken by the Red Army in Manchuria in August 1945 have a significant relation to the fate of the German prisoners in the hands of the Western powers, because they provide another chance to determine the general accuracy of KGB prisoner records.

In at least thirty-five central camps already identified, Japanese prisoners were kept alongside German and other European prisoners. It is highly significant that the death rate reported by the KGB among the Japanese and German prisoners from 1945 onwards was almost exactly the same. For the Japanese the rate was about 9.6 per cent (full term) and for the Germans 9.4 per cent. As we shall see below, the death rate among the Japanese was reported correctly by the KGB, *according to the Japanese themselves*. This provides even more evidence of the accuracy of the KGB figures for deaths among Germans after 1945.

Because the Japanese were kept by the same MVD camp system under the same conditions and in many of the same camps as the German and other European prisoners after August 1945, the fate of the Japanese must be very similar to that of the Germans and other Europeans after August 1945. The fate of the Japanese prisoners has been determined by the Japanese themselves, which enables us to give a definite answer to the question, is that fate accurately described in the Soviet documents?

Beginning about two years after the war, Japanese families began asking when their missing men were coming home. The US military government of Japan, the US State department, and the Japanese, British and Australian governments berated the Soviets for enslaving a million or more Japanese prisoners of war during 1945–50. They accused the Soviets of hiding the fate of these prisoners because they were slaves, or else slave-soldiers impressed into the Red Army to wage war against the democracies. The Japanese and Americans said at various times that some 300,000 to 500,000 prisoners were 'missing' or 'not accounted for', in Soviet camps. They hinted strongly that most were dead. The Soviets angrily denied this, saying that only 10,627 had died.[48] They then fired back the charge that around 100,000 Japanese POWs had died in American, British and Australian camps. The Japanese produced for the UN a list of 253,000 'known dead', whereupon Jakob Malik, the Soviet Ambassador to the UN, denounced the Japanese. Huge rallies gathered in Tokyo, and General Douglas MacArthur, the American commander, said that the missing prisoners were 'the most serious concern' he had ever had in his years of rule in Japan.[49]

Just as they had lied to the public about Katyn for many years, the Soviets kept their records secret while they lied about the deaths of Japanese in their camps. For instance, having said in 1950 that some 3,800 Japanese prisoners died, a few years later they amended this to the much higher figure of 30,000.

However, by careful interrogation of returning Japanese prisoners over many years, the Japanese themselves gradually determined by 1960 that of the 640,000 soldiers in the Kwantung army taken prisoner, some 62,000 had died.[50] The

British, Americans and Australians meanwhile contended in the UN and other places that millions had been taken and many hundreds of thousands had died.

After *glasnost*, Russians working in the Soviet archives found the death certificates and personal dossiers for the prisoners. The deaths recorded there numbered about 62,000. Mikhail Gorbachev in April 1991 and Boris Yeltsin in 1994 each gave the figure of 62,000 to the Japanese government with an apology, and Yeltsin provided a list of the names of those who died. The list and explanation were accepted with thanks by the Japanese.[51]

As the propaganda missiles roared round the world for forty years, these separate records lay undisturbed in the archives in Moscow, Tokyo and probably Washington. And the amazing thing was, these records agreed that 62,000 had died.

And for forty years, no one said so.

In sum, then, these tremendous Soviet archives report in great detail the fates of three ranks of prisoner from twenty-five countries through fifteen years. They are by far the most valuable, precise and comprehensive documents ever discovered in any archive in the world about the fate of prisoners of the Second World War. We know they are reliable because they fit all other known evidence, explain Western historical lacunae, are supported by millions of subsidiary documents, and are confirmed by German, Polish and Japanese reports. Most important, they were kept secret for over forty years because the Soviet leaders feared them. And this was because they believed them. They recorded a huge atrocity committed against many nations.[52]

In contrast, in the West, it is admitted by archivists and historians that the Western archives have been weeded of revealing material.[53] There are no personal dossiers for any prisoners anywhere in the West. The British government withheld documents such as the Phillimore Report from this author when he was researching the Germans in British camps.[54] The Canadian archives contain complaints by the former Empress Zita of Austria that the Canadian troops were behaving like Nazis towards Austrian prisoners in the camp at Aurich. But there are no records of any investigation, just a routine high-level denial that is contradicted by an unpublished Canadian army report. This frankly records 'indescribable filth' in the latrines, complete lack of utensils in the kitchens, 'extremely cold' conditions, and 'poor health' among the prisoners, most of whom had been taken from hospital.[55] As we have already seen, the International Red Cross has several times refused this author access to their Second World War files while admitting three other writers. Following reports in 1991 of atrocities in French camps in 1946, the death records in the archive of the town of Labouheyre were closed to historians. They had previously been open for fifty years. These are only a few of the many examples of how a vast international falsification has been maintained for fifty years. Sometimes the Allies have lied in co-operation with the Soviets, sometimes they have lied to foment hatred of them, sometimes they have lied to cover up their own crimes. They are still at it.

Since there is no doubt of the veracity of the Soviet records, and no doubt as to the veracity of the German reports of the missing, we are led inevitably to conclude that the 1.4/1.7 million known missing German soldiers did not die in the Soviet camps as previously alleged. When the 450,000 German deaths in Soviet hands are subtracted from the overall total of 1.4/1.7 million missing prisoners,[56] we see that the deaths not in the Soviet camps must have been at least one million.

The Cold War is over, the Russians are telling the truth, but in the West, the lying continues. In the last few years, dozens of articles, hours of TV film and two books have been published which perpetuate this cover-up. This is undoubtedly the longest running big lie in the history of the Western democracies.

AND THE CHURCHES FLEW BLACK FLAGS

'The Morgenthau Plan was conceived in sin, died at birth and lived to a ripe old age.'

ANONYMOUS

Two contradictory Allied policies began to operate simultaneously in Germany in the spring of 1945. The dominant policy was vengeance through imposed starvation; the subsidiary policy was relief through imports of food to ward off threats to the occupying armies. The victorious Allies began to punish the Germans for their crimes as soon as the Germans had surrendered. Among the many fantastic crimes of Germany – against Jews, socialists, Christians, Polish intelligentsia, homosexuals – one of the worst was their treatment of the Dutch, whose country they had cruelly invaded in 1940.

One of the reasons for the Dutch famine has never been fully told in the West, perhaps because it is discreditable to Winston Churchill. He imposed a blockade in this war as he had tried to do in 1917, because he believed that the relief proposed by Hoover for the Belgians or Dutch would materially help the Germans. But Churchill was ignoring Hoover's arrangements to protect the food from possible German depredations. The food would be sent by the ICRC in its own ship, guarded through the journey to Belgium by neutral observers. It would be cooked and eaten by the children in the presence of supervisors. And finally, Hoover's master touch: the Germans agreed to match pound for pound everything that Hoover could round up for the starving. Not only would there be no gain to the Germans, there would be a very slight loss. That the Germans were perfectly sincere in this is now certain because of the recent discovery of a secret German diplomatic telegram signed Albrecht in Berlin to the German Embassy in Moscow in February 1941, routinely informing them that the Hoover plan for aid 'against starvation for Belgium has been thoroughly examined by the German government and . . . agreed'. It continues: '. . . it was assured that neither the food envisaged in the plan coming from abroad nor food taken in a similar way from Belgium would be requisitioned for the purposes of the occupying power [Germany] in Belgium.' The telegram referred with apparent pride to the 'already successful deliveries of considerable quantities of potatoes and cereal grains from Germany, which under conditions of war constitute all the greater concession since Belgium, in peacetime drew [much of] its food supplies from overseas'.[1]

All this was jettisoned by the British, who thereby inflicted no harm at all on the German war effort. The people who suffered most were the children in Belgium and Holland.

The situation changed towards the end of the war, as the Germans lost territory in the east. The Dutch grew short of food because the Germans were taking so much away to feed their soldiers and workers. By the end of the war in the spring of 1945, the plight of the Dutch was so serious that the Allies threatened the Germans with war crimes charges if they did not permit Allied airlifts to cross their lines. This the Germans did, at the order of their Nazi civilian commander, Arthur Seyss-Inquart.[2]

Nevertheless, Seyss-Inquart was hanged at Nuremberg, for earlier crimes against the Dutch. No secret was ever made of this trial or execution; on the contrary, the record of the

Nuremberg trials was published in dozens of books in several languages. The German crimes have been recorded in every possible way as a warning against similar crimes. Only Hoover has recorded that the mercy that the Allies had made possible in the First World War was deliberately denied in the Second. Conventional history has spared Roosevelt and Churchill all account of this sad episode.

Even as the gallows at Nuremberg displayed their awful warning, the Allies were depriving men, women and children in Germany of available food. Foreign relief agencies were prevented from sending food from abroad; Red Cross food trains were sent back to Switzerland; all foreign governments were denied permission to send food to German civilians; fertilizer production was sharply reduced; and food was confiscated during the first year, especially in the French zone. The fishing fleet was kept in port while people starved. British soldiers actually blew up one fishing boat in front of the eyes of astonished Germans. 'The people say the sea is full of fish, but they want to starve us,' said Burgomaster Petersen.[3] For several years after the Allied conquest, the Germans subsisted on less food than the Dutch in the hungriest time.

The judgement against Seyss-Inquart was, in sum, that he had deprived the Dutch of food in order to further the German war effort. Yet Churchill and many other Allied leaders also deprived the Dutch of food, in order to further the Allied war effort.[4] Hoover wrote that his wartime efforts 'became a crusade on my part against a senseless stone wall of opposition from Churchill and Roosevelt . . . But we did keep some moral and spiritual lamps alight among our own people during the eclipse of human decency and compassion which swept over the world.'

Hoover went on: 'There were no insurmountable difficulties in carrying out such relief [to Holland] except the attitudes of the British and American governments. There was ample food surplus in countries overseas from Europe.

Shipping was available without diminishing the transportation of the Allies.'[5]

The measure of Churchill's cynicism is that in fact the British and Canadians both broke the ban for sentimental or political purposes. They sent food of course to their own men in German prison camps, and also to Greece. The Canadians justified sending food to the Greeks by saying that the help to the Germans (by reducing Greece's food demands) was minimal, and at that time (1944–45) the food was an important political weapon. It was sent to help lure wavering Greeks to the British side during the incipient struggle for power between left and right. To put it more clearly, it was part of Churchill's plan to extend and protect the Empire by dominating the Mediterranean sea. Mackenzie King was deeply opposed to that, but he gave in to Churchill.

The destruction caused by war had been amplified by the scorched-earth policy of the Nazis in the last days of Hitler's Reich, leaving huge disruptions which the occupying armies tried to correct. A distinguished American member of Hoover's Presidential Mission in 1947 observed, 'That within hours or days a minimum of civil order was restored out of the complete chaos and life kept going amidst the ruins; for this the German people owe the Western victors a debt of gratitude which has rarely been recognized in the distress and disappointment of the following months and years.'[6] That the policy had been implemented entirely for the convenience of the occupying armies soon became evident to all Germans.

'From 1945 to the middle of 1948 one saw the probable collapse, disintegration and destruction of a whole nation.' These are not the words of a revisionist historian of the 1990s, but of an American naval officer who watched German society collapsing under Allied punishment in the Western zone. His papers have very recently been opened to the public at the Hoover Institution in Stanford. He is Captain Albert R. Behnke, USN MC, a medical doctor, who compared the German civilians under the Allies with the conditions in 'heroic Holland' under the Germans, and concluded that 'Germany was subjected to physical and psychic trauma unparalleled in history'. The Germans under the Allies fared much worse than the Dutch under the Germans, and for far longer. 'In the age group 20 to 39, for example, the average [German's] body weight in January 1946 was 137.1 lbs . . . and in December of 1947 it was 132.1 lbs. The average normal weight for men of this group (stature 68 inches) is 154 pounds.' Normal adult German consumers were rationed to 1,550 calories per day (cpd), often receiving far less, whereas in Holland in 1943 they got 1,775 cpd. In 1944, the average Dutch ration was 1,397 and in 1945 it was 1,556. In Germany, for years at a time, the average official calorie ration under the British and Americans was 1,550 per day – often not issued – and under the French, for long periods, 1,400, and sometimes as little as 450.[7] The situation in the British zone was so bad in early 1946 that it drew an angry warning from the wartime hero, Field Marshal Bernard Montgomery, commanding the British occupation in Germany. Montgomery sent a cable to the British Foreign Office demanding immediate and substantial increases in imports, with the warning that 'If we do not we shall produce death and misery to an extent which will disgrace our administration in history and completely stultify every effort which we are making to produce a democratic Germany.'[8] In the British zone for six months in the winter/spring of 1946-47, the ration was around 1,000 cpd.

For long periods in the American zone, the ration was officially 1,275 calories per day. But it was well known that even the official ration was not enough to support health. Herbert Hoover told the President of the United States that 'the 1,550 ration is wholly incapable of supporting health'.[9] One of the

American Mennonites who were trying to feed people in Germany commented in March 1946 that, 'Only if we can be an instrument of bringing food to these at our doorstep can we atone for the sin of which we personally are a part.'[10]

In the east of Germany in 1945, the people starved because the Russians confiscated so much food and virtually all the factories. The French took a terrible toll in their zone, by forced seizure of food and housing, and by physical violence including mass rapes, in Stuttgart and elsewhere. The famine went on for years. The churches flew black flags. The children were too weak to play. The official ration in the French zone in January 1947 was 450 calories per day, half the ration of the Belsen concentration camp, according to the writer and theologian Prince zu Löwenstein.[11]

The Allies had studied German food production during the war, so they knew what to expect when they arrived. They knew for instance that to strip off the rich farmlands of the east to give them to the Poles and Russians deprived Germany of over 25 per cent of her arable land – this while most of the male labour force was imprisoned, and the many other measures we have already seen were imposed in order to reduce German food supplies. Every hope of survival was reduced to the vanishing point for millions of people. There was scant hope from the beginning of the occupation that most of the Germans could survive for long under Allied policies.[12]

It is possible that one of the reasons that prompted Eisenhower's order banning civilian supply of the camps was the threat of a food shortage. Eisenhower was concerned to control very strictly the distribution of food, according to many historians. However, many prisoners and German civilians saw the American guards burn the food brought by civilian women. One former prisoner described it recently: 'At first, the women from the nearby town brought food into the camp. The American soldiers took everything away from the women, threw it in a heap and poured gasoline [benzine] over it and burned it.'[13] Eisenhower himself ordered that the food be destroyed, according to the writer Karl Vogel, who was the German camp commander appointed by the Americans in Camp 8 at Garmisch-Partenkirchen. Although the prisoners were getting only 800 calories per day, the Americans were destroying food outside the camp gate.

To conserve food could scarcely have been the reason for the order threatening death for civilians wishing to feed prisoners, because the Allies' predominant policy in Germany for many months was actually to reduce supplies of food destined for German civilians, as well as prisoners. The rations were to be held at the lowest possible level to 'prevent starvation',[14] or to 'prevent disease and unrest'.

Reparations also reduced the shrunken German food supply. The Allies decided to take huge reparations, amounting to at least twenty billion dollars. All used German prisoners as slave labour, thus subtracting them from the labour force needed to bring in the reduced harvest. The Western Allies had more than three million prisoners in their camps in January 1946, purportedly working for them. Beyond that, about 650,000 Germans had already starved to death in the Western Allied camps. Hundreds of thousands had died in the Soviet camps, and another million were enslaved there. German prisoners who had worked as farm labourers in the UK and France have reported their horror at arriving home in 1947 and 1948 to find their families starving.[15] Unable to feed themselves adequately from home production, the Germans were trying desperately to increase production for export, but they were seriously hampered by the Allied reparations policy. Even as late as 1949, the pace of dismantling was still rising. In that year, 268 factories were removed, in whole or in part. In the

French zone, ten factories were dismantled in 1946, nine in 1947, forty in 1948 and fifty-one in 1949, of which thirteen were shipped whole to France. In the previous three years, nine dismantled factories had been sent to France.[16]

The Poles, Czechs, Russians and others were driving about 14/15 million eastern civilians (expellees) into the occupied remainder of the country.[17] By common Allied policy, no Germans were permitted to emigrate until late 1949, so the catastrophe was intensified, with no end in sight.[18]

One of the most harmful deprivations under the Morgenthau Plan was the drastic reduction of German fertilizer production, some of it on the grounds that nitrogen fertilizer can be diverted to production of ammunition, some because they were by-products of steel and coal production, themselves severely reduced.[19] As we have seen, production of manufactured goods as well as of food, fell drastically, partly as a result of this policy.[20] The total application of the three principal fertilizers dropped from 2,113,000 tons in 1938–39 to 782,000 tons in 1945–46, but the drop in effectiveness was greater than the loss of tonnage, because the effectiveness of the combination of the three fertilizers is largely controlled by the amount of nitrogen. And this drop was catastrophic, 82 per cent, from 563,000 tons to 105,000.[21]

The British and Americans, fearing 'disease and unrest' that might imperil their armies, were forced to import large quantities of food to maintain civil order. The military authorities thought that if they did not do this, the communists would exploit the situation to begin a revolution.

The British especially felt the load, because their zone received more refugees than any other. Also, some of the grain they were getting cheap or free from Canada for domestic use had to be diverted to Germany, so their own ration was threatened.

But not nearly enough was sent to Germany. So it happened that the Allies forced the Germans into starvation, and then in fear of public reaction at home and of communist 'exploitation' in Germany, fed them inadequately while complaining about the cost. They then praised themselves for their generosity.

The famine that began in 1945 spread over all of occupied Germany and continued into 1948. This was camouflaged as much as possible by the various armies and governments. American senators, churchmen and writers, British parliamentarians and church leaders protested, at first to no effect, but later with great success. The soldiers and politicians gradually saw the sense of helping the Germans, who could then help to rebuild Europe. And if West Germany did not starve, it would cease to be a hindrance to the West.

Mixed in with this new attitude, like the salt in the porridge, were the teachings that lie at the heart of Western democracy. The ideas that it is best to forgive your enemy, love your enemy, and do good to those who have hurt you, slowly blended into a new policy which predominated in Allied council chambers and in the ruins of Germany by 1950.

The expulsions

The fate of post-war Germany was largely settled at the Potsdam conference in July–August 1945 by the three principal Allies, the USSR, the USA and Great Britain. They were determined to eliminate the German problem once and for all. One solution was to weaken Germany by annexing her territory. British Foreign Secretary Anthony Eden and Franklin Roosevelt had agreed years before Potsdam that Poland could have East Prussia.[22] But this would mean that a discontented German minority would be left behind, like the Sudeten Germans in Czechoslovakia. Or else that the Allies would have

Okresní správní komise v Kraslicích.

Upozornění.

Byly, opuštěné osobami odcházejícími do sběrného střediska, musí býti zanechány v pořádku a čistotě.

Na jednu osobu přípustno zavazadlo do váhy 60 kg a ruční zavazadlo nejvýše do 10 kg.

Ostatní věci buďtež zanechány na místě v bytě jako záclony, koberce, stolní lampy, nástěnná zrcadla, mycí mísy, součástky nábytku, na stole ubrusy, potom 2 ručníky, v postelích slamníky, prostěradla a alespoň po jednom polštáři a přikrývce, vše čistě povlečené.

Zavazadlo nesmí být baleno do koberců a povlaků.

Bude-li prohlídkou zjištěno, že nebylo dbáno tohoto upozornění, nebude dotyčná osoba přijata do odsunu, nýbrž poslána do vnitrozemí na práci.

Übersetzung.

Personen, welche für den Abtransport bestimmt sind, haben ihre Wohnung in vollster Ordnung zu verlassen.

Gepäck wird für eine Person zugelassen: 1 Gepäckstück von 60 kg und Handgepäck von höchstens 10 kg.

Die übrigen Sachen sind in der Wohnung an Ort und Stelle zu lassen z.B. Vorhänge, Teppiche, Tischlampen, Wandspiegel, Waschschüsseln, Teile der Einrichtung, Tischdecken, 2 Handtücher, in Betten Matratzen, Bettlaken und mindestens je ein Kopfkissen und Zudeckbet alles frisch bezogen.

Das Gepäck darf nicht in Teppiche oder Ueberzüge gepackt werden

Wird bei der Kontrolle festgestellt, dass dies nicht beachtet wurde wird die betreffende Person nicht in den Transport aufgenommen, sonder ins Inland auf Arbeit geschickt.

Okresní správní komise, Kraslice

196-46 Braun, Kraslice.

District Administrative Commission of Grazlitz [Kraslice]

Notice

People selected for transport must leave their homes in complete order.

One piece of luggage weighing 60 kilograms and hand baggage of a maximum of 10 kilograms will be allowed per person.

The remaining effects must be left where they are in the home, e.g. curtains, carpets, table lamps, wall mirrors, wash basins, pieces of furniture, table cloths, 2 towels, and on the beds, mattresses, bed linen and at least one pillow and bedcover, all freshly made up.

Luggage must not be wrapped in carpets or coverlets.

If, on inspection, it is observed that these instructions have not been obeyed, the person concerned will not be taken on the transport but sent to the interior to work.

to abandon one major war aim – self-determination for all peoples. Roosevelt abandoned the principle in a letter to the President of the Polish Government in Exile in November 1944: 'If the Polish government and people desire in connection with the new frontiers of the Polish state to bring about the transfer to and from the territory of Poland of national minorities, the United States Government will raise no objections and so far as is practicable will facilitate such transfer.'[23]

Stalin was determined to retain the eastern section of Poland, which he had seized under his secret agreement with Hitler in 1939. When the British and Americans ratified this seizure at Potsdam, they were thus carrying out one of Hitler's foreign policy aims. The nominal difference this time was that Poland would be compensated for this loss: she got part of East Prussia, East Brandenburg and Silesia. But in fact, the whole country was turned into a province of the Soviet empire, and remained that way for half a century.

So far as most Germans were concerned, Potsdam was a word meaning mainly brutal expulsions of fourteen million or so people from the eastern section of Germany, and the loss of 25 per cent of the country, including much of its best farmland. They were told that the expulsions would be carried out in an 'orderly and humane manner', in the soothing words of the victor.

What 'orderly and humane' meant was visible to the Canadian army officer and writer Robert Greer when he visited Berlin in late 1945:

> There's something I must tell you about before I go to have dinner. It's the worst of all. In driving about [Berlin] on Sunday morning, we came to the Stettiner Bahnhof. It's a complete wreck of course, the great arched glassway broken and twisted. I went down to the ground level and looked. There were people. Sitting on bundles of clothes, crouched by handcarts and little wagons were people . . . they were all

exhausted and starved and miserable. You'd see a child sitting on a roll of blankets, a girl of perhaps four or five, and her eyes would be only half open and her head would loll occasionally and her eyes blink slowly as though she were only half alive. Beside her, her mother apparently, a woman with her head on her outstretched arm in the most terrible picture of despair and exhaustion and collapse I've seen. You could see in the line of her body all the misery that was possible for her to feel . . . no home, no husband, no food, no place to go, no one to care, nothing nothing absolutely nothing but a piece of the floor of the Stettiner Bahnhof and a night of weary hunger. In another place, another woman, sitting with her head in her hands . . . my God, how often have I sat like that with my stomach sick within me and felt miserable and helpless and uncaring . . . yet always I had someone to help, or a bed to rest on and a meal to eat and a place to go. For her there was nothing. Even when you see it it's impossible to believe. What can you do when you have nothing? Where can you go, what can you do, when you have no strength left and hunger is a sickness in your belly? God it was terrible.

Greer saw no men, only women and children. One of the boys was so thin 'you could see the cords of his legs quite clearly. The rest of the skin was tight about the bones. His face was expressionless, his mouth hung open, he was bent with a large bundle, he just tramped along behind the woman and followed where she led with no real consciousness at all. Terrible, wasted half-dead people. Alf took the boy out to the car and gave him bread and cocoa and some stuff we had, and he took it with still no expression. He was so hungry that even the sight of food didn't arouse him. As he left one of the Germans in the crowd handed him a 20-mark note . . . incredible encouraging touch. But the rest . . . I wanted to run from it all.

'That's some of it. The rest is like that . . . all mixed up, all different, yet all with the same terrible helpless almost hopeless sense of destruction about it. British officers in the mess . . . eating meat and cucumbers and lettuce and fried potato admitting that they expected thousands to die this winter.'[24] And these were the lucky ones.

The people Greer described had survived the expulsions in their eastern homelands, where everything was even worse. Some of it was described by the curate of the parish of Klosterbrück in Silesia, who observed in the summer of 1945 that, 'In every town and village in Silesia, the Poles have affixed placards bearing the words, "The harvest is like the seed."'[25] The atrocities of the Nazis would now be avenged by Polish atrocities.

In one Sudetenland village, all the German women were seized, and their Achilles tendons were cut. As they lay on the ground screaming, the Czech men raped them. Some of them were raped many times in a day, day after day. Frau X's eighteen-year-old daughter was raped about fifteen times every day for weeks. This was what the Czechs, Poles and Russians did in 1945.

Hermine Mückusch, grandmother, of Jägerndorf in the Sudetenland of Czechoslovakia, saw scenes like this almost every day in June and July of 1945 as she was herded west on foot with a few belongings. Behind her lay her whole life, all her possessions, her history, her friends, her relatives. She, her daughter and two grandchildren were allowed to take almost nothing. 'It was a terrible sight which our transport now presented. The young mothers with their children sat on the side of the road, dirty and mainly without shoes, thirsty and emaciated. The older children, red in their faces from fever and heat, lay in the grass, asking for something to drink, which we were unable to give them as the Czechs had made no arrangements whatsoever to look after these transports. It seemed that they had deliberately omitted to supply food or drink so that people should perish.' Women were shot at random by the guards, and no medicine was available for them among the expellees. Her mother and her own sister, hearing that the 'transport' was in their village, came to see her. The guard pushed the great-grandmother away brutally, threatened to beat her and sent her away. That was how Mückusch said farewell to her mother and her sister. She never saw them again.[26]

When her grandson got fever, the Czech transport commander, in her words, 'generously' gave her aspirin. In Spornhau, they were led past a garden fête of Czechs under a marquee tent eating, drinking and playing band music, which showed her poignantly how much the war had cost her – and might have reminded her of similar scenes with the roles reversed when the Germans had ruled here. That night they had to stay in a dirty, bug-infested building with no latrine facilities. The people were so exhausted that they literally lay down and died, in their own excrement. 'No one who had been outside could go indoors without horror.' At the beginning of the march, they had with them twenty-seven children. Within fourteen days in the overcrowded hospital, twenty-six children aged one year and under had died. The one who lived was Wolfi, her youngest grandson. 'The bodies of the children were put in adult coffins, five to seven in each, and buried together. They all died with their eyes and mouths open and the certificates stated "starvation" as the cause of death.'[27]

After 9 May, when the Red Army marched into Pribram, one of the women was told to go with a Russian soldier. She knew what he would do, so she refused. He threw her out of the fourth floor window, killing her. In the same camp, another woman was seized and raped so often that she died. Her children were watching and weeping beside her the whole time. In the transport of 1,300 people who had left Pribram for Strahov, about 300 died in a few weeks that spring.

The death rate among the 9,000–10,000 people in the

Strahov stadium can be computed from the number of bodies seen by the inmates every day. They averaged between twelve and twenty per day. The death rate for a few weeks was therefore between 43 and 81 per cent per year. Among the people there was a man with a tiny orphan in his arms. He had found the child lying on his dead mother in a ditch. The author of this account – one of many thousands taken in sworn depositions by the Germans and others after the expellees reached Germany – lost his father-in-law, his sister-in-law, and his fifteen-month old son. He observed that although some Czechs wanted to help these victims, anyone who brought food, shelter or medicine, was shouted down as a Nazi by his fellow Czechs. This man, Kurt Schmidt, was enslaved for a year in Czechoslovakia. He almost died but was finally expelled to Bavaria.[28]

The expulsions in the area round Aussig, Czechoslovakia were deliberately compared to a notorious Nazi massacre by a Czech official in the Czech Administrative Commission in Aussig. Writing in a Czech *émigré* magazine published in London in 1948, he said that the Nazi massacre of Lidice 'lit a torch which roused the whole civilised world against the cruellest [Nazi] tyranny and the debased nature of a totalitarian regime. Truth and humanism were on our side in the world when it happened. It was our right and our duty as soon as the war was over to deal with the criminals who sinned against humanity. But our attempts to settle accounts with these criminals have been overshadowed by even greater acts of inhumanity than those committed by the Nazi gangsters.' He described one of those acts, committed by Czech soldiers on a bridge over the Elbe who had been specifically ordered by their officers to refrain from attacking some German civilians returning from work. They seized 'a mother wheeling her child in a pram across the bridge and killed her with sticks. Together with the child, she was thrown over the railings into the Elbe whilst sub-machine guns fired at her.'[29] A German who had spent four years in a concentration camp for anti-fascist activities was scalped, shot through the stomach, and died in the street. 'He died instantly. There were hundreds of similar instances. Within three hours, more than 2,000 people were murdered.'[30]

A Catholic priest reported that the dead in Dubí near Kladno were thrown into a coffin several at a time and emptied into a pit in Rapice behind the wall of a cemetery. The coffin was re-used.[31]

The curate of the Parish of Klosterbrück in Silesia observed of the Poles and Russians, 'I have heard of cases where the Russians brutally raped mothers whilst their small children were present. After that they took the children on their knee, gave them bread and butter and sugar, and played with them. I am convinced that the Russians would be quite different if there were no bolshevism in their country. They are spiteful in a manner that is different from that of the Poles. The maliciousness of the Polish militia reminds one of the maliciousness of the German SS troops. It is cold and venomous, whereas the Russian maliciousness is somehow warm-blooded.'[32]

But not all the Poles were like that. The priest at Dittersdorf, who had befriended Poles during the German occupation, feeding and clothing them, allowing them to attend services in his church when this was forbidden by the Germans, was assaulted after the war by Poles. One of these men who beat the priest half to death, came to him two days later to apologize. He had tears in his eyes, begging for forgiveness. The bandaged priest forgave him.[33]

One man walking along the road near Lamsdorf with his family was assaulted by Poles, who beat and robbed them. After many incidents like this in the summer of 1945, seven of the eight members of his family were dead.[34] The railway stations and houses in Lamsdorf were posted with signs saying that the expulsions were to be carried out in 'an orderly and humane fashion'.

At Neisse in Upper Silesia, the village priest wrote, 'During the first night of the Russian occupation, many of the nuns were raped as many as fifty times. Some of the nuns who resisted with all their strength were shot, others were ill-treated in a dreadful manner until they were too exhausted to offer any more resistance. The Russians knocked them down, kicked them, beat them on the head and in the face with the butt-end of their revolvers and rifles, until finally they collapsed and in this unconscious condition became the helpless victims of brutish passion, which was so inhuman as to be inconceivable. The same dreadful scenes were enacted in homes for the aged, hospitals, and other such institutions. Even nuns who were seventy and eighty years old and were ill and bedridden were raped and ill-treated by these barbarians. And to make matters worse, these atocities were not committed secretly or in hidden corners but in public, in churches, on the streets, and on the squares, and the victims were nuns, women and eight-year-old girls. Mothers were raped in the presence of their children, girls were raped in front of their brothers, and nuns were raped in front of young boys.' The Russians even went so far as to fuck their victims when they were already dead. 'Priests who tried to protect the nuns were brutally dragged away, the Russians threatening to shoot them.'[35]

Germans who were still alive in the former eastern provinces under Russians or Poles in 1945 faced one of several fates.* Most of the soldiers were sent to prison camps in the Soviet Union, although a few dozen thousand were held in camps in Poland. Most of the civilians, nearly all women and children, with a sprinkling of older men, were expelled from their homes and homeland, usually under atrocious conditions, to starve in shrunken Germany. Several hundred thousand people were seized for slave labour in the USSR; many, as we have seen, to

---

*Much remains to be revealed in Polish archives and among Polish witnesses, who are invited to write to the author.

replace Wehrmacht prisoners who had died en route from the front to NKVD camps, or who had escaped. But many hundreds of thousands of people were forced at gunpoint into former Nazi concentration camps now run by Poles, there to suffer like those people so recently persecuted and murdered by the Germans themselves. Not only in Poland did such things happen, but in virtually every nation in the east of Europe where ethnic Germans were being expelled.

The fate of these German prisoners in Poland and elsewhere has scarcely been described in historical literature. Polish historians have understandably been averse to this harrowing story of vengeance. Not many Germans survived these camps to bear witness. Those who did were so wounded by the experience that they could scarcely bring themselves to speak about what had happened to them. And if a survivor did attempt to tell others, he was hampered not only by remembered terror, but by a lack of documents, by incredulity, by cover-ups, by the widespread refusal to believe in the post-war tragedy of the Germans that persists to this day throughout the west. For instance, bones discovered in 1976 and 1981 in mass graves at Kaltwasser/Bromberg were returned to the ground without any marker when it was decided by a Polish commission investigating Nazi war crimes that the dead had been German.[36] The investigation ended there. Analogous incidents have occurred at Lambach in Austria and at Rheinberg, Erfurt and Bretzenheim in Germany.

There were approximately 1,200 Polish camps east of the Oder–Neisse line, where the children were separated from their parents and all enslaved. According to one eye-witness who survived, in the children's barracks at Potulitz (Potulice in Polish), the death rate was very high.[37] The witness, Dr Martha Kent, née Schulz, was there from 1947 to 1949. She knew the children and watched them die. At the end of two years, so many children had died that the three-tier bunks were taken away and replaced by single bunks, for the survivors. 'Not many children left the barracks alive, but more were added,' Dr Kent said recently. 'More were added than left alive.' It is therefore quite likely that more than two-thirds of the children died in two years. Her experience has been confirmed by the recent extensive research of a German writer, who has described the deliberate starvation of newborn babies in Potulitz. Fifty German women gave birth to fifty babies in one barracks, of whom forty-six died within a few weeks. These were the babies of raping Russians, who were succeeded by Polish men after autumn 1945.[38]

Approximately 37,000 people were enslaved at Potulitz between 1945 and 1949. In Barracks 17, which held at various times between 132 and 238 people, 744 people died in twenty months. The two populations produce death rates between 176 and 318 per cent per year.[39] These rates are both much more than 100 times the ambient Polish death rate. At Graudenz, 62 per cent of the slaves died in a single year, 1945. Overall at Potulitz, about 12,000 persons died among a total pass-through of 37,000 in fifty-three months, approximately six times the ambient Polish civilian death rate in the same years 1945–50.[40]

Dr Kent, an American citizen now living in Arizona, suffers the reticence of all the survivors. She, her mother, younger brother and sister, were sent to Potulitz from captivity in Busckowo. Her grandmother was separated from the family in 1948, and they never saw her again. Her father, older brother and sisters were scattered to other concentration camps, where they endured torture, beatings, and enslavement. Some prisoners were shot.

In 1948, the German children were joined by a new group of healthy-looking girls who, to judge from their shining skin and plump cheeks, had only recently entered Polish captivity. Each of them wore a strange yellow device sewn on to her trouser-leg. Young Martha Schulz, aged eight, whispered to her mother through the barbed wire, 'Who are they?' Her mother replied with a word that Martha did not understand, but thought meant some special work group. Not until many years later, in North America, when she saw her first pictures of the Jews victimized by Hitler, did she realize the girls were Jews. 'It was as if the Poles had learned only one thing from the Holocaust: to sew the Star of David on to the legs as if to say, "You see, we're not like the Nazis."'

After Dr Kent was released, and had emigrated with some other survivors, first to Canada and then to the USA, she found that people refused to believe any stories about atrocities against Germans by the Allies. Once, when she was a student at university in the US, she approached a group of students conversing with a professor. When Kent joined in, the professor said, 'Here's our little Nazi. *Seig Heil.*' Her younger sister once spoke of her family's sufferings in camp to some American students. 'What did you do to deserve that?' someone asked. She answered that she had nursed at her mother's breast. At the end of the war, her sister was one year old, Dr Kent was five.

Dr Kent is only one part of the wave of new evidence now entering the historical record which will probably change the estimates of German deaths in the years 1945–50. Alfred de Zayas has recently added to his pioneering work with his book *A Terrible Revenge*; the American writer John Sack in his book *An Eye for an Eye* has told an appalling story of Jewish vengeance against Germans in Polish concentration camps; and the German writer Hugo Rasmus's new book, *Schattenjahre in Potulitz* tells in detail the story of one concentration camp run by Poles. So far, most historians have assumed that about 2.1 million of the 16.6 million dispossessed Germans died during expulsion, about 12 million arrived alive in shrunken Germany, and the rest, some 2.5 million, somehow evaded expulsion to survive. It now appears that if many of these evaded expulsion, it was only by dying.

In every tragedy of this sort, there are many people who do

not lose their heads, but act from normal courtesy and kindness. So there are moments of relief in these sad chronicles. The priests who reported these incidents were quick to see the hand of God, or of the church, but religious teaching had nothing to do with the kindness that appeared constantly among the pagan Bolsheviks. Many times one reads of a kind-hearted Russian officer who winked at oppressive rules, or who allowed starving refugees some food from his own stores, originally looted from the Germans. Two Jewish girls from Breslau who had been sheltered during the war by a German family in Maifritzdorf at the risk of their lives, went straight to the Soviet commander when he arrived in the village of Maifritzdorf, to tell their story. They were believed and the kindness of the Germans became the kindness of the Jews which then spread to the Russians. The Soviet commander went so far as to give to Chaplain G. of the village a document with the hammer and sickle seal which protected the villagers from abuses which had formerly been inflicted on them.[41]

Among Protestants and Catholics whom I interviewed in France because they had saved so many refugees during the war, I encountered a strange resistance to my inquiries which amounted to hostility. I could not understand this at first, and then it was explained to me by a woman in Le Chambon-sur-Lignon. I had been expressing admiration and praise for the actions of these villagers who had saved thousands of refugees at the risk of their lives. She made me see it had been nothing like what I imagined. 'What we did was normal,' she said. 'It was the Nazis who were extraordinary.' She was very matter-of-fact about having risked her life for others. This was the banality of good.

Many of the priests of the eastern regions, including a high number of resisters against Nazism, were murdered by Poles

and Russians in the spring and summer of 1945. In Upper
Silesia, some forty-five priests were murdered because they
remained with their flocks to the bitter end. In Birkenau, four
priests shared the fate of earlier victims of the Nazis' nearby
concentration camp.[42]

The great Russian writer Alexander Solzhenitsyn, winner of
the Nobel prize, who has contributed enormously to the
destruction of the Soviet regime, wrote a rigorously honest
poem about the Red Army conquest of Prussia in 1945. He
was soon arrested and imprisoned for the anti-Soviet views he
expressed. Solzhenitsyn wrote in one stanza of the poem:

Zweiundzwanzig, Horingstrasse.
It's not been burned, just looted, rifled.
A moaning, by the walls half-muffled:
The mother's wounded, still alive.
The little daughter's on the mattress,
Dead. How many have been on it?
A platoon? A company perhaps?
A girl's been turned into a woman,
A woman turned into a corpse.
It's all come down to simple phrases:
Do not forget. Do not forgive!*
Blood for blood. A tooth for a tooth!
The mother begs, 'Kill me, soldier!'

---

*The italics are a quote from Russian propaganda inciting the soldiers to
vengeance. The first line refers to the address of the house where the women
lay.[43] In the last lines of the poem (not shown), Solzhenitsyn confesses that he
too took advantage of a captive woman.

VI

DEATH AND
TRANSFIGURATION

Various statistics published by the US Army, the US Military
Governor, the State Department, the German and French governments, and by several writers such as Alfred de Zayas, Konrad
Adenauer, Heinz Guderian, Gustav Stolper and the American
authors of the booklet *The Land of the Dead* display a very wide
range of opinion about total deaths in Germany in 1946–50. In
other European countries at the time, there is no such variety of
opinion on census statistics. Whatever caused the strange variations in Germany in the years 1945–50, the Allies were all
agreed on one notion: most of the dead had never died. The
proof that well over a million prisoners of war and civilians
were missing many years after 1945 elicited a simple response:
ask the other guys, not us. The prisoners were missing, not dead.

To demystify these strange transfigurations of the dead and
their statistics, it is essential to remember that Germany for
nearly all of 1945–50 was one great prison. Germans were not
permitted to emigrate until 1949 except for a handful of people
valuable to the Allies. Here is yet another example of how the
Allied policies were not intended only to prevent Germany
from making war, but also to wreak vengeance. Many Germans

wanted to emigrate right after the war but were refused. Emigration would certainly have achieved the allied purpose of weakening Germany, but the people were forced to remain behind in starvation conditions. Mass immigration was controlled and enforced by the Allies. The statistics were all under the control of the Allies. Everything of consequence in the country was controlled by the Allies. When assessing the validity of the figures now being issued by the German government, one must remember that there was no independent German government in those days. All of the figures for 1945–50 were gathered under strict Allied control. Even the German Chancellor, Konrad Adenauer, when writing his memoirs of the period, relied on Allied figures for the number of expellees.[1]

There were three main locales for death for Germans after the surrender. The first was in the POW camps, the second among the expellees at home or on the road from their former homes to occupied Germany, the third among residents of occupied Germany.*

The lowest death rate for residents including expellees already arrived (i.e. not including deaths en route) is offered by the Military Governor of the US zone, who said that in the US zone in 1947, the death rate of 12.1 per year per thousand among civilians was only slightly higher than before the war.[2]

The next lowest are the figures of the German government (from the official agency Statistisches Bundesamt, Wiesbaden, henceforth 'the German government') which show that some 2.1 million expellees died between 1945 and 1950. They also report death rates among residents based on Allied occupation army reports. For 1947, the rate reported today by the German government is 12.1 per thousand per year among the resident population.[3]

---

*Of course, many Germans from the seized territories who evaded expulsion died as well, but figures for them are not available.

In the middle range are the several writers, among them Adenauer, Heinz Guderian and Gustav Stolper, who say that six million people died among the expellees alone. The expellees numbered around 14/15 million total between 1945 and 1950.

The highest numbers are from the French government, which implied that close to 7.5 million died among the expellees only. We shall deal with the two extremes first, and end with a discussion of the middle range figures.

The lowest estimates

The figures reported in the US Military Governor reports have done a lot to determine our view of the history of the period. Widely disseminated, they have been widely accepted. They are at the basis of the belief today throughout Germany and the West generally, that in the west of Germany in 1945–50 no very large number of people died among either the expellees or among the resident, non-expelled Germans of the three Western zones.

The US Military Governor, Lucius Clay, gave the death rate for 1947 in a report dated December 1947. It is 12.1 per thousand per year. This death rate, says the governor, compares 'favorably' with the pre-war rate of 11.9 per thousand per year.[4] If we take this literally, it can only mean the governor favours a rise in the death rate for Germany. If it is not to be taken literally, it would have to be followed by 'in the circumstances', an easy enough phrase to put in. This is a minor example of the sloppy and evasive expression permeating the Military Governor reports on the subject of the health and Allied treatment of the Germans.* The accuracy of the death figure may

---

*There are so many examples of important omissions, evasions and callous indifference in the reports that it is impossible to believe they are all the result of sloppy writing.

114

be judged from the fact that General Clay's own diplomatic advisor, Robert Murphy, had reported independently to Washington just a few months earlier that the death rate in Germany was so high that, in effect, it must exceed the birth rate by two million people in the few years during which the expellees and prisoners were to return. The birth rate in 1947 in Germany was about 14%%.[5] And, as we shall see below (p. 125), Clay's own US Army Medical Officer was at that very moment reporting *in secret* a death rate of over 21.5%% as at May 1946.

A bigger flaw was in the reporting of the condition of prisoners of war. The first Military Governor (Eisenhower) reported that in August 1945 4,772,837 prisoners were on hand, or had been transferred or discharged, without mentioning that the original capture total was 5,224,310. The governor therefore was failing to account for 451,473 people. Recent research has shown why: these prisoners had died in camps commanded by the same governor.[6]

Governor Clay himself inadvertently revealed the deceptiveness of his own figures when he wrote about the death rate in the Soviet zone. Clay wrote of the Soviet zone in 1945 that, 'This low food ration is already having its effect. The death rate in many places has increased several-fold and infant mortality is approaching 65 per cent in many places. By the spring of 1946, German observers expect that epidemics and malnutrition will claim 2.5 to 3 million victims between the Oder and the Elbe.'[7] Clay must have had stars and stripes in his eyes when he wrote that, because he did not mention the death rate in the west although he knew the food situation was just as bad in the British and American zones. He himself had to reduce the ration to 1,275cpd, then it fell even further, to 1,000 for a while. A group of German doctors reported in 1947 that the actual rations issued for three months in the Ruhr section of the British zone for average people amounted to only 800 calories per day.[8] Gustav Stolper reported that the ration in both British and American zones for 'a long time in 1946 and 1947 dropped to between 700 and 1,200 calories per day'.[9] *The ration that Clay said was predicted to kill so many millions of people in the Soviet zone was 1,150 calories per day.* But Clay makes no reference to millions of corpses disfiguring the western landscape under his command.[10]

The kind of reporting we have seen from Eisenhower and Clay has led people to believe that the German death rate in 1947 was 12.1 per thousand per year,[11] *lower than it was for two years (12.2) in the prosperous 1960s.* This notion is reported without comment by the otherwise serious *International Historical Statistics*, edited by B. R. Mitchell. Professor Mitchell does not clearly cite his source, but he has said in correspondence that 'it looks quite probable that [one] is right to disbelieve the official death rate'.[12] The Allied Control Council supervised all the general statistics gathering, including the census in Germany, through the Military Governments. The inheritor of that information is the Statistisches Bundesamt, which today may report 12.2 or 12.1. Which one it believes is hard to say.[13] That the expert Mitchell could not clearly cite his sources for Germany in 1945–50 is symptomatic of the difficulties met by researchers attempting to determine vital statistics in Germany when it was under Allied rule. So the conditions which in the east sent the death rate soaring 'several-fold' according to Clay are reported to have had absolutely no effect in the west. Perhaps he did not notice – or care – because he was still in the grip of his wartime animus against the Germans. Normally a correct if autocratic man, Clay was still meting out harsh treatment to the starving Germans in late November 1945, when he was asked to permit two large shipments of Red Cross food destined for German civilians to enter the country. Clay refused, with the words 'Let the Germans suffer.'[14]

The evidence is abundant in the Military Governors' reports themselves that the governor was interested in giving the Chief of Staff in Washington, the Secretary of State and the President a pleasing portrait of Germany rather than a reliable statistic. It is also clear that the President himself did not rely on these reports. When the Displaced Persons camps were said in the American press to be in bad shape in autumn 1945, Truman did not rely on the Military Governor reports to find the facts, although the governor was in charge of those camps and reported every month. Truman appointed a commissioner to investigate. Similarly, after many senators had angrily denounced American policy in Germany, Truman paid no attention to the Military Governor's monthly reports, with their enormous detail showing that there was no problem. Instead, he asked Hoover to take over and solve the problem. Hoover replied to Truman that he would not go unless he had a mandate to investigate the very conditions in Germany that the Military Governor reports were supposedly describing. Truman let him have his way.

The highest estimates

The death figures of the French government are so high that they verge on the unbelievable.[15] They imply that some 50 per cent of the expellees died in a couple of years, far beyond the normal death rate. Combined with the deaths of prisoners and the unreported deaths of non-expelled civilians, this would mean an overall total of around fifteen million deaths. A cursory reading of the documents about the expulsion shows, however, that this 50 per cent figure does not differ much from the reports of thousands of eye-witnesses who survived the expulsions. As we have seen, in the hospital near Prague, twenty-six of twenty-seven children in one transport died in a few weeks; in another case, the death rate for some weeks was between 43 and 81 per cent per year in one large 'transport'.

In Silesia, some figures given mainly by priests have survived. In Klein-Mahlendorf, according to the parish priest, 175 people died in 1945, whereas normally around 110–115 people died each year. And this happened although the village had already lost about two-thirds of its people through the expulsions. The main cause was the typhus that the Allies feared might spread to their own troops in the west if they did not relieve the starvation somewhat. The 1945 Klein-Mahlendorf total death rate was about 456 per cent of the pre-war death rate.[16]

Of eighteen landowners near Alt-Wette in Silesia who were arrested and forced to work in the mines, twelve died in the first six months, beginning in late 1945.[17] Among sixty-eight villagers of Niederhermsdorf in one rail car, seven died in three days and four nights, plus three more on arrival. This is a rate far above 100 per cent per year.[18]

The people of Lossen suffered abominably under the Russians. Of 770 who returned to the village after the Russian occupation began, more than 100 died in the six months from June to December 1945. This was a rate of around 26 per cent, or 260 per thousand per year, roughly twenty-one times the pre-war rate for the area.[19]

In the villages of Glogau and Kuttlau, the rate was between 100 and 155 per thousand per year for the last half of 1945.[20] At Thomaswaldau, the rate was around 42 per thousand in the last six months of 1945.[21]

These and the French figures must be viewed against figures from Stolper, Guderian and, above all, Adenauer. These seem promising to investigate because they are offered by experts who were there in responsible positions at the time – Stolper with the Hoover Commission, and Adenauer first as Mayor of Cologne, then as Chancellor of West Germany. They reveal a massacre not as huge as implied by the French, but far beyond the belief of any later historian.

The mid-range figures

The mid-range figures from Adenauer and a few others say that some six million expellees alone died, without specifying any unusual number of deaths among the resident civilians. Adenauer wrote in March 1949:

> According to American figures, a total of 13.3 million Germans were expelled from the eastern parts of Germany, from Poland, Czechoslovakia, Hungary and so on. 7.3 million arrived in the eastern zone and the three western zones . . . Six million Germans have vanished from the earth. They are dead, gone. Most of the 7.3 million who stayed alive are women, children and old people.

A large part of the workers were shipped to the USSR for forced labour. The expulsion of these 13 to 14 million brought with it unending suffering. 'Atrocities were committed that are worthy of being put beside those perpetrated by German National Socialists [Nazis].'[22]

All these reports come from staunch friends of the West – Adenauer, Stolper, the French government, and others. We can see they are not lies: are they perhaps incorrect?

One of the leading experts on post-war refugees, author of a standard reference work, *European Refugees*, which is cited by many subsequent authors, is the British writer Malcolm Proudfoot. In Table 40 of his book, Proudfoot gives a detailed survey of the statistics of the German expellees from 1945 to 1950, by which time the exodus had ended for nearly all of them. We can get some idea of the validity of the Adenauer figures by combining some of Proudfoot's basic figures with others from the Allied Control Council, so we can compare the *apparent* growth of the German population between January 1946 and September 1950 with the *actual* census count in 1950.

To Proudfoot's opening population of 60.4 million in January, 1946, we add the births and immigration in the period 1946–50 to find the total possible population for 1950. Births numbered some 5 million, the returning prisoners numbered 4.8 million, and the expellees, according to Proudfoot, added some 8.3 million, making a total potential population before deaths and emigration of 78.5 million. From these we subtract deaths *officially recorded* of 3.85 million and emigration of some 0.6 million.[23] The result is that in September 1950 we should find 74.05 million people. But the census of September 1950 found only 68.8 million. Missing, not accounted for, were 5.25 million people. These are in addition to the officially recorded deaths inside occupied Germany. These are in addition to the six million expellees Adenauer thought had died *before* reaching Germany. What happened to all these people?

Can the statistics be wrong? As we shall see below, the Allied Control Council figures from the census are the most reliable we have on this subject. If these are wrong, then virtually nothing is known for certain on the topic.

Can the expert Proudfoot have misunderstood? There is some slight evidence for that. For instance, he admits that he was working only 'from estimates' in a large number of categories, without specifying *which* categories. Also, he did not refer to the census of Germany that was conducted under the Allies in October 1946, ten months *after* the start-date of his own population tables, although he did end his table with the census conducted in September 1950. Further, Proudfoot reports that the total of refugees in the British zone in January 1947 was 3,201,000, whereas the British themselves reported to the Control Council that just over 3,500,000 had arrived at that date, of whom only 2,800,000 actually remained in their zone, the others having departed for other zones.[24] Clearly, Proudfoot did the best he could with the figures that were available at the time, which have been superseded by papers since declassified.

We have today something Proudfoot did not use in his basic table, the census figures for October 1946, done by the four military governments of Germany who controlled the censusses of 1946 and 1950.

The October 1946 census of all four zones of occupied Germany was carried out 'by Germans under the direction of the Allied Control Council'.[25] The second census, of August–September 1950, was also carried out by Germans under the control of the four occupying powers. An important subset is the births recorded in the relevant period. Statistics concerning the expellees have always been disputed, but we do now know, as a result of the declassification of the Murphy Papers from 1988 on, the number of expellees who arrived in occupied Germany during the period between censusses. There were six million.[26] The number of prisoners discharged into Germany during the period is also known: 2,600,000.[27] This number has been seriously disputed, but the truth has been discovered in the KGB archives in Moscow, recently opened. The numbers of deaths and emigrants are also known.[28] With these figures in place, we can swiftly calculate the missing/unreported deaths.

The population of all occupied Germany in October 1946 was 65,000,000, according to the census prepared under the ACC.[29] The returning prisoners who were added to the population in the period October 1946–September 1950 numbered 2,600,000 (rounded), according to records in the archives of the four principal Allies. Births according to the official German statistical agency, Statistisches Bundesamt, added another 4,176,430 newcomers to Germany.[30] The expellees arriving totalled 6,000,000. Thus the total population in 1950 before losses would have been 77,776,430, according to the Allies themselves. Deaths officially recorded in the period 1946–50 were 3,235,539, according to the UN Yearbook and the German government.[31] Emigration was about 600,000, according to the German government.[32] Thus the population found should have been 73,940,891. But the census of 1950 done by the German government under Allied supervision found only 68,230,796.[33] *There was a shortage of 5,710,095 people*, according to the official Allied figures (rounded to 5,700,000).*

Such a gigantic discrepancy immediately raises questions. The first is, how reliable are the largest figures, the censusses?

The Allies took great care over these figures because the German population was extremely important to all of them. They even recorded the 1,143 people registered as ship crews at sea. All the Allies believed that they were in serious danger of further German aggression, which they judged was prompted (as Hitler himself had said), by too great a population confined to too little land. Therefore, the Allies' discussions centred on population comparisons of post-war Germany with Germany in 1939; of Germany with France; on the German birth rate; on population per square kilometre; on agricultural production per person and per kilometre; and so on. Important Allied policy decisions about Germany in this period were based on these censusses. The Allies disagreed about all kinds of substantive issues and policy in the period, but they agreed on the German birth rates and the base populations assessed in 1946 and 1950.

Of the remaining variables, we know that the arriving expellees were counted at the border and reported year by year

*These results differ from those based on the Proudfoot figures largely because the time period is different.

by the Allied Control Council, whose figures we now have.[34] 'The statistical picture of newcomer-population in the western zones is elaborate and complete,' according to a memo of 18 May 1949 by Brad Patterson, secretary to Robert Murphy, in the preparatory papers to the 1949 Council of Foreign Ministers used by US Ambassador Robert Murphy. Nevertheless there were some slight variations in the figures.

Up to 1995, the prisoner-of-war arrivals were in dispute because the Western Allies said that the Soviets had over 3,000,000 prisoners, when in fact they had only around 890,000. With the opening of the KGB archives, we now know that the Soviet figures are the most solid evidence available in all the prisoner archives. This is a massive correction only possible because of the end of Cold War. All the other figures necessary to calculate the prisoners on hand at October 1946 were supplied by the governments in question.

Of all the remaining variables, the only one seriously at issue is the death figure. Could 5.7 million *extra* deaths have occurred beyond those recorded in German and Allied documents? Either the official death figures are wrong, or the censuses with their subsidiary figures. The question has now become: are those official, published, Allied/West German death statistics reliable?

To begin with, the official West German government death figures are at odds with themselves. As we saw, they reported that the death rate during two prosperous years of 1968–69 was 12.2 per thousand per year. This is higher than the death rate of 12.1 they report for 1947, a year of unparalleled misery, starvation, want and epidemic disease, remembered by Germans as the Hunger Year (*Hungerjahr*). That is incredible. I believe that the explanation for this is simple: the source for the official German figure for 1947 was not German at all, it was the US Military Governor, who reported the 12.1 figure to President Truman. Dr de Zayas, author of the definitive work on the expellees, has several times since January 1994 asked the Statistisches Bundesamt at Wiesbaden to explain the discrepancies and to reveal their sources for statistics in 1945–50, and has received no satisfaction. This also happened to a Member of the Bundestag, a friend of De Zayas, who asked for similar information, and received no explanation of the strange discrepancies. As we have seen, the expert Professor Brian Mitchell has cast doubt on the reliability of the official figures.

The West German government death figures being reported to this day are also at odds with nearly all the other sources that we have, both German and Allied. Let us look at a mid-sized city, Brilon, which had always been prosperous, and in 1945 regarded itself as one of the more fortunate of the German towns. In the first place, it was in the British–Canadian zone, where the policy was, if not exactly genial, at least not fatally indifferent as it was in the French and Soviet zones. And Brilon was also favoured by its location, in beautiful rolling country north-west of Kassel near a formerly prosperous agricultural region not as heavily damaged as most others. This was especially lucky for the 71,000 people of Brilon, because it meant that they could scrounge for food more easily in a productive countryside close by.

According to a report gathered from the town council of Brilon by the Canadian army in 1946, the death rate in the town was 34 per thousand per year for the eleven months between 1 May 1945 and 31 March 1946. The same report shows that the death rate was triple the birth rate (2,224 versus 687).[35] A similar situation existed in the village of Marktoberdorf, near Augsburg, in the US zone, where the death rate in 1946 was 27%%. It was 24%% in 1947, then fell in 1948 to 17%%. But then it rose again, to 24%% in 1949 and 27%% in 1950. The long-term effects of famine may be evident here.[36]

General Mark Clark, US Military Commissioner in the US

zone of Austria, reported in April 1946 that the death rate in Vienna was varying between 27 and 35 per thousand per year. His report stated that, 'This relatively high death rate prevailed during a period when the ration scale was 1,550cpd. With a drop in the ration it is probable that these rates will increase.'[37] And in fact, those rations for Germans did drop by about a third, or more. 'During the first months of 1947, supplies of food for the Combined [US and UK] zone fell again to the low level of the two preceding winters.' Daily rations were often less than 1,000 calories.[38] In Schleswig-Holstein, in the British zone, the daily ration for seven months in mid-1947 was only 1,240 calories per day.[39]

All this had the effect that Clark predicted. We know from the Medical Officer of Health of the US Army that the death rate in the US zone in Germany in May 1946 was 21.5 per thousand per year, *and that it had previously been higher*.[40] Hoover reported to the President that there had been an appalling increase of 40 per cent in deaths of aged people *in only three months*.[41] This is a significant report, since aged people not only constitute a far greater share of the dying than any other sector of the population, they were also a much higher proportion than normal among the population in Germany at that date. On the basis of the report from Clark, and because we know that the rations in the US and British zones did often drop to around 1,000cpd, it is not unreasonable to assume that the higher rate in the Combined (British–American) zone was at least as high as the Vienna rate of 27/35 per thousand per year.

It is impossible to reconcile the official Military Governor and West German figures of low deaths with the figures from the city of Brilon, the Medical Officer of the US Army, ETO, and the census results. Because the Military Governor figures are contradicted by the detailed documentation found in Ottawa and Stanford, and because the Military Governor and official German figures are self-contradictory and self-serving, and because Robert Murphy predicted a huge loss of life in Germany, and because the Proudfoot comparisons show a huge number of Missing/Not Accounted For, and because the Allied censuses show 5.7 million Missing/Not Accounted For, and because Hoover Commission members found 'much lying' going on among the officers of the US military government, and because members of the ACC said that the Morgenthau Plan was being implemented, and because the low official death figures do not accord with the reality reported and deplored in the United States Senate, and because the German government statistical agency has been unable to define its sources, it is reasonable to conclude that the low death figures are not reliable.

In contrast, the figures based on comparison of the censuses, and the figures below from Robert Murphy, are all coherent in themselves, and relate convincingly to each other. They also describe in statistical terms the huge die-off that is reported throughout Germany in anecdotal terms.

As Clay's top diplomatic adviser, Robert Murphy was perhaps the most important American participant in decisions on Germany in this period. But his personal papers at Stanford were classified until 1988, and papers to which he contributed, relative to the Council of Foreign Ministers' conferences in 1947 and 1949, were classified at the State Department in Washington until 1989 – a few more were declassified as late as 1991. These papers together give a high-level and deeply informed view over the whole of the period in Germany. They are especially revealing on the subject of the German population.

Murphy understood both from the census and from direct personal experience what was being done to the people of Germany. He wrote in his Council of Foreign Ministers' preparatory papers, February 1947, that he expected the

Enclosure to Despatch No. 90,
dated Febru..y 20, 1947, from
Ambassador Murphy, London, England.

M E M O R A N D U M

I. Notes on Areas, Population and Population Densities.

The significant statistical data may be summarized
as follows:

Area	Size in Square Miles	Population	Population density—inhabitants per square mile
1939 Germany (excluding Austria and Sudetenland)	181,025	69,000,000 (approx.)	381
1947 Germany (excluding area east of Oder-Neisse)	137,377	69,000,000 (estimated*)	502
1939 Poland	150,470	35,000,000	233
1947 Poland (including area east of Oder-Neisse)	136,153	25,000,000**	184**
Polish-Administered German Areas—1939	39,042***	8,500,000**** (including perhaps 7,000,000 Germans)	218
Polish-Administered German Areas—1947	39,042	5,000,000***** (including 600,000 remaining Germans)	128*****

---

* Preliminary figures from the German census, taken on
October 29, 1946 under direction of the Allied Control
Council, show total population of 65,900,000. This includes about 700,000 displaced persons (UNRRA Situation
Report of October 31). Assuming that all these DP's will
eventually leave Germany, this will leave 65,200,000 inhabitants. German war prisoners still held abroad are
estimated by OMGUS Armed Forces Division at 4,000,000
(consisting chiefly of 3,000,000 estimated held by USSR).
German expellees still to be returned to Germany are
similarly estimated by OMGUS PW and DP Division at
2,000,000. This gives a total eventual population for
Germany, once all DP's have left and German war prisoners and expellees returned, of 71,000,000. However, in
order to be conservative, and in view of the present
high death rate in Germany, a figure of 69,000,000 will
be used. 71,000,000 would give a population density of
517 instead of 502.

* Some observers claim this figure of 25,000,000 for
Poland's post-war population is too high, and that even
if all Polish refugees, troops, etc. return from abroad,
the maximum population will be closer to 20,000,000.
This would change the population density figure from
184 to 147.

*** i.e.

German population overall *to shrink by two million* during the period of the return of the prisoners, roughly the next two to three years. This overall shrinkage would exist after allowing for the net of births, deaths, emigration and immigration including return of prisoners. He wrote that this tremendous loss of life would occur because of the 'present high death rate in Germany'.[42]

Murphy said that after the influx, which he expected to number two million prisoners and four million expellees, the population would rise by only four million. This was only possible if deaths exceeded births by two million in the period, since emigration was not permitted at the time. The period was three years, so Murphy was saying that deaths would exceed births by two million in 1947–50. We know the birth rate for 1946. It was 14%%. Therefore Murphy was basing his prediction on a death rate he knew to be 24%%.[43]

The importance of Murphy's prediction can hardly be exaggerated. It shows that he was basing official American policy on the expectation that this phenomenal death rate, already prevailing nationwide, would continue for three more years. He believed it so firmly that he put it on record to the State Department, to the British, French, Soviet and other American officials in Germany. And he based this on the same statistics that determined all Allied policy decisions for all four powers towards Germany. In other words, by implication, all of the Allied powers believed as Murphy did, that the death rate in Germany was 24%% or higher, and would continue for years at that rate.

The comparison of the censusses has shown us already that some 5.7 million people disappeared inside Germany between October 1946 and September 1950, in addition to those officially reported, and in addition to the millions of expellee deaths and millions of prisoner deaths. But the census of 1950 also shows that Murphy in 1947 was low in estimating future deaths. He had estimated a population for Germany of 69,000,000 once the expellees had arrived and the surviving prisoners were back. The 1950 census showed there were actually only 68,400,000 present, and that many more expellees and prisoners had returned than he predicted. Murphy had predicted that the net 'immigration' would be 6 million, made up of returning prisoners and expellees arriving. In fact, the number who had arrived between October 1946 and September 1950 was 8.6 million, made up of 6 million expellees and 2.6 million prisoners. *Murphy's death prediction was low because the death rate he was using as at October 1946 was too low.* The rate rose during the disastrous Hunger Year, 1947.

The West German government has not accounted for those five to six million people missing *in* Germany, but it has said that 2.1 million expellees died en route *to* occupied Germany from Poland, Czechoslovakia, and the Soviet Union.[44] These deaths, having occurred outside Germany, were not included in the official death figures for Germany as published today, and are therefore irrelevant to the death totals *within* occupied Germany.

Little is known about the fate of the Germans who remained behind in the seized territories. The expellees say over and over in their accounts that, 'Our village was empty . . . all of the villages were abandoned . . .' and so on. Since it was the policy of the Poles and Russians, agreed by the Western democracies, to empty the land of all Germans, and the anecdotal evidence says over and over again that this happened, it is easy to believe that the policy was carried out. It is therefore hard to believe that people stayed behind, unless they were already dying. But the West German government figure of 2.1 million dead and about 12.5 million arrivals means that one must believe that some 2,645,000 persons went on living in these 'empty villages'. Can this be believed? The Poles said that in early 1947 there were only 400,000 Germans left in the land where there had been about 8 million people. The stay-at-homes thus were around 5 per cent of the original population.[45] In Czechoslovakia there were around 250,000 who remained behind in 1950, approximately 8 per cent of the German population in May 1945.[46] It appears more credible that most of the missing died, and their deaths were hidden. The evidence above speaks for itself to the reader. In the statistical tables of deaths that follow, the official figures for expellee deaths and stay-behinds are used but not endorsed by the author.

Summary

In sum, there is compelling evidence from the census and from Ambassador Murphy that between October 1946 and September 1950 in the four occupied zones, some 5.7 million German civilian residents of Germany died but were not reported to have died. Although most of these people died from lack of food, their deaths were not caused by the world food shortage described by some historians. They were dying seventeen months to five years after the German surrender. They began dying when world food production was 97 per cent of normal. They were for a considerable time prevented from receiving charitable help, and from earning their own bread. They went on dying while world food production climbed ever higher. The great majority of the dead Germans were women, children and very old men.[47]

The Adenauer government also determined by survey that at least 1.4 million Germans did not come home from Allied POW camps. They all died.[48]

A further 2.1 million people, nearly all women and children, are admitted by the West Germans and the Allies to have died during the expulsions. Notable authorities, including the first Chancellor of West Germany, have written that at least six

Henry Morgenthau, US Secretary of the Treasury. His Morgenthau Plan for the destruction of German industry led to the deaths of millions of Germans years after the war's end.

The Potsdam Conference in the summer of 1945, where the transfers of millions of Germans from Poland, Czechoslovakia and Hungary were approved. Truman is in the foreground, with his back to camera; Stalin is seated further to the right and Churchill is across the table on the left.

US President Harry Truman (left) greets Herbert Hoover on 28 May 1945, before a 45-minute meeting during which they discussed world food relief.

In September 1945, US Secretary of War Robert Patterson and President Harry Truman controlled the most powerful military machine in human history. They soon used it for a huge food-relief campaign.

Norman Robertson, Under-Secretary of External Affairs for Canada, led the Canadian food aid programme from 1945. Later he became Ambassador to the United States.

William Lyon Mackenzie King, Prime Minister of Canada. He worked with Norman Robertson and Herbert Hoover to bring Canadian wheat to starving people around the world.

Painting by prisoner Kurt Spillman of the French camp at Thorée-les-Pins, near
La Flèche, in early spring 1945. 'We arrived about 6 A.M. in a snowstorm. The dead
lying on the right are comrades who suffocated during the journey. US soldiers look
on as we are beaten by the French support troops.'

US Army camp at Sinzig, on the Rhine near Remagen, spring 1945. Millions of Axis
prisoners were herded into open fields and kept for months without sufficient food,
water or shelter.

Aerial view of the infamous Russian camp at Vorkuta, two thousand miles north-east of Moscow, between the Barents Sea and the northern peaks of the Urals.

On these tiny pages (shown actual size) the names of dead Austrian prisoners were written. Rudolf Haberfellner (now of Toronto) risked his life to smuggle this notebook out of his camp at Novo Troitsk, USSR.

The Allies deprived Germany of chemical fertilizers, so this farmer near Bamburg uses liquid manure. The cows drawing the wooden tanks also provided milk and, when too old to work, meat for the hungry.

April 1946: German engineers are forced to dismantle a power-plant at Gendorf for shipment to Russia as reparations.

January 1946: civilians in Kiel clean up rubble in front of the Empire Building used by the British for their Army Welfare Service.

Demonstration in Kiel against the excessive Allied regulations, which helped cause food shortages in 1947. Signs read: 'We demand control over food distribution'; 'Severe punishment for black marketeers'; 'We demand sufficient food for all'; and 'End dismantling. We want to work'.

Hamburg, 1946: a barefoot German boy scavenges for food.

The British philanthropist and publisher Victor Gollancz denounced Allied crimes in passionate prose. He is seen here during his 1946 visit to Düsseldorf, in the British zone.

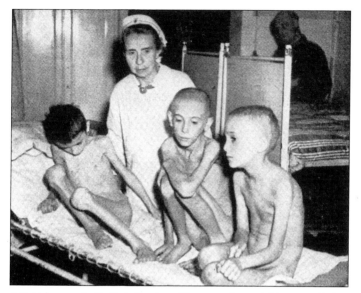

A British nurse in Berlin helps three German refugee children expelled from an orphanage in Danzig, Poland. The boy on the left, aged nine, weighs 40lbs and is too weak to stand. The boy in the centre, aged twelve, weighs just 46lbs, and his eight-year-old sister, right, weighs 37lbs. This picture was first published in *Time* magazine on 12 November 1945.

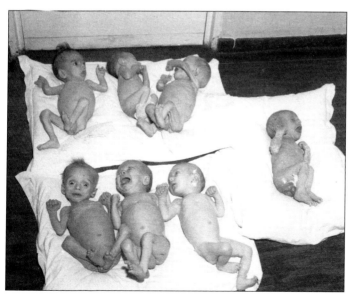

Seven starving babies in the Catholic children's hospital in Berlin, October 1947. The infant on the right is near death.

Canadian poster asking for contributions to help save the lives of children in Germany, undated but probably from 1947.

At Christmas

REMEMBER

THE

STARVING CHILDREN

IN THE

British Zone of Germany

AND OTHER PARTS OF
CENTRAL EUROPE

Thousands of children face death by starvation in the ruined cities. The signs of starvation are written in their drawn faces. Thousands are dying from tuberculosis. Rickets and other diseases of undernourishment are prevalent.

SAVE THESE CHILDREN

while they can still be saved. Support the Child-Feeding Programme of Canadian Lutheran World Relief.

Seven Dollars NOW . . . Saves One Child Through This Winter

Give generously and give quickly. Every day without help is costing the lives of hungry children. Hand your contribution to your Pastor. (If necessary, you may send direct to Canadian Lutheran World Relief, 460 Main Street, Winnipeg, Manitoba.)

(This appeal is being published by a friend of this grand work of saving children.)

In 1946 Mrs Hugh Champion de Crespigny, centre, wife of the British Regional Commissioner of Schleswig-Holstein, helps with the Christmas celebrations of refugee children in the convalescent home established in a wing of their official residence in Kiel.

hildren emerge from ruins. Many families in wrecked German cities lived in damp,
nheated basements for years after the war.

Expellees from the east, who left home with few supplies and little or no transport, pass US Army vehicles.

Displaced women and children move slowly in horse-drawn carts and on foot along the road near Wurzen.

Bunk-beds and makeshift furniture in a crowded barracks for refugees, Germany, 1946.

The first food parcel allowed to be sent from the USA arrived in Berlin at the home of Heinz Lietz on 14 August 1946. Many Germans starved to death when such readily available help was denied.

The original handwritten caption to this photograph reads: 'Bread, the "staff of life" in Berlin. — Thanks to the providence of God and the Dutch Red Cross which brought MCC [Mennonite Central Committee] flour and other nice food to the Mennonite refugees in Berlin.'

An old refugee woman gathers sticks to help cook meagre meals supplied in part by Mennonites from Canada and the USA.

Mennonite Peter Dyck, from North America, helps a young expellee boy from the east.

American Cornelius Dyck, the first member of the Mennonite Central Committee to enter the British zone in late 1946. The Committee provided invaluable help distributing food packages in Schleswig-Holstein, where the population increased by over 70 per cent after the arrival of expellees and refugees.

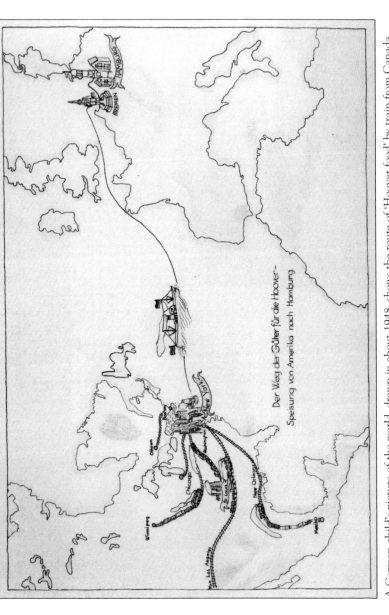

A German child's picture of the world, drawn in about 1948, shows the route of 'Hoover food' by train from Canada, the US and Mexico and then across the Atlantic to Hamburg.

million among the expellees alone died.

At least 9.3 million Germans died needlessly soon after the war, the great majority because of the conditions imposed by the four major victors. This is many more Germans than died in battle, air raids and concentration camps during the war.[49] Millions of these people slowly starved to death in front of the victors' eyes every day for years. These deaths have never been honestly reported by either the Allies or the German government.

TOTALS OF DEATHS

	Minimum	Maximum
Expellees (1945–50)	2,100,000	6,000,000
Prisoners (1941–50)	1,500,000	2,000,000
Residents (1946–50)	5,700,000	5,700,000
Totals	9,300,000	13,700,000

NOTE:

The prisoners' minimum deaths is an unrealistically cautious estimate based on the notion that somehow, no one died who had not been counted missing by Dr Bitter and subsequent surveyors. Those counted as missing numbered 1.4 million military, to whom are here added 66,000 dead paramilitary in the USSR.

The deaths above are not only above and beyond those actually reported, but also most of the victims died after October 1946. Of course there were many deaths in the period from August 1945, when the Potsdam policies took full effect, up to the time of the first census in October 1946.

Between the imposition of the Potsdam Agreements in August 1945, and the first census, October 1946, probably about 1,950,000 German non-expelled civilians died, but only about 1,100,000 deaths were reported.[50] This means that about 800,000 more Germans died and were not reported by the Allies between August 1945 and October 1946.

It is not possible from the figures available to determine how many civilians died in the Soviet zone and how many in the Western zones.

Why did this happen? The answer begins with understanding that most of the deaths were not accidental. A man who studied the cause of these deaths, who knew the famine intimately, and who worked magic to avert the catastrophe, has written of the famine in Germany in 1947: '[Our] occupation has no chance of success if these [famine] conditions continue. This state of affairs has been foreseen, and I have urged repeatedly that priority be recognized for food shipments to Germany. The basis for the priority is the prevention of famine in the US–UK zones of Germany . . .'[51] The man who believed that 'this state of affairs has been foreseen' was the US Secretary of War, Robert Patterson. The man he was trying to move to action was the US Secretary of State, George C. Marshall.

The rest of the answer to 'Why?' is to find out why so many people tried to cover this up. After all, if the Allies did their best to feed the starving civilians, and all the fault lay with the Nazis, or the world food shortage, why cover up the resulting deaths? Why not advertise them as the grim consequence of evil and error? The gallows at Nuremberg, the prosecutions of concentration-camp guards for fifty years, are public evidence of an apparently clear conscience in the West on Nazi crimes. Why hide these millions of civilian deaths, since historical theory, if it pays any attention at all, attributes them to consequences of Nazi policies? The cover-up alone shows that the Allies have to this day a very uneasy conscience on the subject.

Clearly the military camouflaged all this as best they could because they knew their reputations would be damaged if the truth came out. Love of reputation is a minor guarantor of good behaviour but a great source of hypocrisy in any society. The cover-up illustrates another feature: that the perpetrators of the crimes were in profound conflict with people in the West who saw a much better solution than vengeance – like Hoover, Gollancz, Senators Langer and Wherry, along with Dorothy Thompson, thousands of nameless aid workers and a very few honest reporters. Theirs was the conflict between crime and mercy – or good and evil if you will.

Many people representing the West in Germany were deeply distressed at what they saw. People such as Murphy and Behnke reveal in their uneasy words their uneasy conscience. Many such people were quite prepared to hang a Nazi, but it was repugnant to them to starve his child to death without a trial. They were disgusted by Allied co-operation in forcing the expellees out of the east. It might be thought that the Nazis' aggressions and crimes against civilians were the unique cause of this terrible vengeance, but nothing like this was visited on Japan. The Japanese had been waging a war of conquest, enslavement and near-extermination against civilian Chinese and Koreans for far longer, but General Douglas MacArthur, when he was Military Governor of Japan, demanded enough food from Washington to keep civilians alive. 'Give me bread or give me bullets,' he told Washington, and they gave him bread.

At heart the Westerners appear to have reacted in 1945 against the Germans much as they had in 1918, except that their fury was magnified by the desire to have done with the German problem once and for all. This anger went on so long, cut so deep, that it endangered the whole continent, while it exposed the West to ever-increasing danger from the Soviets. While the Soviets pillaged, menaced and murdered in Eastern Europe, while they stole Canada's atomic secrets, subverted democratic governments and spread hatred of the West round the world, the Western democracies fed, protected and befriended them. But the democracies would scarcely recognize those in Germany who had proven at the risk of their lives that they too were enemies of Hitler.

Those few people in the West today who do admit to allied crimes excuse them on the ground of the ferocious hatred roused by the race crimes of Hitler. But the truth is, the Western nations had already inflicted a similar vengeance on the Germans when there was no question of Nazi racism. What happened before happened again.

The pattern began long before 1914. For centuries, various powers in Europe had attempted to dominate or destroy the Germans. One of the classic passages of German history, by Heinrich von Treitschke, describes the result of the Thirty Years' War of 1618–48. 'Then at length the last and decisive war of the epoch . . . broke out. All the powers of Europe took part in the war . . . In a disturbance without parallel, the old Germany passed away. Those who had once aimed at world domination were now by the pitiless justice of history, placed under the feet of the stranger. The Rhine and the Ems, the Oder and the Vistula, all the ways to the sea became captive of the foreign nations . . . The entire life of Germany lay open without defence to the superior civilization of the foreigner . . . Never was any other nation so forcibly estranged from itself and from its own past . . .'[52] These words might have been written about the Germany of 1945, which was also captive of the foreign nations, after Hitler's attempt at world domination was ended by the last and decisive war of our epoch.

The similarities between the events immediately following the First and Second World Wars, are uncanny. After the First World War, Allied promises of just treatment for all peoples after the war were immediately broken; food lay rotting on the docks in European ports while Germans starved to death;[53]

German soldiers were accused of great atrocities such as bayo-netting babies, of burning libraries, massacring civilians; a pogrom against Jews was reported, and vast reparations were imposed on the Germans while the economy of the nation col-lapsed, millions of people starved and communist Russia threatened the whole of Europe. All this happened after 1918, and it happened again, only far worse, after 1945.

There was thus in 1945 among the Allies another motive to secrecy. It was important to hide the punishment because it had already been demonstrated that the earlier punishment had not been a deterrent. In fact, the only lesson of Versailles was that it had helped Hitler to goad the Germans to re-arm in the 1930s.

Two characteristics distinguished the victors of 1945 from nearly all others in modern European history. One is that they refused to allow the vanquished any treaty at surrender. Everything was imposed. The other was that they did not end the killing at the end of the war, but increased it. Above all, what was expected of the Allies, even by their own people, was to end the killing. But in fact, far more civilian Germans died in five years of 'peace' than soldiers in six years of war.[54]

As we have seen, at the Nuremberg trials of the German war criminals, the Soviets saw an opportunity to pin the blame for the Katyn massacre on German scapegoats, to hang them and have done with it. But their case was so patently bogus that the Western Allies objected. All the Allied lawyers and judges knew perfectly well that the Germans were not guilty, but not one of them told the truth: that the only other nation that could have committed the crime was the USSR.

One of the chief objections the Allies had to Nazi policies from the beginning was that, in true totalitarian fashion, the Nazis had persecuted many innocent Germans, beginning with their political opponents, especially communists and Jews, liberal academics, priests, pastors, homosexuals, gypsies, the mentally retarded, and so on. More than three million Germans had been in Nazi prisons at one time or another between 1933 and 1945. Of these, some 800,000 were imprisoned for active resistance to the Nazis.[55] Many others had fled the country. These Germans were the only significant internal indigenous resistance movement in the whole world during the war. Many Soviet citizens resisted the Stalinists, but not at the highest levels, and not until the Germans had taken over their areas. Only in Germany were there any attempts on the life of the leader; only German senior officers secretly delivered important intelligence to the enemy during wartime; only in Germany did senior officers such as admirals and generals risk their lives and their families to bring down the regime. The second-in-command of the Nazi party, Rudolf Hess, defected to the British in an attempt to bring the war to an end in 1941. The British made no attempt to use him to bring down Hitler. They judged him mad and imprisoned him for the rest of his life. The most famous general of the war, Erwin Rommel, was ordered by Hitler to choose between execution and suicide for his part in the resistance. The head of German military intelligence, Admiral Wilhelm Canaris, 'took breathtaking risks to advance the cause of resistance to Hitler'[56] by passing secret information to the Allies. He was hanged by Hitler in April 1945.

Allen Dulles, the head of the American intelligence effort in Switzerland, who ran the only important American spy ring inside Germany, complained strongly about Allied policy in 1943. 'I do not understand what our policy is,' he cabled to Washington, 'and what offers, if any, we could make to the resistance movement.' In March 1943, he told Washington that the Allied policy of unconditional surrender would mean a catastrophe 'for the country and for the individual German. We ourselves have done nothing to offer them a more hopeful meaning for this expression: we have never, for example, indicated that it refers only to military and party leaders.' The reason was clearly expressed by Roosevelt himself during a meeting with his Joint Chiefs of Staff, when he said, '. . . the German philosophy can not be changed by decree, law, or military order . . . I am not willing at this time to say that we do not intend to destroy the German nation.'[57]

Churchmen such as Joseph Cardinal Frings of Cologne, Pastor Niemöller,[58] Bishop von Galen, aristocrats, leaders and officers such as Fabian von Schlabrendorf, were pushed aside, or ignored or treated with contumely by the victorious Allies. The widow of one officer, Col. Georg Hansen, who had been executed by Hitler for resistance, lived in grief and poverty after the war because she was refused a pension and her husband's bank account was for a long time blocked by the Allies. Some, such as Ernst von Weizsäcker, were jailed by the Allies despite much evidence that they had risked a great deal to prevent war. Von Weizsäcker was found guilty and sentenced to five years. After strong British pleas to President Truman, he was finally released, when his sentence was reduced to time already served. He died less than a year later, on 4 August 1951. As the English author Patricia Meehan has shrewdly concluded, 'It was not the imprisonment for years of an innocent man which the [British] Foreign Office deprecated, so much as the incompetence of the American judges. The "Von Weizsäcker Trial" file listed in the Foreign Office index is not, alas, to be found. No doubt it still exists somewhere in the weeders' limbo.'[59]

While the German resistance movement was being treated with contempt by the British and Americans, the Soviets were making considerable efforts to indoctrinate captured Germans with communist ideology. As we saw, they set up a special camp at Krasnogorsk near Moscow where they re-educated willing German prisoners, including the famous Field Marshal, Paulus, who had besieged Stalingrad. The democracies made great efforts to aid every other resistance movement in Europe, none of them able to make a material difference in the fighting, while they refused all help to Hitler's German enemies, who were the only ones with a chance to end the war immediately. After the attempt on Hitler's life in July 1944, which ended in mass executions of resistance leaders by the Gestapo, all Churchill could think to tell the House was that 'the highest personalities in the German Reich are murdering one another, or trying to, while the avenging armies of the Allies close upon the doomed and ever-narrowing circle of their power'.[60]

Sir John W. Wheeler-Bennett, a senior Foreign Office advisor, thought that, 'It is to our advantage therefore that the [Hitler] purge should continue, since the killing of Germans by Germans will save us from future embarrassments of many kinds.'[61]

There was of course a reason for this unreasonable behaviour: the Allies were intent on unconditional surrender, which meant that they would not have to make any deals at all with any Germans, and could then treat the country as they wished. According to this view, all the Germans were so treacherous that no one could trust any of them. It was not just Nazis who were bad, it was all Germans. Any who tried to make peace were simply evil men who had seen the writing on the wall. No one could trust a German who was simply trying to get himself or his country out of a losing war by sacrificing Hitler. There was never any movement on the Western side to a *rapprochement* with any Germans, no matter how opposed they were to Hitler, no matter what they risked in defiance of Nazism, no matter how much they believed in the same ideals as the Allies themselves.

One of the oddities in Western policy was to continue support of Stalin in the USSR and Eastern Europe, while shunning like the plague all Stalinist communists in Germany, who had been by far the strongest of the resistors against the Nazis. Some communist prisoners at the concentration camp at Buchenwald very nearly captured the camp administration; communist and socialist resistors crowded the jails of Germany from 1933 to 1945. Their resistance was on a vastly greater scale than all others. But the Western powers feared them, while they were quite willing to hire ex-Nazis if they seemed useful.[62] These were a few scientists, spies and the like, who were spirited away regardless of their political affiliations. Some of these were taken to the US in 1945–47, then taken by train to the Canadian border at Niagara Falls, where the Canadians allowed them to enter the country illegally, then re-enter the US to comply with American immigration regulations. Some, perhaps many of these people, had been members of the Nazi party. One such was Dr Herbert P. Raabe of Potomac, Maryland, a radar expert who was illegally brought to the US, then 'laundered' along with many others at Niagara Falls, Canada, before being returned to the US as a 'legal' immigrant.[63] At the same time, large categories of resisting Germans, easy for the Allies to identify because many were in Hitler's jails in 1945, were starved along with the rest. These included Jehovah's Witnesses, who had fiercely resisted Hitler, refusing to fight or salute Nazi symbols, and so on.

The German-born Mennonites also resisted, although many caved in to Nazi pressure to join the armed forces. Some stuck to their pacifist principles, and ended up in jail, or else working in hospitals. But when in 1945 the Mennonite Central Committee in Canada and the US tried to send food over to their co-religionists, the Allied military governments refused the necessary permits. For over a year, thousands of men and women, many of whom had bravely (or not so bravely) resisted Hitler, starved while their co-religionists were prevented from helping them. Only in June 1946 were the Mennonites, Quakers and others finally permitted to send the necessary food to Germany.[64] Among the millions of Soviet citizens returned to the USSR were hundreds of thousands of refugees from communist tyranny. These included thousands of Mennonites who were beaten and shot at by British troops trying to force them on to the trains to the Gulag, for example at Liezen in Austria in June 1945.

Thus the democracies went on fighting the Germans long after the war ended, while their leaders promoted the Soviets, lied for them, and aided them in many ways. It has long been assumed that the West was simply too weak to resist the Soviet takeover of Poland and other Eastern European countries, but in fact the West was not helpless in the face of Russian might. At Potsdam, they were not under any threat from the Soviets when they approved the illegal transfers of populations and the seizure of German lands, all actions which were completely against the Atlantic Charter and various UN declarations. The US and Canada went on sending food, machinery and other aid to the Soviets long after their brutal actions in the East were known to Allied leaders.

Herbert Hoover was astonished to find how little UNRRA was doing to feed civilians in 'the seat of Western civilization', west of the Iron Curtain. Only 20 per cent of the world's famine area was being served, and most of UNRRA's food and other aid went to support the communist regimes in Eastern Europe and the Soviet Union itself.[65] The West not only helped them to cover up the war crimes they had committed against Poles at Katyn, the British showed that they apparently approved of Soviet crimes, when they delivered many thousands more victims from their cages into the hands of the same KGB murderers.

Winston Churchill bullied and persuaded the Free Poles who had been his allies in London during the war to return to Poland, assuring them that they would be taken into the new government. In fact, they were immediately arrested by Stalin and never seen free again. It is a fact that the British helped the Soviets to butcher or imprison the Cossacks and White Russians, while they and the Americans were indiscriminately punishing the Christian democratic resisters within Germany.

It has never been explained in the West how it was that their governments could reinforce the regime of mass-murderers like Stalin, Beria, Kaganovich and Molotov, while they were so afraid of truthful, compassionate men like Dietrich Bonhöffer, Cardinal Frings, Helmut von Moltke, Claus von Stauffenberg and hundreds of thousands of other German resisters. Many Western leaders viewed with indifference or approval the starvation of Germans who included friends of democracy and freedom. For instance, when Pastor Martin Niemöller said that he wanted to make a tour of Switzerland and the US in 1946 to 'appeal to fellow Christians and men of good will', he was arrested and returned to a concentration camp.[66] The Westerners had condemned the Nazis for assigning collective guilt to groups for crimes of individual members, but it would be unrealistic to deny that they did the same thing themselves.

All this is scarcely known to the major participants. A whole nation was maimed in peacetime, but when the events are even mentioned by the German survivors, they are immediately hushed up by their own government. No one is allowed to dig for the corpses of the murdered prisoners in Germany.[67] The criminals go free. To defend them, lies are told by historians who also defame the injured. Free expression of historical opinion is curbed by legislation that grows ever more stringent as time passes. No denial of history has ever been so successful.

Never was any other nation so forcibly estranged from itself and from its own past.

Which goes for the democracies too.

VII

THE VICTORY OF THE MERCIFUL

'Erst kommt das Fressen,
dann kommt die Moral.'*

BERTOLT BRECHT, THE THREEPENNY OPERA

We now turn our eyes away from criminals to men of the same nations but not of the same kind. These were the saviours, who came in the wake of war to help others.

There were two extraordinary events in the summer of 1945, apart from the atomic explosions. The first was the imposition of Allied vengeance on all Germans regardless of guilt, and the second was the organization of the greatest act of compassion the world had ever known. All around the world in 1945 there were areas of food poverty, as there have always been and are now. But in 1945, for the first time in human history, there was a concerted attempt by some nations to deal with food poverty around the world. This had never happened before. This was the real news, not the eternal pockets of food poverty. The nations leading this effort were the United States and Canada, helped by Australia and Argentina.

The relief of hunger around the world lay in the hands of a few men in Ottawa and Washington during the spring of 1945.

*'First the grub, then the preaching.'

142

These were the Prime Minister of Canada, Mackenzie King; one of his chief advisers, Norman Robertson, under-secretary in the Department of External Affairs; the new American President Harry Truman; and a man with no office, Herbert Hoover.

In the spring of 1945, Herbert Hoover stood aloof from the many people in Washington who were imposing starvation on Germany. This was why Truman needed him. He was never vindictive. Hoover appealed to a huge constituency of decent, moderate Americans who could not be satisfied by anyone less. Any world relief effort under his command would be effective and credible. Anyone else would begin with a handicap: not being Hoover. In 1945, as before, Hoover was the conscience of the West.

Harry Truman shared Herbert Hoover's generous impulse to feed the starving, whether they were ex-enemy or not. In May 1945, both were caught in the conflicting forces of politics in Washington. Truman needed Hoover's wisdom and experience because starvation threatened both ally and enemy in Europe, but it was difficult for Truman the Democrat to call on Hoover, who was not only a famous Republican but also a political has-been. Roosevelt had cast him into the outer darkness, a policy that remained in force under Steve Early, the press secretary inherited by Truman from Roosevelt. Steve Early and Roosevelt were so opposed to Hoover's efforts to bring relief to starving Belgians and Poles that Early had once given orders over his White House phone to Norman Davis, Chairman of the American Red Cross, to 'Stop that fellow Hoover. We don't want him to get anywhere.'[1]

Hoover was by far the most knowledgeable person in the world on international food relief, but he had been kept entirely out of the allied planning for post-war aid. The planning had been initiated by the British in September 1941, then gradually expanded to include the Americans, Soviets,

Canadians and Chinese. It was the Chinese delegate to the Inter-Allied Committee meeting in Washington in December 1942 who asked that Hoover be called in to advise on some difficult voting procedures, but the Roosevelt administration was so prejudiced against Hoover that it refused.[2]

The State Department also opposed Hoover. This combination made it so difficult for Truman that the preliminary negotiations in spring 1945 to get Hoover's help, through Secretary of War Henry L. Stimson and others, went on for weeks, while both the principals fretted. Truman wanted Hoover to offer his services publicly, so he would not have the onus of inviting him; Hoover needed the President's public invitation in order to be effective once he did accept. This would demonstrate to the recalcitrant Democrats and others that he was not seeking office, but had responded to his country's needs. So many advisers became involved that Truman finally escaped by a simple method: he wrote by hand a letter to Hoover which he posted himself, inviting Hoover to come. The ice was broken. Hoover accepted eagerly and finally went to Washington for a meeting in the White House with Truman in May.

Truman asked Hoover for advice on several subjects, but especially food relief for foreigners, excluding Germans. At that time, the occupied countries were exclusively the province of the occupying armies. All of the relief discussions among the Western Allies had had a meagre result – the United Nations Relief and Rehabilitation Administration (UNRRA). Hoover had a derisive opinion of it, because it was dominated by power politics and lacking in authority. He told Truman that it was 'incapable of administering the larger economic problems of Europe'.[3] Part of the trouble was that the organization was more interested in itself than in its mission. Truman was probably shocked to hear from this expert that UNRRA was grossly inefficient. By the end of its life in Europe in 1947, it had administered the supply of some 24 million tons of food and

equipment worth some $2.9 billion, and had paid substantial
salaries, whereas the American relief work Hoover had administered during and after the First World War supplied almost
twice as much food and equipment, worth more than double
the amount sent by UNRRA. And all the principal officers of
the American Relief Administration under Hoover were vol-
unteers.[4] When Truman met Hoover in May 1945, UNRRA
was then gearing up to its maximum effort, which by spring
1946 still covered less than 20 per cent of the famine areas of
the world. And most of the food was going to areas controlled
by the communists. Germany was totally omitted, and Western
Europe received a relatively small share.[5]

After Truman called on him a second time, in early 1946,
Hoover again agreed to help. He began his world food relief
effort by studying the world food situation from documents
available in Washington that showed there was considerably
more food on hand than the government had previously
thought: the reduction, according to Secretary of War Robert
Patterson,* was only 9 per cent per capita from pre-war. An
amount of 1 per cent per capita at world population levels of
the time meant a difference of enough food to increase rations
from starvation levels of around 1,200cpd to survival levels of
around 2,000 for approximately fifty million people.[6] Hoover
confirmed this in his report in the spring of 1946 when he said
after a world-wide survey that by the methods he suggested,
'over 90 per cent of the gap between supply and minimum
needs of the famine areas would be met'.[7] The Patterson papers
show conclusively that in US Cabinet discussions during one
severe crisis, in early 1946, the best informed Americans,
including President Truman, judged there had been enough
food ever since the end of the German war to feed everyone –
including Germans. The problem that Patterson encountered

*Patterson succeeded Stimson in 1945.

over and over again was what he called the problem of 'priority'. Not shortage.[8]

In the spring of 1946, Hoover continued the policy that had succeeded so well during and after the First World War, appealing to the voluntary generosity of the Americans because he believed passionately in the United States of America. He was convinced that the public opinion in the country normally expressed good-will. The function of government was never to tell people what to think; it was to do co-operatively what the people could not do so well individually.* In the First World War, Hoover raised money for Belgian relief by private subscription as well as by accepting the accumulated savings of the Belgian people. After the war, he raced around the US 'selling goodness' at $1,000-a-plate dinners for Polish relief. He was openly critical of John Kenneth Galbraith and President Franklin Roosevelt for imposing price controls by law during the Second World War, because he had led voluntary price controls in the First, which had kept inflation lower than during 1939–46. Public opinion and the public will were everything to him: they could scarcely be wrong. In any case, where he needed help for a great public benefit, he appealed to the innate charity in Everyman. He was never disappointed by the common man, only by statesmen.

Hoover broadcast an appeal to the American people in March 1946, just before leaving for a round-the-world mission by air to visit the heads of thirty-eight states to discuss ways to feed the starving. Hoover outlined the situation to the Americans, and concluded with the words: 'I can only appeal to your pity and your mercy. I know that the heart of the American people will respond with kindliness and . . . compassion. Will you not take to your table an invisible guest?'[9]

---

*A corollary to this might be that anything proposed that was *against* public opinion did *not* express good-will. Therefore it had to be kept secret.

Hoover's summation of the situation in early 1946 was brief and to the point. 'The net result of our computations was that approximately 313,000,000 people were confronted with the problem of providing overseas [i.e. imports] food for some 1,400,000,000 hungry people in "deficit" countries.' The major surplus countries to make up the shortfall were Canada, the USA, Australia and Argentina. There was a gap in the foreseeable future between the need for 26,000,000 tons of cereals and apparent supplies of around 15,000,000 tons. If the statistics were correct, Hoover estimated that very soon some 800,000,000 people would starve. Most would die.

The Cabinet meeting on 29 March 1946 to discuss the food problem, with Truman, Secretary of Agriculture Clinton Anderson and Patterson, decided that 'the real trouble was one of price, it being more profitable for the farmers today to feed their grain to animals than to sell it as grain. The farmers were holding wheat in an expectation of a price rise.'[10] Truman was lifting price controls so American grain farmers could get a free-market price, which could only be afforded by the richer nations, who were not starving. Later in the year, the Americans also solved the rail-car problem that had been allowed to delay shipments abroad. Patterson was vehement: 'I am impressed by the fact that . . . the percentage of cars now used for grain has fallen 15 per cent below last year. Such a condition seems to me to be one which it is indefensible for this government to tolerate in the face of the imminent hunger confronting the populations of our occupied areas . . .'[11]

In his lengthy correspondence on the matter, Patterson constantly refers to lack of priority, misallocation of rail cars and so on, not to any production shortage. As we have seen, he told Secretary of State George C. Marshall that the occupation would fail if starvation conditions continued. He insisted that the famine had been foreseen, but little done to prevent it.[12]

The American price policy was a great problem for the

Canadians, as Prime Minister King pointed out in a 'most important' Cabinet meeting in Ottawa in September 1946. 'The US are allowing the price of wheat to be sold to England to go from $1.50 to $2. Were we to do the same . . . altogether the result would very shortly be the bursting of the price ceiling with rapid inflation of prices.'[13]

In early 1946, the Canadians still had rationing and price controls, and were generously giving away wheat or selling it below market value to those who needed it most.[14] In February 1946, Prime Minister King was told by Norman Robertson, his senior foreign affairs policy adviser, that 'Though the war ended nearly six months ago, our food industry and Canadian consumers are still on a wartime basis. Thus we rationed meat when others [i.e. the Americans] were dropping controls. We cut our rice consumption in half. We slashed sugar and butter rations last year and took another big slice off butter consumption a few days ago. We have always lived up to our commitments. We are the only country in the world which has done so.' This was done because 'the people of Canada will wish to make new efforts to help meet a world shortage and will expect the government to give advice and direction as to the form those efforts could most effectively take'.[15]

The Americans, who in autumn of 1945 had promised to ship 225 million tons of wheat abroad, had vastly exceeded their target by June 1946.[16] Patterson was especially pleased by this achievement. He wrote a letter to Truman on 8 July 1946 outlining what the United States had done to relieve suffering around the world. It is an extraordinary document, showing the man in charge of the greatest war machine that had ever existed delighting in how he had used his enormous power to feed the starving.

He told Harry Truman that 'It gives me a great deal of personal satisfaction to be able to say to you that . . . by the middle of this month we will have loaded and shipped the surprising total of 417,000,000 bushels [of wheat] which is 17,000,000 more than were ever committed by this government. It is all the more remarkable because the requirement presented to the US representative on the Combined Food Board a year ago was 225,000,000 bushels for the year and remained at that figure until late Fall of 1945. Thanks are due to you for the vigorous way in which you supported the [War] Department and its efforts and to [others including] Herbert Hoover . . .' He was especially grateful to Col. Monroe Johnson and Captain Granville Conway, 'without whose able handling of the transportation problem our job could not have been done'.[17]

By the end of 1946, Hoover was proclaiming triumph over 'the greatest famine in world history'. He claimed that hundreds of millions of lives had been saved in the first world-wide famine relief effort in human history. Only Germany was left out. For the rest, it was an amazing creative achievement, following on the most destructive war that mankind had ever known. How did he do it?

Hoover travelled 35,000 miles and visited twenty-two countries in the spring of 1946, arranging for food collection and distribution. He travelled by a slow propeller-driven plane. He was seventy-two years old. He co-ordinated supplies, improved transport, borrowed from people in early-crop areas to feed others who repaid the loan after their own crops came in; he appealed directly via radio and print to Americans and Canadians to reduce consumption of luxury foods, he helped to reduce spoilage, he improved pricing policy, he humbled himself to beg in countries that had surplusses not yet reported, he reduced reserve supplies, always co-ordinating with the President's team. Together, Truman, Anderson, Mackenzie King, Hoover and Patterson vastly reduced the gap in supplies.[18] By the end of the year, the gap between need and production had vanished, although, as the situation in Germany showed, production did not necessarily fill the evident need.

Hoover's unshakable commitment was essential to success. For instance, he flew to Argentina for talks with the dictator Juan Perón, overriding the strong objections of the US State department. But Hoover knew that Perón had over 1.6 million tons of surplus food. He went to Perón's inaugural dinner because 'I was resolved . . . to eat even Argentine dirt if I could get the 1,600,000 tons.'[19] He ate the dirt, and Europe got the food.

Prime Minister King invited Hoover to Ottawa to make a speech at the end of his world tour in June 1946. Hoover was generous in his praise of the Canadian people: 'To Canada flows the gratitude of hundreds of millions of human beings who have been saved from starvation through the efforts of this great Commonwealth of the north.' He described the crisis, and then explained how it had been met. 'In these two months since those estimates, the world has developed even further additions to world supplies. The Latin American states have greatly reduced their import requirements during the crisis months.' But he warned that the children were going to suffer terribly even if they did not die. 'Millions of mothers are today watching their children wilt before their eyes.' The proof was in annual mortality rates that in some cities were as high as 200%% per year. Children's TB cases in Kiel in 1946 climbed to 70 per cent more than in the previous years. Hoover called for a renewed effort to save the children.[20]

King wrote in his diary that Hoover told him in confidence that in certain areas, not including Germany, he 'had found the reports about starvation much exaggerated. When he got down to discuss with technical officers the actual situation, he found it in many countries quite different from that which the politicians had been stating it was.'[21] This did not reduce the importance of the work, but it certainly made Hoover's task easier, both because some people had actually more food than he had been told, and because the rich had more surplus.

The situation in Germany was in fact worse than press

reports indicated. A year after the war had ended, the Canadian Military Mission in Berlin sent a telegram to External Affairs in Ottawa saying that they had spoken to the British Food and Agricultural Division that morning, who reported that no imports had been programmed beyond the month of May. The date of the telegram was 9 May 1946.

'Bread and potatoes constitute nearly two-thirds of civilian ration,' said the Canadian telegram. 'British zone was consequently faced with the prospect of being reduced from slightly over 1,000 to about 450 calories [per day]. There was therefore justification for statement that famine was just around the corner.'[22]

Patterson prompted Truman to turn to Hoover once again at the end of 1946. After a talk with Hoover in December, Patterson noted for his files, 'I said that . . . he had been of great value to us in obtaining sufficient food for the United States zone in Germany earlier in the year; that we had difficult problems relative to food at the present time, as to getting an adequate supply to maintain a 1,550 ration in Germany and Austria because of transportation troubles, as to the possibility of raising the 1,550 ration to 1,800, this being primarily a fiscal matter . . . I stated that we would be going to Congress next month for additional funds to support the army food programs in the occupied areas.'[23]

When Truman's third call to Hoover came, in January 1947, Hoover was ready. He was well aware that he might be loaded with much responsibility and little authority, so he refused Truman's first offer by returning the President's letter with amendments giving him the right to investigate the effects of American policy on Germany. This was the first time that such a mandate had been asked of the powerful Executive branch. Truman sent Hoover's letter to the State Department, the same department that had authorized the illegal, secret and unilateral denunciation of the Geneva Convention,[24] which was supposed to have the force of constitutional law in the US, as we have seen. The Department had also resisted Hoover's snooping before.

If there was not absolute dread in the State Department at the thought of the energetic, truthful and compassionate Hoover poking into this sordid affair, they had more *sang froid* than it is reasonable to assume. One likely reason that Truman at first resisted Hoover's request was that the State Department advised him to do so. Truman sent back to Hoover an equivocal version of the requested mandate. That was enough for Hoover: he would interpret the mandate as broadly as possible. Thus began a mission that extended a mercy while it investigated a crime. He brought back to the US thousands of pages of army and US Military Government documents relative to the effect of American policy on Germany, all of them still in the Hoover Institution archives in Stanford, California.*

Hoover and travelling US diplomat Will Clayton met in January 1947 to discuss the disaster in the British–American zone of Germany, where industrial production had been forced down to 28 per cent of 1938 output. Food production in France and the UK had actually dropped in the preceding year, partly because of the fall in German industrial production which in turn was caused in part by the destruction of German factories and machines, and partly because of the cutbacks in fuel production. It was precisely oil production that Henry Morgenthau had fought bitterly to ban in 1945, among 500 other banned items.[25] The enforced reduction in oil production was particularly damaging to the farmers, because it meant that their tractors were useless, and other machinery endangered. The reduction in coal meant that it was much more difficult to transport food to processing and preserving centres.

*They are at the foundation of this section of the book. To my knowledge, they have never been used *in extenso* by any writer before to describe Germany as it then was.

In 1945–46 the democracies were concerned about starvation around the world, excluding Germany. After that, the problem was the politics of hostility towards Germany. The 9–10 per cent reduction in world food supply, if shared equally in the world, would have meant a drop in North American consumption from the existing average of about 3,300cpd to about 3,000cpd.[26] Since the long-term optimum for health in an active adult is around 2,000 to 3,000cpd, depending on activity, temperature and so on, the new level would have been healthier than the old.

In Germany, pre-war consumption had been about 3,000cpd, and the nation on average had been 81–85 per cent self-sufficient in food production.[27] It was never necessary to make war to get food, or to get 'land for the German plow', as Hitler had said. This was underlined by the result of the survey conducted by the US Army in summer 1945. The army discovered that the Germans had never been seriously short of food during the war, and that their requisitions from foreign countries had been 'minor'.[28]

The exclusion of Germany from world relief was thought at the time to be entirely the fault of the Germans themselves. It has been repeatedly stated by Western historians that if Germany was short of food, this was neither the fault nor the intent of the Allies. The argument is simple: 'The war was the culprit, and the Germans had started the war, so they should suffer first and most. In difficult circumstances not of their own making, the Allies generously fed the Germans from their own resources. This they did at their own expense, many hundreds of millions of dollars per year for each of the US and UK. Far from vengeance, this was an unprecedented act of generosity.' In the words of the British Select Committee on Estimates in London, 'It is probably without parallel in history that twelve months after the end of a war, Great Britain should be paying eighty million pounds a year towards the upkeep of her principal adversary.'[29] It makes a creditable ending to a grotesque war. But is it true?

A few facts support the theory. Many of the Allies in the summer of 1945 had no intention of imposing mass starvation on Germany. A Canadian on Eisenhower's staff, Lt. Gen. A. E. Grasett, was asked to report on the wheat situation, and wrote in June 1945 to his chiefs at SHAEF that 'the wheat that will be arriving should be adequate to prevent starvation', among the German civil population.[30] Much wheat was sent to Germany intended for relief of German civilians. But many people in high places, from Morgenthau down, were determined to impose a harsh vengeance on Germany in the guise of preventing a resurgence of German power. This would be easier to carry out if the public believed that there was a world food shortage from 1946 on.

The statistics of world food production do not bear out the official history. The food production of the world measured in calories per capita in October 1945 by the US Office of Foreign Agricultural Relations was 90 per cent of pre-war levels.[31] Food production in the world for 1945–46 per capita *outside the US* was about 12 per cent below pre-war levels.[32] Distributed according to need, this food would have been easily adequate to feed everyone, because the pre-war average was well above basic human need. For 1946–47, world production was up by 7 per cent, meaning that, overall, it was very close to pre-war levels.[33] It also means that much of the 3 per cent shortfall was low production in Germany. However, in Europe, the '1946 harvest was surprisingly good', according to the World Food Appraisal report of the UN, issued in December 1946. Wheat and rye production was up one-third, to 80 per cent of normal, potatoes up 18 per cent, and sugar-beets up one-third to 66 per cent of pre-war level.[34]

Since production in 1944–48 was running far higher than it had before the war in the main producing/exporting countries,

Canada and the US, the critical factor then and later was the availability of the Canadian-US surplus.[35] The United States, Canada and several other major exporting countries began 1945 with a surplus of food. As Robert Patterson wrote to Mr Justice Byrnes on 27 December 1944, US food production in 1944 equalled the all-time high set in 1942. The 1944 crop was 10 per cent higher than any year prior to 1942. Wheat, corn, rice and many other crops broke all records. The fact was, Patterson said, there was 'a surplus of food [in the US]'.[36]

World food production was virtually normal in 1947, except in Germany. Since the rest of the world was so close to normal, it is clear that the reason for German starvation was not that there was a fatal world shortage of food. Allied policies were responsible for nearly all the excess deaths. The worst of the policies of the four occupying powers was the confiscation of 25 per cent of the arable land of the country, together with the forced expulsions of nearly all the inhabitants into the damaged and shrunken remainder. But this was not all. Another part of Allied policy prevented the Germans from manufacturing goods to pay for food imports; another part prevented them from collecting food or cash in return for the billions of dollars' worth of goods that were confiscated surplus to reparations; another part prevented them from producing sufficient food for themselves; another part prevented international relief agencies from providing them with food during the most critical first year to year and a half of peace; and later, another part ordered food to be supplied to them free by Allied taxpayers. Hoover later wrote that under President Roosevelt, the American policy had 'accumulated blunders in administration which by January 1946 had endangered the lives of millions of people all over the world'.[37]

*

155

What was the Germans' agricultural capability in the summer of 1945? The British Foreign Office said in 1947 that the area occupied by the British and Americans was capable of producing about 1,750cpd for the local inhabitants, which was the production before the war. Ambassador Robert Murphy agreed.[38]

Lt. Col. Grasett reported in June 1945 that the US–UK–French zone had been 60–70 per cent self-sufficient before the war. This meant a potential of 1,800 to 2,100cpd for those zones. Grasett added the amazing fact that the cropland planted that spring was 97 per cent of normal despite the bombing, lack of labour and military campaigns that had just rolled through.[39] However, both Hoover and the Foreign Office reported that German farmers in the combined British and American zones actually produced food enough *for only about 1,000cpd in 1946 and 1947.*[40]

It is clear from this that if the Germans in the west, unburdened by refugees, had produced as much as their land would grow, very few would have starved. But they didn't even get above 1,000cpd production despite tremendous incentive. Why not?

The British Foreign Office reported in July 1947 that this catastrophic fall in production was due to lack of labour, lack of implements, lack of fertilizer and the increase in demand for food caused by the refugees.[41] Robert Murphy agreed.[42] The most important of these – labour, fertilizer and surplus mouths – were caused by Allied policies.

The industrial production on which farming depends had been around 105 per cent of pre-war levels in late 1944 and early 1945,[43] showing that once the war production had been eliminated in May 1945, there was sufficient to supply the existing level of farm production. In spring 1945, about 60–70 per cent of the pre-war livestock were still alive.[44] It is clear that when the Allies took over in May 1945, *the potential for agricultural production in west Germany was much higher than the food the Germans received.* The potential was almost enough to maintain life; it was certainly enough to sharply reduce epidemic disease, which occurs in starving populations.

This food potential had been achieved during the war despite the absence of most of the German male labour force, despite reliance on inefficient prisoner labour, despite the bombing, military campaigns, and shortage of oil and transport.

What finally assured the prolonged starvation of Germans was the enforced reduction of industry. By autumn 1945, industrial production was deliberately reduced to around 25–30 per cent of pre-war levels,[45] thus preventing the chance of buying food imports. This was not a consequence of the bombing or the military campaign. The most heavily damaged area of Germany was the Ruhr, where less than 30 per cent of the plant equipment and machinery was destroyed by war. In Germany as a whole, 80–85 per cent of the machinery and plant survived intact,[46] but in 1946 in the US zone, exports were forced down to only 3 per cent of pre-war levels.[47] The Allies slowed oil production to a trickle, closed down factories, kept the male labour force imprisoned, confiscated or destroyed factories and machinery, imposed restrictive financial measures, reduced the postal service, and so on.

Food production and food imports came under specific attack when the fishing fleet was prevented from going to sea for a year, and the Western Allies drastically cut the production of fertilizer.[48] By false accounting, the Allies also refused to credit the value of some German exports to the German account, making it impossible for Germans to earn foreign currency to buy food. Baldly stated, many valuable goods were stolen, beyond the reparations agreed among the Allies.[49] All foreign governments and international relief agencies, including UNRRA and the Red Cross, were prevented from assisting

Germans for the first critical year. By the time such pacifist organizations as the Mennonites of Canada were permitted to send food to their co-religionists in Germany, in June 1946, the overall death rate in Germany had risen to more than double the normal rate.[50] So much food was confiscated by the invaders that the ICRC was moved to complain in August 1945.[51] The ICRC had over 1,000 boxcars and 400 trucks actually shipping relief food into Germany despite war damage in the spring of 1945. At least three trains reached Ravensburg, Augsburg and Moosburg, but were refused permission to unload by the Allies, who sent them back with their food to Switzerland. From there, the Red Cross returned the food to the original donors.[52] An exception to the general rule appears to have been the arrival in Lübeck in autumn 1945 of three Swedish ships loaded with relief supplies intended for Germans. It is not clear, however, that the supplies were actually distributed to Germans.[53]

As a result of the seizures of land and the expulsions in the east by Poland and the USSR, about twelve million starving, penniless refugees poured into the remainder of Germany. In the British zone between January 1946 and January 1947, more than 1,700,000 of these helpless people were imposed on the twenty million original inhabitants.[54] Such were the avertable calamities in the three Western zones that created the situation Hoover was trying to correct.

Despite all the catastrophes of war, despite the loss of food from the seized lands and the loss of the food production of the Soviet-occupied zone, in the spring of 1945 the western Germans had at least a hope of maintaining themselves without any imports. If the Allies had not impeded them, there can hardly be any doubt that they would have found a way to feed themselves a meagre diet on their own land. Many lives would have been saved.

Another very odd aspect of all this is the fact that although the British and Americans undoubtedly did send much wheat to Germany in 1945–48, the Germans themselves rarely got more food than they produced themselves. Herbert Hoover and assorted British officers all said at various times in 1945–46 that the Germans were producing around 1,000 to 1,100cpd, but they often received less than that. The ration actually received for long periods in the British–American zone was around 1,000cpd and sometimes no more than 900.[55]

The Germans themselves had of course recognized the desperate plight of their children. They set up feeding programs in the cities, but the scarcity of imported food limited their scope terribly. For example, from 31 October 1945 to 31 March 1946 the welfare authorities of the city of Kiel organized feedings for 1,000 schoolchildren, who got a warm midday meal of 500–600 calories. Parents paid 10 pfennig, but money was also contributed by the British soldiers of Sperrzone F. At first only 6 per cent of the city's children could be fed, despite the fact that 20–25 per cent were undernourished. Thus the aid went only to the neediest. In order to help as many as possible, each 'class' was fed for only ten weeks, then replaced by another.[56]

By 1946, the Germans were dying in such large numbers, probably about double the pre-war average, that the ban on private aid was slowly relaxed.[57] Early in the year, the Allies set up CARE (Co-operative for American Remittances to Europe), covering twenty-two independent US charities. CRALOG (Council of Relief Agencies Licensed for Operation in Germany) was set up in February to supervise sixteen American independent charitable organizations.[58]

The Germans in the three western zones co-operated through their own large charitable organizations such as the Hilfswerk der Evangelischen Kirchen in Deutschland, Deutsche Caritasverband, Arbeiterwohlfahrt and Deutsche Rote Kreuz (whose work had been curtailed immediately after the war because of suspected Nazi elements in the administration).

These organizations banded together to form the Zentral-ausschuß zur Verteilung ausländischer Liebesgaben, with headquarters in the seaport city of Bremen.[59] The Zentral-ausschuß authorized the delivery and distribution of foreign aid that had finally begun trickling in. According to the German author Gabriele Stüber, the reliable infrastructure of these German welfare agencies helped to ensure an equitable distri-bution to those in greatest need.

The grisly mortality rates for children quoted by Hoover to Mackenzie King certainly applied to the Germans ahead of all others. Yet Hoover had to beg the American Military Governor, Lucius Clay, to improve the official ration, which had been cut from slow starvation, 1,550cpd, to 1,275, effective from 1 April 1946.

Hoover was typically generous when the autocratic Lucius Clay swallowed his pride to make his own appeal to him for help. Hoover replied: 'Feeding the enemy requires no debate with me, since it must be done for many reasons.' He urged Clay to restore the 1,550 calorie level, promising to do his best to arrange immediate help. But as Hoover wrote: 'The General apparently determined to take no risks and held to the reduced 1,275 calories – which was below the endurance level.'[60] Even this might not be maintained, and in fact was not, as Patterson was 'deeply disturbed' to note in May 1947. He told Anderson that the situation in both Germany and Austria was 'extremely critical'.[61] He also told Secretary of State George Marshall in June 1947 that the 'average ration for the last six weeks has been 1,200 calories, and in many places it is as low as 900 calories . . . this is slow famine . . . the British ration [in the UK] is 2,900 calories per day, the average American consumes 3,300 . . .'[62]

Clay did lift one restriction that had prevented Americans from sending CARE food-relief packages to Germany. As

Hoover pointed out, some Americans imbued with 'the spirit of the Morgenthau Plan' had 'invented the warning that [relief] packages would all go to the "upper classes" so our military authorities had refused to allow the distribution of CARE packages . . .'[63] The many letters of thanks received from the grateful recipients demonstrate that the CARE packages were not going to the 'upper classes'. Even the smallest CARE packages lifted the spirits of the parents and children. To receive even one half of a CARE package so cheered Deacon Wilhelm Lorenz in Kiel in the British zone that he wrote, in May 1947:

> You will think it is not very much since it is intended for the sixty-five students and seventy small children we have in our care. Quite the contrary. For us it is a great deal to get our hands on such a thing in these scarce times. We are able to create with it much joy. For us even the smallest help is worth while.[64]

In happy contrast to the situation in Germany, conditions in Holland, Belgium and France 'are much better than had been anticipated', Mackenzie King was told by the former Premier of France, Léon Blum, in August 1946. King had no trouble believing this, because he had already heard from the Canadian Military Mission in Berlin that the Belgians were flourishing. They had eggs and steaks, and queues for food were small and rare.[65] According to the United Nations, 'the United Kingdom, although a major food importing country, still maintained a diet which though much less varied than in normal times, reaches about 90 per cent of the pre-war calorie level.'[66] Germany and Italy were much worse off than the others.[67]

The US Secretary of Agriculture Clinton Anderson had told Truman the same thing in March 1946. He said that 'the food situation had been thus far nearly normal in the Scandinavian countries, Britain, Holland, Belgium and France. As for Italy, one of the principal troubles was faulty distribution . . . the situation was not good in Germany . . . [General McNarney felt] deep concern about the food situation in the United States zone in Germany'.[68]

The first few CRALOG packages arrived in the US zone in February 1946.[69] The Evangelische Hilfswerk distributed packages in the US zone in April 1946, but it was not until October 1946 that the Hilfswerk distributed parcels in the British and French zones.

In the US zone the military government would not allow other aid organizations outside CRALOG members to operate. Robert Kreider, representing the Mennonite Central Committee as a member of the first CRALOG delegation, came to Berlin in March 1946 and later worked in Stuttgart under the US military government. For a pacifist Mennonite like Kreider it was an unusual experience:

> We were assigned billets in a requisitioned apartment house, issued mess cards, PX* cards, clothing ration cards, photographed for our military pass, issued currency control booklets. Never in my life have I felt so enveloped in the military . . . I am confident that our civilian dress and status will have its rewards as we proceed with our work. It is best that we be not too closely identified with the conquering power. Frequently I experience sharp pains of conscience in regard to our comfortable existence. In the officers' mess we eat far better than we did at home, and then on our doorstep are the German people who live on a 1,275-calorie-a-day ration. Only if we can be an instrument of bringing food to these on our doorstep can we atone for the sin of which we personally are a part.[70]

*'Post Exchange': the US military retail store.

In the Mennonite archives at Goshen, Indiana, is a letter from Kreider describing the relations between the US military government and the efforts of the Mennonites. 'The AMG (American Military Government), apart from the Welfare Branch, apparently is none too keen on CRALOG – as military men only tolerating this civilian group . . . we are happy to co-operate fully with the other agencies in this joint relief distribution effort of CRALOG. As demonstrated by our work in England, France, Italy, Belgium etc. – our relief concerns go far beyond the needs of our own group. In Germany our concern is beyond the needs of our own people.'[71]

The Mennonites, through the Evangelische Hilfswerk in particular, helped to supply school feeding programs. Twenty tons of Mennonite flour went into a feeding program for 72,000 children in Greater Hesse, who received *Brötchen*, or 100-gram rolls, which the children said were 'better than cake!'.[72]

Cornelius Dyck arrived in Kiel in the British Zone as a CRALOG representative for the Mennonite Central Committee of the US and Canada in late December 1946. By 13 January 1947 he had arranged facilities to feed 5,000 children in Kiel aged from three to six.[73] A further 6,000 were fed from Swiss aid. The German Red Cross, with foreign help, took on another 2,500. Food was given out in the form of a warm meal (usually soup) served in the local schools. But before the children could even walk the snowy streets to school for food, the Swiss had to distribute 1,000 pairs of shoes to the barefoot. Huge kettles left kitchens set up in the dismantled Germania-Werft factory and were carried in trucks fuelled by British gasoline. Sometimes in this particularly severe winter of 1946–47 the kettles had to be dragged by hand through the snow near the schools when the trucks got stuck in unplowed drifts. At the end of the initial feeding in April it was decided to continue feeding 7,500 especially undernourished children in Kiel. As late as 1949, more than a third of the schoolchildren in Kiel were barefoot.[74]

Similar programs were set up in Lübeck, and Krefeld in the British zone. In the French zone there were a number of child-feeding projects in the cities and in the Saar area where 9,000 children were fed by the Hilfs-Ausschuß, a committee with representatives from at least four German agencies. In Ludwigshafen 8,000 children between the ages of six and fourteen got a 300–500 calorie meal six times a week.

By the summer of 1947 the Mennonite Central Committee was reaching approximately 80,000 people in feeding operations in Germany. Of the more than 5,815 tons of food, clothing, Christmas bundles and other supplies sent to Europe by American and Canadian Mennonites by the summer of 1947, nearly 4,000 tons went to Germany.[75]

Other donations arrived from the United States and Canada, especially from Lutheran Church members, and citizens of German background, and various non-denominational charities like the Save the Children fund. Sweden and Switzerland and later Denmark[76] made large contributions. British relief agencies belonging to COBSRA (Council of British Societies for Relief Abroad) had been working along with the French *Mission Militaire de Liaison Administrative* in the British 12th Army Group area even before UNRRA teams arrived. By the summer of 1945 COBSRA had 1,500 relief workers operating in the British zone, but their contribution was directed towards supplying and helping displaced persons rather than German civilians.[77] In the summer of 1945, Eisenhower had forbidden the North American Quakers to come to Germany to help orphans who were wandering the streets 'unaccompanied'. He had also recommended to the War Department that this policy be kept secret.[78] But finally, one year later, Canadian, British and American Quaker personnel were allowed to take care of the children. It is painful to imagine what happened to the orphaned children in the year when help was banned.

In July 1946 the Irish Red Cross initiated a programme to

bring more than 400 German children to Ireland for a three-year period of recuperation. In 1948, 100 children were given a six-month holiday at Glencree in Ireland, special preference being given to children aged between five and eleven whose fathers were dead or missing due to the war. Some of these children later reminisced that they had at first refused a banana or an orange because they had never seen one before, and remembered how they had thought that chocolates were shiny buttons.[79]

In the spring of 1947, in the midst of the worst food crisis since 1945, a new programme entitled Hoover Aid ('Hoover-Spende') was planned to broaden the scope of the school feeding operation to more children throughout Germany. Many mothers and fathers breathed a sigh of relief at the assurance that their children would at last be fed. The programme was massive: over 4.6 million schoolchildren in the Bizone (newly combined British–American zone) would be involved, 2.8 million in the British zone and 1.8 million in the American zone. The price per meal was to be between 15 and 25 pfennig. But then the disastrous news came: not enough food was available. The number of participants was cruelly cut, from 4.6 to 3.55 million, 2.15 in the British zone, and 1.4 million in the US zone. For some areas in the British zone such as Schleswig-Holstein, which had abandoned its own school feeding programs to make way for the Hoover-Spende, the new guidelines meant that at first *fewer* children could be served than under the old programme. According to the new quotas, of the 500,000 schoolchildren there, only 50 per cent could be involved at one time. These quotas were especially hard on those Stadtkreise and Landkreise which were coping with a huge influx of expellees from the east, many of whom were children.

By June 1947 it was decreed in Schleswig-Holstein that only children who were at least 15 per cent underweight or had severe health problems would be able to take part. In March the following year, meals were reduced from six to five days a week in order to be able to accommodate more children. Schleswig-Holstein was not the only area forced to reduce the numbers fed in 1947–48. In Niedersachsen, 52.8 per cent of the schoolchildren, i.e. about 500,000, were categorized as in bad health, but of these only 330,000 children obtained a meal supplement under the Hoover Plan.[80]

The need for extra feeding for children persisted for years. In Bonn in 1949, after the currency reform, 19,000 meals were still being given out every day at a cost of 15 Dpf per meal and the kitchens were not closed until April of that year.[81] As late as the summer of 1950 the state health department of Schleswig-Holstein felt the urgent need to continue the school feeding program because 60–70 per cent of their school children were still undernourished.[82]

The Allies set up various agencies to 'control' relief into Germany, but clearly a large part of their purpose was not to control but to eliminate relief. One Quaker said, 'The US Army made it difficult for relief.' This is a forgiving under-statement considering that they were physically barred for a whole year when the starvation was most acute.[83] As we have seen, thousands of truckloads of supplies from Switzerland, Sweden and Ireland were refused entry in 1945 and 1946.[84] A few were sneaked in illegally simply through the benevolence of the local Allied commander. The Swiss Relief Fund started a private charity to feed a meagre meal once a day to a thousand Bavarian children for a couple of months. As soon as the US zone occupation authorities discovered what was going on, they 'decided that the aid . . . should not at once be accepted'.[85] The army informed the ICRC that 'public opinion in the US would not allow' private charity to go to Germany. They offered no evidence for this. All the evidence of the elected representatives of the people of the US, in the speeches of Senators Wherry, Langer and others, had shown just the opposite. While the local army officers were telling this lie to the Swiss, Secretary of War Patterson, in charge of that very army was, as we have seen, working as hard as he could to get food to Germans. And in the UK 'even the concept of voluntary aid via food parcels from Britain's civilians was anathema to Whitehall' in October 1945. Such aid to Germans was forbidden.[86]

The modern historian comes away from these documents and interviews under the impression that for a significant time after 1945, the hidden purpose of the armies, CRALOG and other such supposedly charitable agencies was to camouflage the elimination of charitable aid to Germany. It was not therefore any paucity of private aid that caused the Germans to starve, but the bureaucratic entanglements the private agencies had to fight. In the hungriest year of all, 1947, CRALOG's top ten voluntary agencies sent to Germany about 26,000,000 lbs of relief material all told.[87] Even if all of this had been food, which was not the case, it would have supplied perhaps eight ounces per year per person in the western zones. This cynical tokenism was why Kreider's conscience bothered him.

The high prices caused by low industrial production were an important cause of European urban food shortages in 1947. This low production was in large part a result of low activity in Germany. The farmers of Europe simply withheld some of their surplusses from the market because the people in the cities were producing so little of value to trade. Will Clayton and Hoover had discovered that the farmers were hoarding food while people in the cities were starving.[88] The British Foreign Secretary, Ernest Bevin, blamed the price rise for the suffering in Britain and for the need to impose bread rationing in peacetime. 'The rise in prices has thrown us a year out [in recovery],' he told Will Clayton in June 1947.[89] Short of exports to earn foreign currency, Britain simply could not afford to pay for all the foreign wheat that she wanted and that was available.

A memorandum by Will Clayton sent to Under-Secretary of State Dean Acheson on 27 May 1947 predicted that in Europe 'millions of people would soon die'[90] unless the Allies faced the 'grisly facts' of their occupation policies.[91] Clayton is here saying, a little more vaguely, what Robert Murphy had already said of the Germans with more detail in his secret reports to Washington of that same spring.

As a humanitarian with a clear world view and strong sense of history, Hoover was under no illusions about the cause of Germany's plight. He had visited Hitler in his new chancellery in Berlin in 1938, which was apparently a massive stone and marble building. But Hoover visited it again in 1946, and saw what the Allied bombs had revealed: the marble was ersatz, merely plaster of Paris spread on nets of twine that now hung in shreds from the gaping roof. 'Having seen the results of Hitler's vengeance on the Poles and remembering the millions who had died in his rape of Europe . . . I had no pity for his ending.'[92] But he also knew that it was pointless to continue the vengeance, for this meant that 'mass destitution and prevention of sheer starvation had become the burden of the victors. No man with a vision that the world would have to bury the hatchet sometime if civilization were to survive, had sat in on these decisions' to starve Germans, he wrote.[93]

The Canadians, like the Americans, were exceptionally farsighted and generous, giving away billions to the British, French and others. The total Canadian aid to the UK in

1939–50 is unmeasurable in precise terms, but in 1997 dollars, it probably amounted to well over $100 billion.

This was done even though the Canadians had a very wry view of the likelihood of a massive outpouring of gratitude. They did not even expect that people would remember the help once it had ended. Prime Minister King in 1944 received from Norman Robertson the comment that 'Canada's main contribution to the rehabilitation and settlement in Europe will be in the field of UNRRA, where we shall probably be the main source of supply of many of the basic food products so desperately needed. This should have a most favourable effect in advertising Canada, but by the time Stage III [of the relief program] is reached, UNRRA's free distribution of food will probably be over and nations and people have notoriously short memories in cases of benevolence.'[94]

But there were millions who did remember, at least for a while. Hoover received birthday greetings from a whole schoolful of children and teachers in July 1948:

Dear Mr Hoover
We have learnt that on August 10 you celebrate your 75th birthday. For many years you have devoted your work and care to ease the lives of poor suffering fellow-creatures, so that your name is now known all over the world and particularly the countries of Europe which have most suffered in and after the war – among them our poor Austria – are all greatly indebted to you for your having started the 'CARE parcel action'.

The school, a seminary for young students thinking of the priesthood, had been closed in 1938 by the anti-Christian Nazis, who were trying to destroy the church. The school reopened in autumn 1945, 'although we have become very poor . . . all appliances for teaching, our whole library, all our linen, and nearly all the furniture has been destroyed during the Russian occupation, neither our teachers nor our pupils will lose heart . . . Our whole establishment, dear Sir, comprising 250 students and 16 teachers, join in sending you their best and heartiest wishes with the expression of their most devoted thankfulness.' It was signed by F. Seidl, Direktor, the Fürstbischofliche Knabenseminar of Graz, Austria.[95]

One letter of request, dated 5 February 1948, shows that the Germans were starving even at that date, almost three years after the war's end, and while the Marshall Plan was getting under way. Aloyus Algen of the Rheinland wrote to the Committee of the American Aid to Children, as follows:

Dear Mr Hoover

With this letter I take the liberty of asking you for a parcel containing underwear, shoes and food. We are six persons in our family and if we do not get help, we will perish, since we are poor and haven't anything to eat or wear. You can hardly imagine how close to death we are. If only you could send a pair of shoes to each of us (size 6, 7, 9, 11, 13), some shorts and underwear for men and stockings.[96]

Hoover's estimate that the food campaigns had saved 800 million lives from at least one fatal famine shows the astounding scale and compass of the work. Even 10 per cent of that number of lives saved was more than had been lost in the entire war, the most devastating in human history. Yet today, as Robertson had calmly predicted, this immense, unprecedented charity is largely forgotten.

Among the millions of refugees who surged through Germany in 1945 were thirty to forty thousand ethnic German Mennonites, who had been savagely persecuted under Stalin then ordered to leave the USSR by the retreating Wehrmacht.

Some of these ended up in Berlin in 1946, where they were cared for in part by the Canadian Mennonites Peter and Elfrieda Dyck.[97] These people gave the Christian feast of the Eucharist a new meaning one day, in a German commercial bakery which they paid to bake their bread from flour sent from Canada. One of the baker's apprentices noticed bits of printed paper whirling around in the dough in the blending machine one morning. He switched off the machine to discover remnants of Bibles. Aware of Hitler's persecution of the churches, the Mennonites in Saskatchewan who had made the flour had also stuffed Bibles into the sacks to make sure they fed the soul along with the body. The German baker threw up his hands and exclaimed 'Mein Gott!', thinking the flour was spoiled. But Elfrieda and Peter Dyck told him to turn up the heat a few extra degrees, and bake away. As Peter Dyck commented, 'To feed on God's word didn't hurt anyone. It usually doesn't.' And he told the puzzled baker, 'Read Ezekiel, chapter three.'*

All of the astonishing generosity of the majority of the American people issued finally in the Marshall Plan, which has dominated much of Western thinking about Allied policy in Germany in 1945–50. It is widely judged to be a fine example of the spotless virtue of the West, one of the proofs of the far-sighted wisdom that animated Allied governments in their European policies. All over the West today, the belief prevails that the Americans generously helped the Germans 'get back on their feet after the war'. According to this widespread belief, the German economic miracle was, to an important degree, America's doing.

Here was a generous policy openly debated and heartily approved by public opinion. Marshall Plan funds were even

---

*'Moreover he said unto me, Son of Man, eat that thou findest; eat this roll, and go and speak unto the House of Israel. So I opened my mouth and he caused me to eat that roll . . . and it was in my mouth as honey for sweetness.' (Ezekiel 3: 1–3)

offered to the Soviet Union, which haughtily turned them down. Then, at considerable cost to the American taxpayers, Europeans were offered funds for reconstruction and development, on a matching funds basis, i.e. that the European nation had to put up as much development capital as was taken from the Marshall fund. The policy passed Congress, and was signed by President Truman in April 1948, becoming effective in a remarkably short time with little opposition. It was strongly supported by public opinion, which had been demanding just such a turn in policy since 1945. There is no doubt that in 1948 it helped re-elect Truman and most of those Senators and Congressmen who supported it. The Marshall Plan was a great expression of the public opinion that is commonly supposed to be free, wise and kind. It was never regretted and nowhere deplored. Except by Stalin.

The Germans were at first excluded, but within a year, the plans were expanded to include them. This was one small part of the German 'economic miracle'. Although they needed more, it was understandable that they would receive less than any other nation, around half per capita of the sum allotted to the UK, and less than 60 per cent of the amount the French got. Between 3 April 1948 and 30 June 1952, the Germans got $39 per person, the French $72, and the British $77. (The equivalent in today's money is probably above ten times the amounts shown.[98]). The effect was magical. The change in Germany, with this and with currency reform, was almost miraculous. According to General Maurice Pope, who was with the Canadian Military Mission in Germany in 1948, following the end of the blockade and the currency reform 'conditions improved overnight . . . [soon] the modest corner grocery store was displaying delicacies of all kinds and at quite reasonable prices'.[99] Within months, the German economy was plainly reviving; within a year it was expanding faster than any other European economy; and within a decade Germany was close to the richest country on the continent. Soon after that the Germans possessing almost no natural resources and very little land, were the richest people in Europe. They paid back to the US nearly every dollar they had received in aid.[100]

The Germans actually received about $1.4 billion, and they repaid around $1 billion, leaving them with $0.4 billion in outright gifts. Britain received eight times as much, about $3,176,000,000; the French $2,706,000,000 and the Italians $1,474,000,000. Only the Germans paid back any of their Marshall Plan money.[101]

The German repayment was not their only contribution to reconstructing the damage they had caused. Reparations probably exceeded by far the initial estimates of $20 billion to go to all Allies. Not only were some of the 'reparations' no better than theft, they also went on under cover as late as 1948. Officials in President Truman's administration denied that reparations were continuing, but Herbert Hoover told the Governor of New York, who was then campaigning against Truman, that he had evidence that the process was still going on. Hoover also said that the reparations policy had cost the American taxpayers about $600,000,000 per year for food because the Germans were not allowed to manufacture enough for export to buy the necessary imported food. According to Hoover, the destruction or removal of factories for reparations from Germany kept the Germans 'in degeneration and idleness'. American, British and French manufacturers enriched themselves at the expense of their fellow taxpayers, who were paying some of the occupation costs.[102]

Herbert Hoover's team in Germany in 1946 found much lying going on about economic conditions among US occupation officers. A US Navy intelligence officer in Berlin told the Hoover Famine Emergency Commission in 1946: 'The figures on economic output can be believed only one-fifth – the rest is doctored to make a good impression with top levels. The lower personnel is permeated with Morgenthau people.'[103] Secretary of State George Marshall himself was party to the cover-up, according to the expert and eminent American author John Gimbel in his pioneering study of US policy in Germany, *Science, Technology and Reparations*. The sub-title is significant: 'Exploitation and Plunder in Post-war Germany'.

At a meeting of Foreign Ministers in Moscow in 1947, Molotov told George Marshall to his face that the Americans were taking valuable reparations without reporting them in the official reparations account that all the Allies were supposed to keep. Gimbel writes, 'Marshall responded angrily – a manner quite uncharacteristic of him, as an esteemed observer commented.' Marshall angrily told Molotov – and the world – that the Americans were giving away for nothing the most valuable part of their reparations, the documents, patents, processes, technical know-how, samples, blueprints and so on, which they were taking from the Germans. Marshall's State Department estimated the worth of the American haul at the time at an incredibly low figure, around $10 million.[104]

Gimbel has combed the Hoover and National archives and discovered a long history of falsification and cover-up on this subject. He concludes that Marshall's angry statement in Moscow was 'distorted, misleading and propagandistic'.[105] The State Department then and later refused to place a value on the reparations, but they can scarcely have been less than the Soviet reparations, because the motive was the same, the Western businessmen avaricious, the resistance weak, and the Western Allies occupied much the richer part of Germany. The American Colonel Gerald B. O'Grady, chief industry officer for OMGUS* in Württemberg-Baden, said, 'I totally disapprove of such robbery . . . practically none [of the investigators] are here in the interest of any government, but for

*Office of the Military Governor – United States.

purely personal gain.'[106] One German estimate that Gimbel
quoted was that the Allies took between $4.8 billion and $12
billion *in intellectual property alone*, apart from the seizure of
foreign assets and shipping, and the machinery, food, timber
and coal that flowed out east and west.[107]

Gimbel is very clear on the myth-making that went on:
'Historians of the Marshall Plan have fallen into a familiar
trap. They have [described] what *must have been* the reasons for
the origins of the Marshall Plan . . . by extrapolation, rather
than by interpretation of documents, sources and contemporary
evidence . . . government officials were not averse to misleading the public. State Department and other officials often
simply told the Congress, the press, the American people or
whomever, *what they wanted to tell them* at a given time, and
they often did so without regard for what was true and accurate.'[108] And of course historians using the 'must have been'
theory uncritically accept whatever story has by then become
predominant.

To revise history this way largely means to ignore the evidence. The creation of the world food shortage belief
depended, and still depends today, upon aversion to the facts. It
might be called a world truth shortage. One of the most important sets of papers bearing on this post-war food problem has
been ignored by historians.[109] This is in the collection of the
papers of Robert Patterson, who as Secretary of War in 1945–47
had a great deal to do with solving the food problems abroad.
Much of this material was declassified for the first time in 1993
during research for this book.[110] Nowhere in the hundreds of
pages of letters, memos, notes of meetings, or draft manuscript,
is there anything to show that Patterson or his Cabinet colleagues thought the shortages in Germany were caused by a
world shortage of food.

The Western Allies understandably exaggerated the amount
of money it was costing US and British taxpayers to feed the

Germans a starvation diet. Freely to feed a vanquished enemy who had committed such horrors was unprecedented among the nations, so they were proud of their magnanimity. But, as Gimbel found, 'the *actual* costs of the German occupation to the British and American taxpayers were much smaller than those to be found in the heavily inflated figures that circulated publicly and in the Congress at the time'.[111] The Western Allies hid what they were doing under a false accounting system: 'Germany's exports of coal, timber and "invisibles" . . . were never classified as reparations and they have not been regarded as such by historians.'[112]

German reparations, taken by every ally as soon as the war ended, were astronomically high. By the most conservative estimates, they amounted to at least US $20 billion, which would be somewhere in the region of many hundreds of billions in 1997, given the inflation and increase in economies since 1950.[113] Soviet Ambassador Ivan Maisky told Churchill in 1945 that the Soviets expected to take $10 billion of the $20 billion in overall reparations which the Soviets judged they could pay.[114] The minimum worth of German reparations to the US was probably around $5 billion.[115] The British and Americans between them took at least $10 billion in reparations for war damages, the French less. No one can be sure of the amount the Germans actually 'owed', because war damage could only be assessed according to the damage itself, and to the degree of war guilt. Certainly the amount was huge, and certainly the Germans have repaid well over $100 billion since 1945, and are still paying the relatives of some of the Nazis' victims.

The main point of reparations was to restore so far as possible the well-being of Germany's victims, but since this was neglected in favour of punishing Germans *en masse*, Hitler's victims suffered further. We see here again Chekhov's Sakhalin discovery, which had been repeated in the Gulag and then in

Hitler's slave camps: a starved hen lays no eggs. The more the Germans were punished, the less they restored the economy of Europe. There was almost universal agreement among the American government experts in 1948 that the Marshall Plan could not succeed without 'major industrial production from Germany', as John Gimbel said.[116] The significant measure for reparations, therefore, was how much Germany could contribute to restoring the European economy, whether by reparations or by trade. Only the first option was chosen.

The Americans took from Germany at least twenty times the amount the Germans retained under the Marshall Plan. They took possibly far more than that. It was at least $1 billion more than the whole Marshall Plan devoted to the UK, France, Germany, Italy and Austria. Clearly the Marshall Plan was generous and far-sighted, a typically American good idea, which would not have been possible without German money.

Reparation was only one aspect of the policies that the Allies tried to pursue. Many skilled Americans and British made energetic efforts to teach Germans democracy during the first years of the occupation, but failed because of German bitterness caused by the policy of vengeance. This attempt and failure had their parallels in the French zone as well. In the French zone, the starving Germans were offered tickets to performances by French artists. Fed even less than the starvation rations in the neighbouring zones, the Germans did not respond enthusiastically to a lecture by a novelist, or a concert by the likes of Edith Piaf. In the summer of 1945, the British wisely installed Konrad Adenauer in office as Lord Mayor of Cologne, but then ordered him to cut down Cologne's famous trees to feed the furnaces that winter. When Adenauer refused, the British angrily kicked him out of office.

The reason for the failure was clearly expressed by an editorial in the *Marburger Presse* in 1949, commenting on the six German workers who had just been sentenced to prison for refusing the help dismantle a factory in Dortmund. 'The Allies criticize us Germans for deferring to authority, try to educate us to be democrats, but demand respect for Allied authority.' The Germans felt that the dismantling had gone much too far, and that to resist it showed democratic reaction to oppression.[117]

The Germans missed the point. There was no democracy because the Allies ruled by force; the Allies ruled by force to make sure the Germans did not rule *them* by force. Nevertheless, the Allies were not wholly hypocrites: if the *Marburger Presse* editor had been able to look forty years into the future, he would have been astonished to see Germany largely democratic, and Allied troops protecting it.

But the Americans also missed the point. Democracy is not rule by fear. The more a government rules by threat of force, the less it is democratic. 'Seek not to enslave hearts, and all hearts will be yours,' Voltaire said.[118]

In that same small city of Marburg in the American zone in 1945, prisoners returning from the American prison camp nearby told of trucks taking away fifty starved bodies every night to a secret burial site hidden from the Germans. A huge influx of expellees from the east arrived, virtually all of them women, children and old, feeble men. They added to the housing problem, subtracted from the food supply and could scarcely find work. Wild rumours spread around the country because all the press, radio, teaching and publishing were controlled by the Allies, and so were not fully believed. Gimbel notes: 'The American occupation gave rise to a strain of anti-American sentiment among even the most democratically-inclined Germans and provided them with a convincing rationale for that sentiment.'[119] The Germans demonstrated throughout the British and American zones for an end to demolition and the restrictions on manufacture for export. The British played an ambivalent game, especially with the coal miners, trying to increase their production while simultaneously reducing their food rations. In 1946 and again in 1947, the standard of living of the coal miners actually deteriorated, despite increased production. The major reason was that the British were paying only $10.50 per ton while the European market price was more than double that, sometimes triple. If the Germans had received full value for their work, there would have been little need for subsidies from the British taxpayers.[120]

The Germans felt that the Americans were hypocrites, beginning with President Truman at the top and going right down to the lowest private in the occupation forces. The Americans talked a lot about the spirit of justice, love, and forgiveness, but it was not much in evidence among the Americans in Germany, at least not those in OMGUS.[121]

What you learn from studying history is how little mankind learns from studying history. The learning is bound to be minimal wherever history is managed to benefit the mighty. After fifty years all officials in the West are still denying the mass deaths in the French and American prison camps; only in Germany are the deaths of the two million expellees remembered and mourned. No one anywhere has remarked on the fact that five to six million more people disappeared entirely from the German population without note, or explanation. No historian, whether British, French, Russian, American, Canadian or German – not even a German historian – has remarked on this. Millions of people disappear under the Allies' rule, and *no one notices*.

Victorious generals are always in training to fight the last war, and diplomats may be no better. One of the effects of the Morgenthau Plan was that the West, chiefly the US, went on fighting the war long after they had won. While the democracies were concentrating primarily on the vanished German danger, they continued to help the Soviet Union. Western policy was anarchically ambivalent for the first few years after the war. The West gave the Soviets great help as part of the momentum of the wartime alliance; the West also began to oppose Soviet expansionist ambitions. Despite the great tension over Poland and Eastern Europe, the Allies were still sending massive quantities of supplies to the Russians in late 1946. The Canadians sent over 1.6 million tons of wheat in three months during that summer, the Americans more than that, and the Argentinians contributed greatly as well. From Canada went electrical machinery, steel rails and so on; from the USA, all kinds of supplies except weapons were sent. But at the same time, the Americans especially put up fierce resistance to attempts by the Soviets to expand their influence into Azerbaijan, Japan and the Dardanelles.

All this help given the Soviets was free. It was the physical expression of the overall policy of trying to get along with the Russians to build a better world. This was happening at the time when the Russians were spying on Canada's top-secret, atomic program, the most advanced in the world at the time after the Americans. In September 1945, Igor Gouzenko defected to the Canadians, taking with him documentary proof of the Soviet treachery. Eventually twelve persons were convicted of spying, the most dangerous spy success against the West of the twentieth century, except perhaps for the Rosenbergs in the US. The stolen secrets enabled the Soviets to build their first atomic bomb. The tranquil flow of aid and the court case went on simultaneously.

To experience is to learn, whether the experience becomes history or not. In 1997 the human race is experiencing events similar to those we experienced in 1945. Now it is democracy's greatest enemy that lies broken, while America's leaders prepare to fight shadowy enemies. They see the danger of the drug lords, terrorists, crackpot dictators and jungle leaders who defend their ancient territories against 'natural resources' companies from the 'advanced' countries. At the beginning of the Cold War, the United States was the greatest creditor nation the world has ever known, and now it is the world's greatest debtor. Along with Canada, the US is technically bankrupt, while its leaders maintain enormous defence budgets to fight no serious enemy.

It appears that the tremendous centralizing tendencies of modern industrial life have degraded many of the more civilizing instincts of the Anglo-Saxon peoples. Fighting totalitarian states, they have grown more totalitarian themselves. Since the 1930s, the rise of prisonership in the USA has been absolutely phenomenal. Proportionally the US now has more people in jail than Tsarist Russia did in one of its most repressive phases. The US has more people in jail per capita than Nazi Germany did in 1939, and that includes concentration camps.[122] This has happened partly because we have failed to defend freedom of expression. The crimes against the Germans by the Americans and the French, and by the British against Mennonites and Russian prisoners, are only a few of those covered up – think of the denials, lies, censorship and so on practiced by the French in Algeria and Indo-China, by the US in Cambodia and Vietnam, by Canada in Somalia and Vietnam. Soon, according to former US Attorney General Ramsey Clark, we shall see proof of more crimes committed by the Allies in and after the Gulf War.

Surely there is something significant in the fact that so many Second World War fighting men and leaders stayed in power after 1945, or came to power as a result of wartime fame. They brought their attitudes with them, and influenced all the politics of the post-war era. Their names are legion – Truman, Churchill, De Gaulle, Macmillan, Eden, Eisenhower, Marshall, Smith, Dulles, Kennedy, Bush. Even as late as 1996, the

Republican Party presidential candidate Bob Dole was renowned for his heroism in the Second World War.

War is born of propaganda. That is why the first victim of war is truth. We are still victims of propaganda about the Second World War.

VIII

HISTORY AND FORGETTING

For most of my life I hardly thought about the flaws in our democratic system. I thought things were bumping along not too badly until I encountered the crimes of Eisenhower and De Gaulle. Even then, I did not imagine that these crimes revealed anything important about our society today because, after all, they occurred almost half a century ago, under the tremendous force of hatred caused by war. It was only when I interviewed Drew Middleton, a star reporter for the *New York Times*, that I began to see how events of long ago were affecting our lives today. In Middleton's office in New York in 1988, I told him I had discovered that the US and French armies had committed enormous atrocities in Europe in 1945. Because he had written stories in 1945 denying this following his visits to the prison camps, I wanted his reaction.

Middleton said, 'I'm not surprised that you were able to dig up some bad things from that time.' He then admitted that he had never visited a prison camp. He did not want to read my manuscript. What Middleton told me basically was that, yes, he had lied in 1945 and no, it did not matter to him or the *New York Times* if I exposed this.

I was deeply impressed by Middleton's indifference. He didn't want to read my manuscript, nor did he threaten me with a libel action, or bring one after the book came out. He was calm in the face of what I had thought for him would be a disaster. I began to see then that the *New York Times* is so powerful it does not need to threaten people even when it is facing exposure. Middleton's sense of security, his sense of the *New York Times*' power, took my breath away. But worse than that, Middleton did not *care* about this atrocity. He did not care in 1945; he did not care in 1988. As we now know, hundreds of thousands of prisoners had died at the hands of his government in one of the worst atrocities in Western history, the *New York Times* witnessed it, then denied that it had happened. And has gone on denying it into the 1990s.

This seemed to me to be more than a routine journalistic slip. And to be worth some reflection, in the great tradition to which the *New York Times* aspires.

In the opinion of nearly everybody in the West, the Second World War was a good war. It was necessary to defeat the utter evil of the dictators. If anyone in the post-war years doubted this, they were reminded of the pictures of emaciated bodies in Hitler's death camps.

Lofty were the aims of the Allies, noble were their ideals, eloquent the expression of these ideals in such documents as the Geneva Convention, the Atlantic Charter, and the UN Declaration of Human Rights. All these were in the tradition of the liberal reforms which had succeeded in the West for many years, yet all these noble declarations were being broken by one branch of government while they were being written by another. Or, like the Geneva Convention, they were broken as soon as they became applicable. People who say anarchy is impractical are ignoring modern government where anarchy is normal, in the sense that government is constantly changing course, covering up, contradicting and reversing itself and doing these things simultaneously. The Allies clearly did not intend to keep their word in the 1940s. Why not? And why give it?

The answer to the first question is of course that people often don't keep their word, because normal human frailties prevail over the noble resolve to correct them. The more interesting question is, why make such declarations? For one thing, it is reassuring to hear them. And probably it is fun to make them. Think of the well-dressed gentlemen, arriving by limousine in English castle, French château or American office block with polished secretaries to sit about a gleaming table making high-toned statements about lofty purposes until lunch. Surely, to a kind of mind that is quite common, this is highly important. But there is another reason, maintained by a delusion prevalent in the West.

That delusion is that the 'good war' led to a good peace: after a 'period of adjustment', Germany was 'put back on her feet' by the Marshall Plan, so she could become a servant of the West during the Cold War. She was, however, not to be trusted because she was still deeply guilty, as she remains today. According to the delusion, the discovery of the death camps had converted Nazi war guilt to collective German guilt.

This is not the record. The record shows very clearly that the Allies were planning a devastating treatment for Germany before Nazi racist crimes were fully comprehended in the West. The Allied policy of starving the Germans was in fact decades old – in 1918/19, after the First World War, the Allies had maintained the sea-blockade, causing the deaths of close to a million Germans. Even the threat of unconditional surrender was not new: the commander of the American armies in France, General Pershing, had advocated imposing unconditional surrender on the failing Germans on 30 October 1918.[1]

One of President Wilson's closest advisers told him at the same time that 'he would disappoint his own people if he accepted less than unconditional surrender'.[2] While the death camps were still mainly a horrifying rumour in the West, in 1943 the Allies were discussing at Washington and Tehran annexation of the eastern quarter of Germany, which, as the Allies well knew, would produce starvation conditions. The Morgenthau Plan was devised and signed in August–September 1944, long before the full horror of the camps was visible to reporters and soldiers. But historians wishing to question the evidence of Allied atrocities keep citing the camps. Stephen Ambrose has recently written: 'Clearly Eisenhower was appalled by what he saw' at several camps.[3] He goes on to exculpate Eisenhower for the mass crimes committed in the American POW camps.

Where the German death camps had most influence was clearly not in the planning but in the execution of plans. The war criminals would be tried regardless of what horrors were actually uncovered in the camps. But the possibility of mitigation of Allied war hatred resulting from the work of leaders who actually practiced the noble ideals – Herbert Hoover, Victor Gollancz, the Bishop of Chichester, Norman Robertson, Rabbi Baeck, Robert Patterson – was postponed by the astounded revulsion felt throughout the West – and in Germany – against the slaughter in Belsen, Buchenwald, Dachau and Auschwitz. This revulsion turned into the sense of collective German guilt, which is still very powerful today. As late as 1996, a book by Daniel Jonah Goldhagen accusing Germans of total collective guilt for war crimes was causing a sensation throughout Western countries.[4]

Certainly Germans *en masse* were collectively guilty for some Nazi crimes because they gave Hitler a plurality of votes in the last election before he became Chancellor. They were collectively guilty of vicious crimes of aggression against countries who had given them no *casus belli*, such as Czechoslovakia,

Denmark, Norway, Holland, Belgium, Luxembourg, Yugoslavia, Greece and the Soviet Union. How many Germans were guilty of racist crimes is in dispute, but one thing is for sure: as a people represented by their national government, they have collectively accepted this guilt, and this is recognized through-out Germany and the world. They have paid enormous compensation to the victims, offered humble apologies to the survivors, condemned the crimes in many books, films, cere-monies and monuments.

This sense of collective German guilt is useful in a specially morbid way to her former enemies because it effectively seals off all discussions about the mistreatment of Germans in 1945. Time and again, when anyone reproaches the Allies for their treatment of German women and children in 1945, the reply is heard, 'But look what the Germans did.' This is a common refrain today in Germany itself. But for much of the war and a long time after, it was actually forbidden in the American press to mention the German resistance. President Roosevelt for-bade the press to print news of the German resistance, a directive that was enforced even after the war by the American occupation authorities.[5]

Guilt pervades Germany like a religion. It is the 'Canossa Republic', penitent in pain before its judges.* Guilt is so pow-erful that it has caused the Canossa Republic repeatedly to deny any intention of reclaiming sovereignty over the eastern lands, although it is a well-established UN principle that no government has the right to waive the claims of individuals to their property. Nor may it impede their right of return to their former homeland. There was wisdom in this renunciation, because the decline of nationalism in Europe has meant the

---

*At Canossa in 1077, King Henry IV knelt in the snow for three days as he begged Pope Gregory to release him from excommunication. The phrase was first used by Paul Boytinck in conversation with the author in 1995.

opening of borders to trade, travel, culture and friendship. But that decline of nationalism, like the renunciation, affects the Canossa Republic more than anyone else. Poles and Czechs make it difficult or impossible for individual Germans to buy back their ancient lands. Even Václav Havel, willing to apologize for Czech crimes, cannot contemplate reparations or restoration of stolen property. The Canossa Republic leads the way, but it is hard to discern anyone following it on the path of reconciliation.

It is especially shocking that for many decades the Canossa Republic has failed to ensure historical recognition of the expellees' suffering, as if to prevent future generations from knowing anything at all about the true history of their forebears and their country. It is true that for a few years, under Adenauer and soon after, the West German government helped with the publication of documents on the expulsion, but for many years now German schoolchildren have been taught little or nothing of their ancestors' tragic sufferings after the war.

The Allies' war aims, which included the right of self-determination for all peoples, apparently guaranteed the homelands of the eastern Germans. But all the Allies actually did was to include a phrase in Article XIII of the Potsdam Protocol stipulating that the 'population transfers' should occur under 'humane and orderly conditions'. As the phrase was being typed into the Potsdam agreement, its nauseating hypocrisy was visible to all: millions of miserable, dying expellees were crowding into the remainder of Germany, but the Western Allies were actually *preventing* help from reaching them. As we have seen, the ICRC, the Quakers, the Mennonites, the Lutherans and many others were not allowed to operate in Germany until many months later. In a memorable phrase, Conor Cruise O'Brien described this sort of thing as a slick coating of the 'hypocrisy and cultivated inattention' that our leaders apply to reduce the friction between our admirable principles and our self-interest. The quote is worth expanding: 'The traditional [Western] ethic will require larger and larger doses of its traditional built-in antidotes – the forces of hypocrisy and cultivated inattention combined with a certain minimum of alms.'[6]

Robert Murphy protested eloquently in a Memorandum to the State Department in October 1945, months after Potsdam: 'In the Lehrter Railroad station in Berlin alone our medical authorities state an average of ten have been dying daily from exhaustion, malnutrition and illness. In viewing the distress and despair of these wretches, in smelling the odor of their filthy condition, the mind reverts instantly to Dachau and Buchenwald. Here is retribution on a large scale, practiced not on the *Parteibonzen* [party big-wigs], but on women and children, the poor, the infirm . . .'[7] Article XIII made no difference at all, other than to history. But history is not idle – in other words, the expellees will not go away. On 26 August 1994, the UN Sub-Commission on Human Rights adopted Resolution 1994/24 re-affirming 'the right of refugees and displaced persons to return in safety and dignity to their country of origin and/or within it, to their place of origin or choice . . .' The language plainly covers the rights of the dispossessed Germans.

Nevertheless, in agreement with the Allies in 1990, the Canossa Republic recognized the Oder–Neisse frontier, as part of the final settlement to free Germany of the Allied presence. In the words of Alfred de Zayas, the German government 'yielded to international pressure and relinquished its legal claims to the centuries-old homeland. These were claims that for decades after the war had been reaffirmed both inside Germany, and to the rest of the world. But that was the old German generation speaking, through earlier governments that still felt morally obliged to the expelled and the dispossessed. Forty years of re-education have resulted in a different perspective. Renunciation was to be expected. Today, the West either ignores the historical record, or accepts the euphemisms about the expulsions propounded by Polish and German apologists.'[8]

This 1990 agreement itself may have been illegal, or *ultra vires*, since it is clear from many UN resolutions that a crime or abrogation of rights is not made legal even if approved or committed by a government against its own citizens. Such arguments might be seen as 'only legalistic', but the creation of the Israeli state and the modern North American aboriginal land claims were at the beginning more *de jure* than *de facto*.

When the state of Israel was founded in 1947, all of the Jewish occupants under the Romans had been dead for almost two thousand years. In North America, not a single Iroquois, Chiapas, Sioux or Cree is left alive of those who were the defeated or defrauded original occupants. Is it legal and just for the German government to banish the claims of living citizens who had been expelled and despoiled? And to do this without even trying to obtain compensation or recognition? Germany in its guilt and poverty found it possible to make apologies and to pay billions of dollars in reparations to the Allies, plus a hundred billion Deutschmarks in restitutions to victims of Nazi atrocities, as well as giving up all claim to some 25 per cent of their national territory, not to mention all the personal goods, land title, factories, schools, houses, farms and so on pertaining to those lands. Millions of German victims of Potsdam have made enormous reparations and humble apologies. They have all been deprived of their human rights, of the right to be judged as individuals, of their right to dignity and equality, of their private land and personal possessions.

As it was in the beginning in 1945, so it was at the end in 1990, our governments and their clients dealt away rights that normally we expect them to uphold. Hardly anyone in the

Western democracies even noticed what was being done. Here was German guilt sealing off discussion of the issues of the expellees and other Allied crimes. The only government that could protect their rights signed them away.

We see today great institutions of public opinion – among them *Le Monde* and the *New York Times* – feverishly denying the Western Allied atrocities of the post-war period against Germany. For most people in the West, the denials rest on delusion, not evidence. The question never even becomes, '*Did* the Allies do such things?' because the answer has been planted in everyone's heads already. 'No, the Allies did not, because they could not.' For instance, the eminent British historian Michael Howard, reviewing for the *Times Literary Supplement* a book about Allied atrocities against Germans, admitted that although he was 'an innumerate historian' unqualified to judge the crucial statistics in the book, he could 'apply the criterion of inherent probability' to refute the book.[9] The French press and TV rose with rhetoric uncomplicated by evidence to denounce recent allegations that mass crimes were committed by the French army against the Germans. Stephen Ambrose also attacked a book about allied misdeeds by concluding that 'when scholars do the necessary research they will find [this book] to be worse than worthless'.[10] The answer is known before the evidence is consulted. In other words, belief is everything, evidence means nothing.

Count Nikolai Tolstoy, the renowned English writer, has been driven bankrupt and forbidden to publish on the subject of British treatment of prisoners of war under Lord Aldington. His books have been withdrawn from British libraries. His attempts at redress in British courts have been constantly frustrated in the UK, although the denial of his rights has been condemned by the European Court of Human Rights at Strasbourg. The alleged libel against Lord Aldington was converted by the courts and government into a libel against the history of the state. Against which there is no appeal.

The books of former US Attorney General Ramsey Clark have revealed tremendous civilian deaths in Iraq during the Gulf War which have never been admitted by any of the Allies who caused them.[11] No major publisher in the English-speaking world has dared to bring them out.

My fellow author Alfred de Zayas, a graduate of Harvard and of Göttingen, spent years researching and writing his book *Nemesis at Potsdam*, about the expulsions from the east of Germany. And then he had to spend ten years sending it round to almost a hundred publishers in the West before the manuscript was finally accepted. The president of one of the biggest houses in New York returned the manuscript with the note that he would never publish a book sympathetic to the Germans.

It is no good to respond that all these authors got published, and so freedom of discussion exists. The full weight of official disapproval has stifled the discussion by shrinking the audience. And once that happens the authors may be silenced by financial distress.

There is an astonishing contrast right now between Russia and the West. We condemned them for many decades precisely because they denied democracy and suppressed discussion. Now, they have demolished suppression, opened their archives, and published the truth about their crimes. They have even admitted that some allegations of German crimes were never true. Public discourse is free and informed on all those topics. And we say, 'Good for you, democracy now has a chance with you.' But in the West, the archives are very often managed in order to present a view of history acceptable to the established authority. Photographs and documents of Allied atrocities have 'disappeared' from archives, and this goes on to the present day. 'In my thirty years as a scholar of American history,' said one American professor, 'I have never known the archives to appear to be so much of a political agency of the executive branch as it is now. One used to think of the Archivist of the United States as a professional scholar. Now he has become someone who fills a political bill.'[12] Many people who have cast doubt on German crimes have been fired from their jobs, vilified, deported, jailed or censored, while anyone who denies our post-war crimes against the Germans is published and praised by press, academe, army and government.

Freedom is diminished when discussion is suppressed, dissidents are jailed, when in fact history is genetically altered, as Stalin showed every time he hid public documents or altered history in the books. If we are to regain the freedoms that we fought for in the war, the official sanctioning against authors must stop, the arrogant abuse of public trust in the archives must end, and full disclosure prevail.

Democracy is generally believed to be the best government because it expresses the public opinion that is normally free, wise and kind. If this were not so, who would defend democracy? If the general belief were that public opinion were normally slavish, stupid and cruel, no one would think democracy was worth defending. And without that faith, democracy dies. Hitler's brilliant propaganda chief Joseph Goebbels said of the German people, 'You can't change the masses. They will always be the same: dumb, gluttonous and forgetful.' Contemptuous of their forgetfulness, he said anything he liked because he believed they were always unaware of what he had said before.[13] We shudder to think that Goebbels' observation might be even slightly true in the Western democracies; on the other hand, our pleasing assumption about democratic public opinion has never been tested.

Public opinion can be discerned but dimly, in primitive jousts such as elections, in referendums or in the tiny samplings passing grandly as public opinion polls. None of these has ever tested us for our freedom, wisdom or kindness. The goodness of public opinion is by and large an article of faith.

But it is a faith that was justified in 1946. Herbert Hoover made many public appeals by radio to the decency, compassion and common sense of the American and Canadian people and was never disappointed. Can anyone in his right mind imagine Henry Morgenthau going on radio with a forthright appeal to the viciousness, vengefulness and hatred of the American people?

To do their good deeds in the post-war period, men like Marshall and Hoover, Gollancz and Mackenzie King walked in the open, but their opposites like Morgenthau, Buisson and Eisenhower had to operate under camouflage. Surely this can only be because the widely-based institutions of Western democracy – parliament, literate education, a free press, the rule of law – foster the normal human sympathies that make mass crimes abhorrent. This is why freedom of discussion in democracy is so important; it is a constant corrective to the cruel tendencies in people. Without freedom of discussion, democracy first grows arrogant, then brutal. And the discussion of Allied war crimes has been circumscribed by lies, propaganda and suppression for fifty years.

On no subject is the Western cover-up more profound and tragic than the refusal of Western public opinion-makers to incorporate the fate of the German expellees into the history of the Second World War and its consequences. This of course effectively denies redress not just to the German state, but especially to the millions of robbed and maimed individuals who are still alive. The cover-up is definitely part of that series of misdeeds which Adenauer condemned roundly in 1949, and which continue to haunt 'the uneasy conscience of the West'.

Speaking to the Swiss Parliament in Bern, Switzerland, in March 1949, Adenauer compared the expulsions to the misdeeds of the Nazis, and concluded, 'The expulsions resulted from the Potsdam Agreement of 2 August 1945. I am convinced that one day world history will pronounce a very harsh verdict on this document.'[14]

History and forgetting

For a long time it puzzled me that we scarcely honour those who implemented our noblest ideals after the Second World War. As nations, we showed wonderful generosity and great skill. But memory of this has almost disappeared, except in the minds of a few survivors, and even they do not usually remember much.

Mackenzie King's kindly assistant Norman Robertson was right about the brief life of gratitude: I interviewed two Polish generals in Moscow in 1993, and asked them what they remembered about Hoover. They said he was a great policeman – they meant J. Edgar Hoover, of the FBI. Yet their lives had been saved by Hoover food when they were young in 1946, and probably their fathers' lives before them, during Hoover's relief campaigns in 1919–21.

The post-war era was not the only time that the Western democracies have aided the unfortunate in far parts of the world. While doing the research for this book, I visited a friend who lived near a village called Durham, in Ontario, where I encountered one of those humble books that are sold even in hardware stores because they are local history by a local author. This was a history of Durham County. I normally buy such books, because there is usually something interesting in them, so I took it back to the farmhouse where we were staying, intending to present it to my hostess, and then to skim through it. In the book, I read of the sermon given by a local Protestant minister in about 1890, appealing for funds to help the starving people of a province in British India.

Durham at that time was many days by sea from London, plus several days by train via Toronto. India was almost beyond imagining to the pioneer farmers of Durham. We can be sure that not one of them had the least intention of going there. Nobody in Durham knew any Indians. Why then did anyone appeal to them? In this remote part of the Empire there were white human beings giving help to distant brown people to whom they had no connection except human sympathy. Sympathy, and a common bond of Empire. They gave – and all of this has disappeared from history. Except in Durham.

Similarly, the French today remember the race crimes of the Vichy government, and pay no attention to the heroic sacrifices of millions of French people as they saved scores of thousands of Jewish refugees from Nazi death camps.[15]

Why do we not remember the heroes of love as well as the heroes of hate? Partly because we love heroes, and heroics itself has come to mean bravery in battle. Still, it is puzzling that those who crowned world-wide defeat of the Axis with the world-wide victory of compassion, who validated our war by carrying out our wartime aims, are not honoured like wartime heroes. Hoover estimated that the food relief campaign after the war saved 800,000,000 lives. Even if he over-estimated by ten times – impossible for this extremely intelligent and informed man – that is many millions more lives saved from immediate death than were lost to untimely death. In that post-war campaign, peoples who had been divided were re-united, ideals for which millions died in war were finally implemented, making the victory not just a triumph of arms but the coronation of civilization. Without the work of millions of people after the war, the victory itself would have been turned into a gross and tragic failure. Yet as we can see by a computer check in one of the world's great libraries* roughly 850 books about Hitler have been published in English, but only 80 about Hoover. Killer Hitler outsells saviour Hoover ten to one in the West.

I have thought about this for years, trying to find the answer to this question, and it has always evaded me. I thought I was going to have to finish this book without even suggesting an answer. The reason I could not understand was simple: I was a young and therefore idealistic person during the Second World War. I saw my brothers and sister and father go off to fight the Hun for great reasons. They were defending democracy, Canada, the British Empire, self-determination and fair treatment for all peoples. We were the just of the world, arrayed in a death struggle against the cruel barbarian.

For many years, until I began to study the post-war period, I really believed that these were the reasons we fought Hitler. Therefore I took it for granted that we were forgetting our most important ideals when we neglected the heroes who had enacted them. Now at last I think I understand: the reason for our forgetfulness is not that we forget the ideals that we value. The ideals that we remember are those we value. But they are not the ideals I thought – democracy, self-determination for all peoples, and so on. No, the ones we remember are the ones we *do* believe in – victory, strong leadership, courage, hard labour in the common cause, self-sacrifice for the common good, and so on. What we remember is what we value. The rest is a noble sham.

But not quite.

After all, if we had not believed the noble ideals, we would not have fed the starving after the Second World War, would not have helped Europe. We do believe in them, but not much. Our leaders tell us we believe in these things to mask in lovely

*The Robarts Library, University of Toronto.

high-mindedness our pursuit of our normal self-interest. Where there is no evidence demonstrating our high-mindedness, we may make it look better by contrasting it with the crimes of others. The world does not lack for dreadful criminals – the Japanese under the Empire, the Soviets, the Iraqis. And of course the Germans.

And we accept all this with shy eyes, because our leaders are encouraging us in the happiest of human pursuits, creating a good opinion of ourselves.

We have still to learn that our ideals will inspire no one if they do not inspire us. Nobody pays any attention to a teacher who has not learned his own lesson.

The struggle between crimes and mercies is not won, or lost, or over. As Solzhenitsyn said of the Russian guards round the Gulag – inside each one of us sits the soldier with his eye on the good woman, and his finger on the trigger.

APPENDICES

1: The Death Rate and the Totals

NOTE: *The double percentage point sign at the end of a number, e.g. 23.5%%, indicates per thousand, not per hundred.*

We can establish the death rate used by Robert Murphy for 1946 in Germany starting with several well-known facts: that emigration was forbidden at the time, and that immigration was compelled, in the form of expellees and prisoners arriving. But Murphy anticipated that the population of Germany would decline by two million despite immigration and births. His prediction means that in a period of two to four years, German deaths would outnumber births by two million.

As we have seen, the official death rates for Germany have been falsified, but Murphy's statistics make it easy to determine the true rate. We begin with the birth rate since this rate does not directly reveal statistics that, like deaths, are dangerous in themselves, so we can be fairly sure that it was reported reliably. The rate for west Germany was 16.1%% in 1946, and for east Germany it was 10.4%%.[1] Pro-rating for population size, we see that the overall German average was therefore 14.47%%. Thus there were born each year in Germany around 940,000 people. For Murphy's prediction to have come true in one year, the deaths would have had to have been 2,000,000 plus 940,000 equals 2,940,000, producing a rate of 45%%. For two years, the rate would have had to have been 29.8%%, for three years 24%%, for four years 22%%, and so on. It is clear that no one participating in the 1947 CFM meetings thought that it would take more than four years to bring back all the expellees and prisoners, so we will stop the calculations there.

It is clear that the death rate when Murphy was writing was between 22%% and 45%%. We have found no evidence anywhere that a death rate as high as 45%% had ever prevailed for long in a major part of Germany, except for Königsberg for a few months in 1945–46. The highest rate we have found was the city of Berlin at around 41%%. Furthermore, to have used such a high rate, Murphy must have thought that all the expellees and prisoners would be home in one year, i.e. by 1948, which was clearly not the case, if only because the French and Russians, the major holders of POWs in 1947, said they had no intention of returning all their prisoners that year. Since that high rate of 45%% is nearly impossible, we should give great weight to the fact that the Soviets, British and French all said that they would return their prisoners by 1949. And nearly all were returned.

We should also give great weight to the fact that the rate of inflow of expellees when Murphy was writing in 1947 meant that nearly all of them would be in Germany by 1950. And the Allies expected the situation in Germany to stabilize sufficiently by 1950 so that a further small flow of expellees would have no material effect on the economy. And this is what happened.

The rate consistent with the virtual completion of immigration in 1950 is certainly the most likely. That rate is 24%%.

It lies to the conservative side (i.e. implying the fewest deaths) of the range from 22%% to 29.8%%.

Since we know from comparing the censusses that Murphy's prediction was actually cautious in the sense of predicting fewer deaths than did occur, it is reasonable to conclude that he was cautious in selecting his time frame to determine the death rate, i.e., it is reasonable to assume that his death rate was on the cautious side of the 20–30%% range. That also is consistent with the death rate of 24%%.

That is the death rate used as a benchmark to check the results of the census calculations.

Analysis of additions to population, October 1946–September 1950

Prisoners of War	Totals	Returned
American	333,525	333,525
Soviet	1,131,000	1,000,000
French	657,000	600,000
British	510,000	510,000
	2,631,525	2,443,525
Prisoners in other countries (e.g. Yugoslavia, Poland)	235,000	200,000
Total Prisoners		2,643,525
Total Expellees		6,000,000
Total Arrivals (rounded)		8,600,000

SOURCES: *American* – according to the Office of the Chief Historian, European Command, Frankfurt, 1947; in the Center for Military History, Washington. Also Patterson Papers, LC. Both courtesy of Dr Ernest F. Fisher, Arlington. *Soviet* – according to Maschke, Bulanov Report and Soviet delegate to CFM, 1947. Allow deaths and holdbacks of 131,000. *French* – according to Buisson, Appendix 4. Less deaths estimated by author of 57,000. *British* – according to UK delegate to CFM, 1947.[2] *Yugoslavia, etc.* – according to Maschke, Vol. XV, p. 296. Allow for deaths and holdbacks of 35,000.

2: OTHER DEATHS AMONG GERMANS

Beyond the deaths totalled in the text, there were certainly other deaths among the Germans after May 1945. Those who died included some prisoners who had not been covered in the Adenauer–Bitter survey that showed 1.4 million missing soldiers, paramilitary personnel and civilians. Also, there were probably more than the reported 2.1 million deaths among the expellees. And there were many Germans who died in Germany during the first year and a half of Allied occupation, from spring 1945 to October 1946.

Estimated deaths among German civilians, May 1945–October 1946

The Murphy estimate of two million deaths to come soon after 1947 is based on his knowledge of 'the present high death rate in Germany'. *Murphy knew the death rate for a considerable period leading up to October 1946.* This rate was 24 per thousand per year.

The conclusion from this death rate is simple: at the very minimum, about 1,900,000 persons of the *c.* 65 million German population in the Occupied Zones died in the period August 1945–October 1946.[3] But the official West German figures for deaths in the three western zones was 786,000.[4] No comparable statistical summaries have been published for the Soviet zone but conditions there, e.g. rations, were not greatly different from those in the west. The Soviet zone had about 39 per cent of the population of the western zones, so the estimate of deaths there is about 306,000. Thus, in the period August 1945–October 1946, when the death rate of 24%% derived from Murphy's figures shows that the death toll must have been around 1,900,000, the official reports show only about

1,092,000. Once again, many people are probably missing/not accounted for. If Murphy was correct in these figures which were never disputed by any of the occupying powers, then between August 1945 and October 1946 about 800,000 Germans died but were not reported dead in the Allied statistics.

As we have seen, hundreds of thousands of other Europeans died in the camps. The Soviets alone reported the deaths of some 160,000.

The figure of 1.4 million missing was based by the Adenauer government on research work done by the Committee on prisoner of war questions (Ausschuß für Kriegsgefangenenfragen) headed by Dr Margarethe Bitter of Munich in the late 1940s. Dr Bitter told the author in 1991 that her survey covered some 94 per cent of all families in the three western zones, plus about 30 per cent of the 19 million people in the Soviet zone. Rüdiger Overmans has written that no one from the Soviet zone responded. Both agree that no one was surveyed in the seized territories, where at least 1 million and perhaps as many as 4.5 million Germans avoided expulsion. An unknown number of prisoners is therefore missing from those families.

The survey when completed *pro rata* should show between 1.7 and 1.9 million missing. The author has taken the lower figure as sufficient for his purpose.

3: THE FATE OF THE EXPELLEES

NOTE: *This is a point-form summary of the evidence concerning deaths of Germans, mainly expellees, from August 1945 to October 1946, some of it from documents newly declassified in the US.*

1) The French delegate at the Council of Foreign Ministers in April 1947 said that 4.5 million expellees had arrived (as at

October 1946) and that 2 million were expected to come in the near future.[5]

2) US Senator Homer E. Capehart said in the US Senate on 5 February 1946 that already 3 million expellees were Missing/ Not Accounted For.[6]

3) The members of the Committee Against Mass Expulsions in New York said that on the basis of the 1946 census, around 4.8 million expellees were Missing/Not Accounted For. This was published in their book *The Land of the Dead*, with an Introduction signed by nineteen prominent Americans, among them H. V. Kaltenborn, Dorothy Thompson and John Dewey. They estimated that 4.8 million had died by the end of 1947. (Infant mortality in Brandenburg province was estimated at 80–90 per cent in autumn 1945. Infant mortality throughout Germany for the year to the spring of 1946 was reported to Hoover to be 30 per cent.[7])

The Catholic bishops of the United States, meeting in Washington on 16 November 1946, said that, 'We boast of our democracy, but in this transplantation of peoples we have perhaps unwittingly allowed ourselves to be influenced by the herd theory of heartless totalitarian political philosophy.'[8] The Catholic bishops were on strong ground, for accusations of this same crime of deportation of peoples had been levelled by the Allies themselves against the Nazis at Nuremberg. Count Three of Section J of the Indictment against Göring, Ribbentrop and others, reads: 'In certain occupied territories purportedly annexed to Germany, the defendants methodically and pursuant to plan endeavored to assimilate those territories politically, culturally, socially and economically into the German Reich, and the defendants endeavored to obliterate the former national character of these territories . . .' The CAME authors added, 'It is inconceivable that the United

States government would endorse policies for which the Nazi leaders were tried and hanged under American auspices.' Yet that is what happened.[9]

4) Finally, for the Polish-administered areas of (former) Germany: the Soviet delegate said at the Council of Foreign Ministers meeting in April 1947 that 5.7 million expellees had (probably as of October 1946) left Polish-administered areas since Potsdam, and 400,000 remained behind. This is amply confirmed by the report of the Canadian Legation in Warsaw at 25 January 1949. The Canadians were told by the Poles that as of June 1947, only 289,000 ethnic Germans remained in the former German territories taken over by Poland.[10]

Murphy said that there had been originally 7 million potential expellees there, which would mean that the Missing/Not Accounted For were 0.9 million from 7 million in two years. Pro-rating to all of the 14/15 million refugees, we see a total of Missing/Not Accounted For of over 2 million from July 1945 to October 1946. Many millions were still left to endure the hardships of the trek after that.[11]

4: How One Writer was Spied on

Following the publication of *Other Losses* in 1989, as I travelled for further research and for publicity, I slowly realized that I was being spied on, presumably by Canadian, American, British, French and Russian agencies hostile to the disclosures in the book.

In the autumn of 1989, my wife Elisabeth and I were staying in the villa of friends in the south of France. The phone was making strange sounds, so that it was difficult to hear. I called the telephone company, and they said they would send a repairman. The following day, as Elisabeth and I were leaving the house, we noticed that a man in a suit with a briefcase was standing in the driveway. I asked him what he wanted and he said he was looking for the Villa Autran. I said that it was the villa he had just seen us leaving, that we were the occupants, and asked him if he had come about the phone. He said yes, and I told him the villa was open and he could go in and fix it while we were out. That night, the phone worked fine.

The next day, I saw a blue and yellow phone company truck in the road just past the driveway, and a man in uniform with tools hanging from his belt. Suddenly I remembered the incident from the day before, so I asked the uniformed man if he was the regular repairman for the area. He said yes, except when he was on holiday and someone else took over. I asked if he had been told to fix my phone and he said no. Then I remembered that there had been no telephone company truck in or near the driveway the day before.

Elisabeth and I talked it over and could not make it out. I saw no point in calling the phone company because they could say only that they knew nothing about it.

A few days later I was on the phone – the same phone – to my publisher in Toronto, Nelson Doucet. I told him about a discovery I had recently made about the prisoners, and my opinion of it. I also told him this was secret.

A few days after that, I was talking by phone – again, the same phone – to a British journalist who told me, 'But you think . . .' and went on to repeat what I had told Doucet. I was dumbfounded. How had he known that? Elisabeth and I discussed it and I said the place was bugged, but she pooh-poohed the idea. I could hardly believe it myself. For that to be true, I thought, the French would have to know about my book, which had not even been published in France. Then they would have had to realize I was in France, and then track me down. And the villa we were in was not rented – it was borrowed, and the phone was in the name of the owners. To the

French police, I believed, I was just a tourist who had been there many times before, and represented no danger. Why then would someone bug my phone, and keep recording all the calls – always in English – and analyze them? Above all, why phone the British journalist and tell him? This was the most preposterous thing of all. But then, how did he know what I had told Doucet in confidence? Did he guess? Did someone phone him? Did Doucet blab? But Doucet is a discreet, loyal and courageous publisher. I could not imagine him doing such a thing. The whole affair seemed so bizarre that I simply had to dismiss it. So I did nothing about it for five years.

Then, in 1994, I met a man I shall call Jean le Spy, who had been a very senior officer in a big security organization in a Western democracy. He knew about me. He said that after the publication of my book *Other Losses* in September 1989, 'You were targeted right away.' Le Spy knew what he was talking about because he had been in one of the agencies that had done the spying. I told Le Spy the story about me and Nelson Doucet. He explained how it was done. He said that the Americans were 'on to you as soon as you published'. He told me that as soon as I had arrived in Paris, the French police, who had been warned by the Americans, entered my hotel room and copied or read what they wanted and bugged the room. From then on it was easy to trace me in France.

He then explained the phone calls. The Americans routinely listen to all the international calls that interest them. They tape-record these calls, which are listened to by computers which are able to recognize key words. The computers are so sophisticated now, he said, that they have syntax built in. They notice the use of a word such as, say, 'Burns', which may be a name or a verb, and they can distinguish between 'fall' as a verb and 'fall' as a season. If a phone call contains the key word or clusters of key words that interest them, the tape is turned over to a human being for analysis. The Canadians do the same thing. The French do the same thing. The British, Norwegians and others do the same thing. Since the Americans and Canadians (and presumably the others) are forbidden by their laws to bug their own citizens without a court order, they must either get that order, listen illegally, or not listen at all.

Not to listen is, for these spies, inconceivable. So, Le Spy said, the Americans listen to Canadian calls, and the Canadians to American calls, all the time. The Canadians then offer the Americans everything they have and vice versa. Technically, no law is broken. And this is so routine now that the word Le Spy used to describe it is that 'they publish this', meaning they exchange it regularly in an organized and pre-arranged manner, but, of course, always within narrow and secret limits.

This capacity naturally applies to all information that is transferred digitally or by satellite, such as bank transfers, faxes, e-mail on the Internet, TV signals – anything. So far as I know, this has never been made public before. So far as I can judge, it is against the law.

In my case, the line of communication is easy to see. The computers downloaded my Doucet call to tape, flagged it and passed it to an expert, who then informed the various American, Canadian, French, German and British writers, State Department employees, academics, print and TV journalists and army officers who were busy rebutting my charges.

This is only one of many bizarre incidents. My mail has been opened, and the contents removed. At Heathrow, my hand-luggage was taken from me by an official of British Airways as I was boarding a flight to Moscow. When I pointed out that I had been promised by BA in Toronto that I could take the luggage, by hand, and that in fact I had just arrived from Toronto with the luggage under the seat, the official quickly said, 'If you want to get on this flight, check the bags.' I checked them. When I arrived in Moscow, my Russian collaborator and researcher Alexei Kirichenko told me that he had been warned by a former KGB officer that a CIA man in Washington had just phoned him to say, 'Tell Kirichenko not to work with Bacque, as he is a very dangerous man.' Reassured, I worked with Kirichenko anyway. I invited him to stay at my house in Toronto to collaborate on a project. He arrived with no type-writer and no notes and nothing done. When I saw the childish scribbling he had done for a draft of a section in our projected book, I said, 'Alexei, this is no good at all. You told me you had written five books.' He admitted then he had written none. One day just before his departure, I was out of the house, leaving him there. When I returned to my study, I could smell his strong body odour in the room. This was odd, as it was clear to both of us that there was no book to work on. The next day, after he left, I received a call from a Toronto lawyer warning me that Alexei had evidence that I was planning to steal his work from him.

The next time I used my copying machine, I discovered it was out of paper, though it had been loaded when Alexei was there. Clearly, he had been using a lot of copy paper while I was out. The lawyer then phoned *Saturday Night* magazine to warn them that I was planning to steal Kirichenko's work. They also phoned my book publishers, Stoddart/General. Later on, the incoming editor of *Saturday Night*, Ken Whyte, refused to publish an excerpt from my new book, even though it proved by my research in the KGB archives in Moscow that my earlier work for *Saturday Night* had been absolutely correct. He did this despite the fact that John Fraser, his predecessor, had paid my way to Moscow and back to do that research, thereby acquiring exclusive rights to the work. Whyte then published an attack on me by a British journalist, and refused to print even a mild letter from me rebutting the incorrect criticism by the journalist.

Work commissioned from me by the *Globe and Mail*, the

Times Literary Supplement and the *Ottawa Citizen* has been refused. My letters to the editor have been refused by such papers as *Le Monde*, the *New York Times*, the *Toronto Star*, the *Globe and Mail*, and *Saturday Night* under Ken Whyte. Although my previous book was an international best-seller, the manuscript of *Crimes and Mercies* was turned down by fifteen different publishers. And let us remember that this has nothing to do with the quality of my writing, or of my research, or of any anticipated financial loss.

Are these rejections a conspiracy? Or did fear outweigh greed in editorial offices throughout the West? Or was it a sudden attack of editorial likemindedness? Whatever, for three years I suffered the censorship by rejection slip of the proscribed writer. There is no freedom of the press in the West, only freedom to own the press.

When I said to Le Spy, 'Why would they go to all this trouble over a book of history?' He said, 'They wanted to know who you were working for. Especially when you went to Moscow.' I said, 'It's obvious who I work for. I work for my readers.' He just laughed.

5: LOCAL DEATH RATES IN GERMANY, 1946–50

Most of the reports show a high death rate. Few of the towns reporting give complete statistics. Most of the towns that report death rates near or below the 12.1%% rate reported for 1947 by the Statistisches Bundesamt also display characteristics that demonstrate their unreliability, e.g. Karlsruhe and Bonn.

Death statistics for one Austrian and nine German cities and towns for certain critical years appear below. Four were issued by the authorities in the places concerned, the rest by other authorities and observers as listed. Those that accord with the general death rates calculated in Chapter V are in

Table A. Those in conflict appear in Table B with the author's comments.

TABLE A

Place	Year	Population	Deaths	Death rate
Bad Kreuznach	1946	26,096	1,010	38.7%%
(French zone)	1947	27,233	743	27.3%%
	1948	26,768	637	23.8%%
	1949	27,000 (ca)	569	21.1%%
Berlin	1945–46	2,600,000		46.2%%
	1947	3,000,000		28.5–29.0%%
Brilon	1945–46	71,110	2,224	31.3%%
Königsberg	1945–47	100,000	75,000	750.0%%
Landau	1946	19,910	787	39.5%%
(French zone)	1947	20,802	563	27.0%%
	1948	21,694	513	23.6%%
	1949	22,426	462	20.6%%
	1950	23,188	485	20.9%%
Marktoberdorf	1946	4,318	119	27.6%%
(US zone)	1947	4,557	112	24.6%%
	1948	4,648	80	17.2%%
	1949	4,913	121	24.6%%
	1950	5,085	138	27.1%%
Vienna (Austria)	1946	1,900,000		27.0–35.0%%

Comments on Table A

Brilon: City officials in 1995 were asked by the author for death statistics of their city for 1945–49, and replied that they were understaffed and could not fulfil the request. The author, during research in Ottawa, came upon a copy of a three-page report made by the official of the City of Brilon in 1946, and given to the Canadian Military Governor. This shows the death rate reported above. A copy has been sent to Brilon.

Landau: 1946 population averaged from (January 1946) 19,370 and (October 1946) 20,450. 1947 population averaged from (1946) 19,910 and (1948) 21,694. All statistics from Landau Town Archives, Landau, Rheinland-Pfalz.

Berlin: Among the 3 million people of Berlin the death rate in May of 1946 was three times the pre-war rate, i.e. around 37%%. In 1947, according to Chancellor Adenauer, it was around 29%%. (Adenauer, Speech to Swiss Parliamentary Chamber, March 1949, and Ernst-Günther Schenck, *Das Menschliche Elend im 20. Jahrhundert. Eine Pathographie der Kriegs-, Hunger- und politischen Katastrophen Europas*, p. 68.) In Königsberg, taken over by the Soviets, over 70 per cent of the population died in two years (ibid., p. 79).[12] Cannibalism was reported to have occurred among some of them. Similar conditions prevailed in other areas of East Prussia, West Prussia, near Frankfurt-am-der-Oder and in many Silesian towns, according to Dr Schenck.

Marktoberdorf: Complete statistics for this small town near Augsburg are available from the Bayerische Statistisches Landesamt and from the Statistical Service in the Rathaus of Marktoberdorf. Average for five years equals 24.2%%.

Augsburg: The Augsburg city archives do not have any figures for 1946, and statistics for only three months of 1947 and three months of 1948, and again none for 1949 and 1950.

TABLE B

Place	Year	Population	Deaths	Death rate
Bonn	1939	100,788	1,278	12.7%%
	1947	101,498	1,062	10.5%%
	1950	115,394	1,233	11.0%%
Karlsruhe	1946	175,588	1,980	11.3%%
	1947	184,376	1,975	10.7%%
Karlsruhe (churched)	1946	175,588	2,039	11.6%%

Comments on Table B

Bonn: The official figures purport that the death rate in the prosperous and mainly peaceful year of 1939 was 21 per cent higher than the disastrous year of hunger, 1947. A parallel anomaly exists between 1947 and 1950. Also, the subsidiary figures for 1947 for men (44,048) and for women (55,825) do not add up to the total population given of 101,498. In view of the conditions of the years 1939, 1947 and 1950, the author finds that the official death toll for 1947 is incredible.

Karlsruhe: Because the official report from the authorities of Karlsruhe seemed odd to the author, his assistant conducted research at the offices of the Catholic church and two of the three Protestant churches, which shows that among the churched alone, the deaths totalled 2,039. It is impossible to know now how many dead Karlsruhers in those years were members of churches, but since the church burials alone exceed the deaths recorded in the town archives, we know that the town archives are not dependable.

SOURCES:
Local governments except: *Berlin* – 1945–46, from Maurice Pate, 'Reports on Child Health and Welfare Conditions', FEC Papers, Box 15, the Hoover Institution at Stanford. Also Konrad Adenauer, speech to Swiss Parliament, March 1949, in *Erinnerungen 1945–53*, p. 187. Also Gustav Stolper, *German Realities*, p. 33, and Herbert Hoover, who said 41%% in 1946 in his *American Epic*, Vol. IV, p. 164. *Königsberg* – from Ernst-Günther Schenck, *Das Menschliche Elend im 20. Jahrhundert*, pp. 78–80. Population in 1939 was 368,000. *Vienna* – General Mark Clark to Herbert Hoover, 15 April 1946; FEC Papers, Box 16, the Hoover Institution at Stanford.

General comments

The statistics that indicate a death rate of normal proportions from 1946 through to 1950 have one characteristic in common: they show a near-normal death rate in circumstances that were agreed by everyone to be abnormally harsh. In fact, some of them, e.g. for Bonn, indicate that fewer Germans died while starving, cold, despairing and exposed than died when the country was prosperous, comfortable, peaceful and well-fed in the late 1960s – the years of the *Wirtschaftswunder*, the 'Economic Miracle'.

The British Army reported that the death rate in North Rhine province in 1946 was about 12%%. It fell during the year until it hit only 8%% in September. The death rate in Hamburg in 1946, according to official British Army reports, was 14.9%%. Having started near 20%% in January, by the end of the year, it had declined to only 12.63%% annually.

In an overall report by Herr Degwitz to the 5th Sitting of the Zonenbeirat on 10 and 11 July 1946, the death total in the British zone was 5,800 per month more than the deaths in the same area in 'normal times'.[13] Given that the death rate in Hamburg, the principal city in the British zone, was 12.03%% in 1938,[14] this means the death rate in the zone in 1946 was around 15.5%%. The increase may seem minimal, but it must be remembered that it rose through 1947 as conditions grew worse. And modern readers can get the scale of death by remembering that it is about 50 per cent higher than one experiences in modern society. In other words, it means that for every two persons you knew who died recently, you also would have to mourn the death of yet another.

In April 1947, the Canadian Army General Maurice Pope, Head of Mission in Berlin, reported to Ottawa that among the elderly, who constituted a high proportion of the war-ravaged population, 'the death rate is high, and the suicide returns do not show much improvement'. He concluded, 'To sum up, the situation is bad, as it always has been.' A few weeks later he reported five 'authenticated' deaths from starvation in Hamburg.[15] The 'authenticated' is revealing. As many writers said, the Allied officers knew almost nothing of the true conditions among the German civilians. The 'authenticated' almost certainly refers to deaths counted in a hospital. But of course very few sick Germans ever got to a hospital in those days. As the US Surgeon General reported in October 1947, 'The alarming scourge is tuberculosis . . . In the British zone, as a whole, there are known to be 50,000 open cases and only 12,000 available hospital beds, while the less serious cases number about 150,000.'[16]

The German doctor, A. Lang, Professor of Physiological Chemistry at the University of Mainz, told an American officer in April 1948 that the death rate in the Pfalz was only around 13%% in 1947. However, he did not cite the source of his statistics. If these had been gathered, like the 1946 census, by 'Germans working under the direction of the Allied Control Council', then one explanation of the low figures could be that

215

the results had been adjusted to provide a more favourable picture of the conditions under the Allied occupation. Pfalz was in the French zone, where rations were consistently lower than in the British–American zone, so one suspects that the death rate must have been higher, as for instance it demonstrably was in Bad Kreuznach. But one other explanation might be that the people of Pfalz, living close to the land, were able to scrounge for themselves to augment the official ration better than people in big cities. The Pfalz was largely rural, lacking any big city, small in population (under one million), and also very low in expellee population. Still, it is hard to conceive of a disparity so great that the people in Bad Kreuznach, so close to the Pfalz and also in the French zone, were dying twice as fast as the rest of the population. The statistics are also very hard to reconcile with those from the town of Landau, right in the Pfalz.

On the subject of health, the American Military Governor Lucius Clay revealed an interesting comparison of the Soviet with the western zones. Clay writes that in 1945, the agricultural production in the Soviet zone was just under 80 per cent of pre-war normal for some grains, and as high as 90 per cent for grain west of the Elbe, plus about 75 per cent of the normal livestock harvest.[17] At the same time, food production in the west was only 57 per cent of the pre-war per capita production. An interesting sidelight on the Clay statistics is that since the agricultural work in all the zones was done exclusively by Germans, and mainly by hand, this superior production in the Soviet zone suggests that at that time the people in the Soviet zone were at least as healthy as Germans in the west.

In sum, then, the figures of local origin generally conform to the overall statistics derived from the census comparisons and presented in the main text. The few that do not conform in general display other characteristics that make one distrust them *a priori*.

6: SOURCES

The chief archival sources are the KGB Archives in Moscow, also called the Central State Archives (formerly the Central State Special Archive, CSSA); the Archive of the October Revolution, Moscow; the Red Army Archive at Podolsk, near Moscow; the National Archives of the US in Washington and College Park, Maryland; the National Archives of Canada in Ottawa; the Dokumentationsstelle, Bretzenheim, Germany, the Library of Congress, Washington, and the Hoover Institution Archive at Stanford. Much of the research material used in this MS has never before been published. Some of it – at Hoover, Washington and in Moscow – has only recently been declassified.

Sources for deaths of German civilians, 1945–50

The papers of Robert Murphy, former US Ambassador in London, also former political adviser to the US Military Governor of Germany at the Hoover Institution Archive, Stanford; the reports of the US Military Governor (first Eisenhower, then Lucius Clay) from archives in Abilene and in Washington; thousands of pages of documents of the Hoover Famine Emergency Committee at Stanford; Canadian Army reports on conditions in Germany; archives in German villages and towns; the census reports of 1946 and 1950 done by the Allied occupation armies that are still in archives in the West and in Moscow; reports from the official German government statistical agency, the Statistisches Bundesamt at Wiesbaden; and the Robert Patterson Papers, Manuscript Division, Library of Congress, Washington. In addition, as a result of the publication of *Other Losses*, my publishers and I have received thousands of letters, diaries, books, documents, phone calls and visits from former prisoners and civilians describing events occurring in Germany from 1945–50.

Sources for prisoners of war

The material drawn from Soviet sources is new to readers in both East and West. Briefly, the central source is the CSA in Moscow, the most important archive in existence about Second World War prisoners. Restricted to a few highly-placed Soviet specialists for many years because it contained state secrets, it was opened to Western researchers for the first time in 1991. The Soviet regime had long before then revealed many atrocities committed against Soviet citizens by Stalin, Lavrenty Beria, Lazar Kaganovich and others. But these newly opened archives document vast crimes against prisoners from twenty other countries around the world, including Japan, Germany and Italy. Here, in grey cardboard boxes, repose millions of individual dossiers, one for each of more than four million prisoners taken to the Soviet Union.

Without the Seal of Secrecy
Edited by Dr G. F. Krivosheyev. This book includes the Red Army's full report on the fate of all prisoners including those taken by the Red Army. It is authoritative.

German POWs and the NKVD
Master's thesis by Captain V. P. Galitski. Captain Galitski, of the Russian Navy, spent fifteen years working on the research for this thesis in Moscow and elsewhere. He visited Toronto in 1996 to give a speech on the topic for the Mecklenburg Historical Society at Massey College, University of Toronto.

Spravka: the Kashirin Report
In 1993, I received a six-page report in Russian from the Russian Army historian Andrei I. Kashirin, whom I also interviewed at length with his colleagues in Moscow. I am satisfied that this report represents to the best of his ability, which is professional, the fate of prisoners of war in the USSR, comprehending other earlier reports. This Kashirin report records the fate of all prisoners in Soviet captivity from 1941 to 1952.

The Bulanov Report
This one-page report by Colonel Bulanov prepared in the NKVD and dated 1956 gives detail of the fates of three ranks of prisoner from seventeen countries over a period of fifteen years. It was the NKVD under Lavrenty Beria that ran the prisoner gulag (Gupwi) and kept the records.

(The above summary reports agree on all prisoner information essential to this book. The reports below are subsidiary to them.)

The Petrov Report
The background is that in June 1943, Lt. General Ivan Petrov, chief of the department for prisoners of war in the MVD/NKVD, reported on prisoner deaths to the Party meeting among officers of his department. Because this was a Party meeting, the report was not censored by Beria, and was certainly the truth as Petrov knew it. He said that up to May 1943, a total of 193,003 Wehrmacht and German-allied prisoners had died during the whole war. However, Beria had previously told Stalin that as of 26 February, some 33,000 prisoners had died for the whole war. Beria's figure of 33,000 dead at 26 February taken with Petrov's, means that some 160,000 prisoners died in the next couple of months out of a total holding of 257,000 (62 per cent), *against Stalin's orders*. This was due

to the fact that the Red Army was not ready to receive such a huge surrender.

After the initial disorganization at Stalingrad, the NKVD and army co-operated very closely, and prisoner care improved radically. As the army entered Germany, if prisoners died or escaped, German civilians were rounded up to replace them. The count arriving at the NKVD camps was always the same as those leaving the front.

The West German Survey of Missing Prisoners
See Appendix 7 below.

7: GERMAN POST-WAR SURVEYS OF THE MISSING

Some Western historians who have never consulted the Soviet archives contend that nearly all of the missing Germans have been shown, by diligent research, to have been taken prisoner by the Soviets. One of the Germans most knowledgeable on this subject is Dr Margarethe Bitter, who was a founder of the first committee to investigate the fate of the missing, the Ausschuß für Kriegsgefangenenfragen. The results of the Ausschuß were based on a partial survey begun in 1947 of living Germans only. The Ausschuß could not survey the whole country door-to-door, so they put up notices in public places asking families and friends of missing persons to tell the committee the date and place where that person had last been known. The committee covered the US zone of Germany thoroughly, the British zone probably adequately but not thoroughly, the French zone inadequately and the Russian zone scarcely at all. It is not known what percentage of the expellees was covered. (In this book, it is assumed that all were covered, which reduces the number of the missing.)

Left completely uncovered were the citizens of such

countries as Italy, Hungary, Austria and Rumania, which had supplied over 2 million soldiers to the Axis, and about 1.9 million prisoners to Allied cages. In one Red Cross survey of an American camp for Germans near Marseille in 1945, over 12 per cent of the 25,000 prisoners were Yugoslav, Hungarian, Rumanian, Italian and Swiss.[18]

In all, the Ausschuß covered only some 58–68 per cent of the potential recruiting sources of the German army. Thus the Adenauer government's final estimate of 1,400,000 missing Germans was too low by scores of thousands. Adding in the losses among German allies, we see that the true total of missing Axis prisoners must have been above 1,600,000.*[19]

The American professor Arthur L. Smith Jr. has said that the Ausschuß found that 90 per cent of the addresses of the missing showed they had last been seen in the east, and were therefore presumed to be in the hands of the Soviets. He wrote: 'It is very important to note that this German committee under the very able direction of Frau Doctor Margarethe Bitter, arrived at its conclusions totally independent of the influence of the American Military Government.'[20] Yes, indeed, so free was it of that influence that the Ausschuß was not permitted to see the only records that might have revealed the truth. These were the records kept by the Americans of the conditions and deaths in the US camps. If, as Smith says, there was no disaster in the western camps, and nothing to hide, why were all the records hidden from the Ausschuß? If there was nothing to hide, why were so many of the records destroyed? Why were the rest classified for twenty-five years? Sixteen miles of paper, viewed

---

*This does not take into account the men who were missing but never reported as such because their families had been wiped out. In the firestorm raid on Dresden, for example, probably more than 100,000 people, nearly all civilians and refugees, died in one night. Similarly in Hamburg, scores of thousands of civilians died in one night. Some whole families were undoubtedly wiped out, and thus could not report a soldier gone missing in captivity after the war.

edge-on, came home from Europe in the army's files after the war, but these few feet of prisoner records were so dangerous they had to be extracted specially and burned. Many of these were being destroyed by the Americans at the time Dr Bitter and Dr Adenauer were working on the fate of the missing prisoners.[21]

Smith's statement about Germans 'missing in the east' is not correct, according to Dr Bitter herself. She said recently that, 'We didn't know where they were. They could have been among those who were captured by the Americans . . . They put them in fields in very bad conditions and many died. I don't think the Red Cross examined those camps.'[22]

Kurt W. Böhme, a German author who has taken the side of the Western Allies in this dispute, confidently asserts that 91.2 per cent of the missing were *Ostvermissten*, or missing in the east, because that was their last mailing address. However, his own statistics disprove this because of the long time lag between the last known address and the end of the war.[23] Almost two-thirds of these addresses are from 1944 or earlier, anywhere from four and a half months to a year or more before the end of the war. This fact affects drastically the usefulness of the addresses, because for more than a week at the end of the war, millions of Germans fled the eastern front to the Western Allies.[24] The round-ups of these soldiers escaping to the west also continued for weeks after the end of the war on 8 May.

8: THE PRISONERS AND THE CENSUS

Professor Dewey Browder of Austin Peay University in Tennessee disagrees with my conclusion that an unusually high number of deaths occurred in the US zone in 1945–50. According to German documents he obtained from the

Statistisches Bundesamt which were published in 1952,[25] the census results for 1946 included those Germans held abroad as prisoners.

If this were true, those prisoners who did return in 1946–50 should not be added to the population expected to be present in 1950. This would mean that the death toll as presented in this book would be reduced by the number of prisoners who were counted as part of the existing German population in 1946. However, the record referred to by Professor Browder does not state the total number of such prisoners, so no estimate can be made of the numbers affected. Professor Browder also cites the death rate of 12.1%% for Germany in 1947 frequently published by the Statistisches Bundesamt, and already discussed above.

The author believes that the documentation from the KGB archives, the US State Department and the Murphy Papers is comprehensive and fully reliable. Murphy states clearly that the prisoners are not included in the census figures, but are apart from them. Murphy's words are:

> Preliminary figures from the German census, taken on 29 October 1946 under direction of the Allied Control Council, show total population of 65,900,000. This includes about 700,000 displaced persons [DPs] (UNRRA Situation Report of 31 October). Assuming that all these DPs will eventually leave Germany, this will leave 65,200,000 inhabitants. German war prisoners still held abroad are estimated by OMGUS Armed Forces Division at 4,000,000 (consisting chiefly of 3,000,000 estimated held by USSR). German expellees still to be returned to Germany are similarly estimated by OMGUS PW and DP Division at 2,000,000. This gives a total eventual population for Germany, once all DPs have left and German war prisoners and expellees returned, of 71,000,000. However,

in order to be conservative, and in view of the present high death rate in Germany, a figure of 69,000,000 will be used.

The French delegate to the CFM conference of April 1947 also believed the prisoners were not counted in the census. He stated: 'Lastly, according to data which the four Delegations have just exchanged, we may estimate at two million the number of prisoners who will have to be repatriated.' He then adds them to the 66 million 'inhabitants which Germany has today' and adds as well the 'two million people of German race . . . to be transferred to the interior of Germany'. He concludes that, 'in sum . . . Germany would have about 70 million inhabitants'.

The delegate was speaking in March 1947, when he believed that the population of Germany stood at 66 million. Since he added the prisoners to the 66 million to arrive at the eventual population, it is clear that he did not think they were counted in the census.

And finally, the well-known expert on Germany Dr Gustav Stolper, who was on the Hoover Commission fact-finding team, wrote in *German Realities* that the 1946 census showed that, of the total population of 65,900,000 persons, '1,125,885 were prisoners of war, displaced persons and civilian internees'. He is in agreement with other contemporary authorities in saying this. Ambassador Murphy says that 700,000 of these 1,125,885 were displaced persons, leaving 65,200,000 Germans. The discrepancy of some 200,000 is discussed in detail in Note 29, Chapter VI. However, it is clear that no prisoners of war being held outside Germany in 1946 are included in the population total used in this book. In the unlikely event that some prisoners being held inside Germany in 1946 *were* included in Murphy's 65,000,000 census total, they did not exceed 300,000 in number, or about 3 per cent of the total number of the dead.

NOTES

CFM   Council of Foreign Ministers
CRS   Congressional Record of the Senate
CSSA   Central State Special Archive (Moscow)
FEC   Famine Emergency Committee
HIA   Hoover Institution Archive (Stanford)
LC   Library of Congress (Washington)
NAC   National Archives of Canada (Ottawa)
NARS   National Archives and Record Service (Washington and Maryland)
OMGUS Office of the Military Governor, United States
PRO FO Public Records Office, Foreign Office (London)
RG   Record Group

Further publication details of works cited can be found in the Select Bibliography.

Foreword (pages xiv to xx)

1   See Chapter III.
2   Dmitri Volkogonov, *Lenin*, p. 29.
3   Victor Gollancz, *Our Threatened Values*, p. 96.

Chapter I: A Piratical State (pages 1 to 15)

1. Women in Quebec and Switzerland were enfranchised several decades later.
2. K. A. Jelenski (ed.), *History and Hope*, p. 29.
3. George H. Nash, *The Life of Herbert Hoover*, p. 70.
4. Herbert Hoover, *Memoirs*, p. 166.
5. Ibid., p. 162.
6. Nash, op. cit., p. 358.
7. The stance and manner are described by Nash in *The Life of Herbert Hoover*, p. 84. The passage paraphrased here was, in Nash's original, used to describe an earlier meeting also addressed by Hoover.
8. Nash, op. cit., p. 85.
9. Hoover, *An American Epic*, Vol. IV, p. 17.
10. Hoover, *Memoirs*, p. 176.
11. Ibid., p. 168.
12. Ibid., p. 170.
13. Nash, op. cit., Chapter 4; Hoover, *Memoirs*, pp. 152ff.
14. Minutes of British War Cabinet Meeting No. 122, held on 18 April 1917, microfilm in National Archives of Canada.
15. Hoover to the Acting Secretary of State, Paris, 25 December 1918, in Paris Peace Conference, 1919, II, pp. 477–8; quoted in Edward F. Willis, *Herbert Hoover and the Russian Prisoners of World War I*, p. 22.
16. Vernon Kellogg quoted in George J. Lerski, *Herbert Hoover and Poland*, p. 20.
17. Hoover, *Memoirs*, p. 360.
18. Martin H. Glynn, 'The Crucifixion of Jews Must Stop!' in the *American Hebrew*, 13 October 1919, pp. 582–3. Glynn was the fortieth Governor of New York State, from 1913–14. In 1919, the year he wrote the article, he was a member of President Wilson's industrial conference.
19. Francis William O'Brien (ed.), *Two Peacemakers in Paris*, pp. 166–7; Hoover, op. cit., p. 358.
20. O'Brien, op. cit., p. 186.
21. Ibid., pp. 186–7.

22 Hoover to Wilson, March and April 1919, quoted in O'Brien, op. cit., p. 115.
23 O'Brien, op. cit., p. 129.
24 Ibid., p. xlii.
25 Ibid.
26 Balfour is quoted in Nigel Nicolson, *Portrait of a Marriage*, p. 143.
27 O'Brien, op. cit., p. 156.
28 Hoover, *Memoirs*, p. 345.
29 Ibid., p. 341.
30 Ibid.
31 Ibid., p. 342.
32 Ibid., p. 344.

Chapter II: The Beginning of Wisdom? (pages 16 to 40)

1 Babinski to King, 18 July 1945: Mackenzie King, *Diaries* (microfiche, University of Toronto Library), p. 696.
2 Richard Overy, *The Road to War*, p. 188.
3 Winston Churchill, *The Grand Alliance*, p. 370.
4 'An Analysis of American Public Opinion Regarding the War', a confidential report by George Gallup, American Institute of Public Opinion, Princeton, September 1942 (NAC, W. L. M. King Papers, 1940–50), pp. C258805ff.
5 *Life* and the *New York Times*, quoted in Paul Kennedy, *The Rise and Fall of the Great Powers*, p. 478.
6 Quoted in Gary Dean Best, *Herbert Hoover: The Post-Presidential Years*, Vol. II, p. 321.
7 See Arthur L. Smith, *Churchill's German Army* (Beverley Hills, CA: Sage Publications).
8 King, *Diaries*, p. 916.
9 Ibid., p. 75. Sir William Mulock was a Canadian Cabinet minister, and Sir Wilfrid Laurier Prime Minister of Canada from 1896 to 1911.
10 The Americans sent more than 400,000 jeeps and trucks; 13,000 locomotives and freight cars; 90 cargo ships; 4,000 bombers; 10,000 fighters; and over 7,000 tanks (FEC Papers,

HIA). The British and Canadians sent over 5,000 tanks; 7,000 aircraft; machinery, steel rails, wheat and much else.

11 W. Averell Harriman, *Special Envoy to Churchill and Stalin*, p. 277.

12 So many thousands of miles of Canadian rails were sent to the USSR that prisoners of war were still building the BAM (Baikal–Amur) line in Siberia with them in 1949. Letters to the author from Hans Wollenweber (1993), Fred Pichler (1992), and others.

13 State Department Memo (Division of Financial and Monetary Affairs), 19 February 1945 (E. E. Hunt Papers, Box 47, HIA).

14 John Charmley, *Churchill: The End of Glory*, pp. 804–5.

15 See Henry C. Morgenthau, *Germany is Our Problem*.

16 Fred Smith, *United Nations World*, March 1947 (UN Library, New York). See the Epilogue in Bacque, *Other Losses*, second edition, for a fuller account of this meeting.

17 Smith, op. cit.

18 Memorandum of conversation, Lord Keynes, 26 November 1944, NARS.

19 Alfred Grosser, *The Colossus Again: West Germany from Defeat to Rearmament* (London: Allen & Unwin, 1955), p. 18.

20 Quoted in John Morton Blum, *Roosevelt and Morgenthau*, p. 591.

21 Cordell Hull, *The Memoirs of Cordell Hull*, p. 1614.

22 NARS, RG 226, Box 176, Folder 2327.

23 Henry L. Stimson and McGeorge Bundy, *On Active Service in Peace and War*, p. 580.

24 Martin Gilbert, *The Road to Victory*, p. 995.

25 According to Jean-Pierre Pradervand, Chief Delegate of the International Committee of the Red Cross in France, the Americans never informed him that they had camps in France in 1945. However, at least one camp, near Marseille, was visited in 1945. The author has several times requested ICRC permission to visit their archives in Geneva to check on this and other mattters, and has been repeatedly refused.

26 Memorandum, 'Handling of Prisoners of War in the Communications Zone', by Lt. Col. Henry W. Allard, June 1946 (Archives, Fort Leavenworth, Kansas).

27 For more, see Bacque, *Other Losses*.

28 Armando Boscolo, *Fame in America* (the words are in Italian, and mean 'Hunger in America'), plus interviews with several ex-prisoners. Because the records have been destroyed, or are still withheld, it is impossible to determine the death rate. However, it certainly did not rise to the levels experienced in the camps in Europe.

29 See John Gimbel, *Science, Technology and Reparations*; also Balfour and Mair, *Four-power Control in Germany and Austria*.

30 Speeches of Senator Kenneth S. Wherry, CRS, January–March 1946. For other sources, see Chapter V.

31 Gilbert, op. cit., p. 965.

32 Senator William Langer, CRS, 29 March 1946.

33 CRS, Vol. 92, Pts 1–2 (29 January 1946), p. 509.

34 With thanks to Prof. Pierre van den Berghe.

35 Victor Gollancz, *In Darkest Germany*, p. 45.

36 Ibid., p. 78.

37 Ibid., p. 77.

38 Hilldring to State, RG 59, 3726A, NARS Washington.

39 Gollancz, op. cit., passim.

40 CRS, op. cit., p. 515.

41 Albrecht is cited in various speeches of Wherry *et al.* in the CRS for January to March 1946. His predictions are partly confirmed by experience recorded in the FEC Papers at Stanford, notably Murphy's prediction that deaths would out-number births by at least two million, and in Gustav Stolper, *German Realities*.

42 This means most children under ten and people over sixty. The rough estimate for children under ten is as follows: in normal times, 90 per cent of those born survive to the age of ten. Since about 900,000 babies were born per year, this means about nine million potential total. If 90 per cent survive, that equals approximately eight million alive after ten years. If half die, that equals four million dead. If only 10 per cent of persons then between the ages of sixty and eighty had survived from among those born in 1865–85, the potential was around fourteen million born, 1.4 million still alive, with half dying gives a total of 700,000. See Adenauer, op. cit., and population tree in Gustav Stolper.

43   Senator Wherry, quoting Probst Grüber (CRS, op. cit., p. 515). Thanks to Paul Boytinck.

44   This and the quotes from Johnson are from the CRS, op. cit., pp. 514–16.

45   The words in quotation are the paraphrase by F. Roy Willis of the report, in Willis, *The French in Germany*, p. 124.

46   Ibid.

47   See Appendix 5.

48   Montgomery to Mackenzie King, 24 October 1945, in King, *Diaries*, p. 1028.

49   Field Marshal the Viscount Montgomery of Alamein, *Memoirs* (London, 1958), p. 415.

50   In *The Progressive*, quoted by Senator Wherry (CRS, op. cit., p. 517).

51   See Chapter V.

52   As, for instance, US Navy officer A. R. Behnke.

53   Senator Wherry, CRS, op. cit., p. 518.

54   Ibid.

55   Senator Langer, CRS, March 1946, p. 2801.

56   King, op. cit., p. 841.

Chapter III: 'From There No Prisoner Returned' (pages 41 to 63)

1   For the Soviets, see: *Spravka*, by Russian Army historian Col. Andrei Kashirin, Moscow, January 1993; also G. F. Krivosheyev (ed.), *Without the Seal of Secrecy: The Losses of the Soviet Armed Forces in Wars, Military Campaigns and Conflicts*; also Captain V. P. Galitski, *German POWs and the NKVD*; also the report of the Chief of the Prison Department of the Ministry of Internal Affairs, Colonel P. Bulanov ('the Bulanov Report'), corrected by Pogachev, 28 April 1956. In IP, OIe (transliterated from Cyrillic letters) in the CSSA, Moscow.

For the captures of the Western Allies in north-west Europe, see: 'Report on Totals of Prisoners of War Taken', SHAEF G1, 11 June 1945, 383.6/1–3, NARS Washington; for Canadians distinct from British, see report of General H. D. G. Crerar covering operations of First Canadian Army 11 March to 5 May 1945, in MG 26 J-4, Vol. 410, File 3978, Sheet C288484, NAC; for Allies in Africa/Italy, see Eisenhower, *Crusade in Europe* and Col. Dr Ernest F. Fisher, US Army historian.

The Western Allies overall took 'about 8,000,000 German soldiers' according to A. T. Lobdell, Commanding Officer of the German prisoners in Iowa, Minnesota and the Dakotas. Since the Axis armies captured were composed in the West of about 85 per cent Germans, this means that the total prisoner take (which is the chief concern here), was around 9.4 million persons. Memo to Governor Dwight Griswold, 9 January 1947, in RG 260 OMGUS, Bundesarchiv, Koblenz. One of the US Army historians gives the total for Germans held in north-west Europe alone in May 1945, as 7,005,732 – see Oliver J. Frederiksen, *The American Military Occupation of Germany, 1945–1953* (Historical Division, HQ, US Army Europe, 1953), p. 89. This excludes Italy and the prisoners held in North America captured in North Africa and Sicily.

2   Most of those captured in the West were Germans who were held in Italy, western Germany and France. A few hundred thousand were held in the UK, and about half a million in North America. The Soviets distributed theirs, including a million non-German Europeans, through a system with some 6,000 sub-camps, spread throughout the whole USSR. See Galitski, op. cit.

3   The first was found by Jakob Zacher in the archives of Langenlonsheim. Copies available in Dokumentationsstelle, Kriegsgefangenenlager Bretzenheim, Bretzenheim/Nahe.

4   The witness has asked that his name not be revealed.

5   Brech to the author, letters and interviews, 1990 and 1991.

6   Brech's camp at Andernach was in the Advance Section zone of the Army, where the conditions were described by the Medical History of the ETO as typical of conditions through-out US camps in Europe.

7   This exemption was meaningless, because the prisoners were not registered by name for many weeks, so no one in the US command, much less a German civilian, could find out who was inside. Only by a chance sighting through the wire could

a civilian find a family member. An exception to the strict order not to allow civilians to provide food seems to have occurred in the camp at Emmering near Fürstenfeldbruck, when in May 1945 the local clergy and civilians assembled supplies from their own meagre stores and were permitted to deliver them to the prisoners. See a series of articles on the camp in the *Emmeringer Gemeinde Spiegel*, March 1986.

8 Hansy Scharf of California, interview with the author, 1991.

9 Berwick has said that he never ordered anyone to shoot at prisoners. This author accepts that statement without question.

10 Interview with Herr Tullius in Bretzenheim, July 1991.

11 Interview with the author, 1991.

12 Tagebuch with the author.

13 Interview with the author, October 1996. Dr Allensworth dissociates himself entirely from the author's overall criticism of US policy.

14 State to American Embassy, Paris, 12 May 1945, in 740.62114/5-445 State Department Archives, Washington.

15 Town of Bad Kreuznach, post 60, file no. 6754 06 WASt: War Graves lists for 1954 and 1963. Also cited in G. Maria Shuster, *Die Kriegsgefangenenlager Galgenberg und Bretzenheim* (Stadtverwaltung Bad Kreuznach, 1985).

16 Shown to the author by Heinz Bücher of Büdesheim, who is writing a history of the camp at Dietersheim.

17 Captain Berwick has told the author that: 'I take issue with the accounts of starvation at Camp A6 [Bretzenheim].' He met every day with the German *Lager* captains (leaders of each cage within the enclosure), and does not remember any complaints that food was insufficient.

18 The names of the prisoners are Paul Bastian, Konrad Schildwachter, Paul Kaps, Walter Drechsel, Erich Werner, Dr Herbert Bolte, Rudi Sauer, Gerhard Wolter, Winfried Punder and Rolf Freyer. Civilians who commented on the camp were Frau Grünwald, Frau Bastian, Frau Lambert and Frau Blank, all of Bretzenheim.

19 Letter of Herbert Peters of Hilden, Germany, to his son. In the author's possession.

20 Letter of recommendation, 8 July 1945. Signed Lt. Roy D. Schneider, HQ Dispensary, Detachment B, 50th US Field Hospital. In possession of Rudi Buchal, Grossenhain, Germany. Copy with the author.

21 Paul Bastian, interview with the author, 1991; Konrad Schildwachter, letter, November 1990.

22 Quoted in 'Menschen in Lagern an der Nahe und im Hunsrück' in *PZ-Information* 8/86 (Bad Kreuznach: Pädagogisches Zentrum, 1986) p. 46.

23 Other US soldiers at the camp – Bill Dodge, Tiller Carter and Frank Borbely – all said that Captain Lee Berwick's figures on the camp were probably accurate in their opinion.

24 Most of the records referred to here are filed under HQ 106th Infantry Division, Office of the Surgeon, APO 443 US Army, Annual Report Medical Activities 1945, signed Belzer, dated 18 September 1945. They are from Record Group 332 at or around Box 18, others from RG 112 at and around Box 313. All were at NARS Suitland until the recent move to College Park, Maryland.

25 The number varied during the period, which lasted from about mid-April to 10 July 1945. Enclosures actually in use varied during the period from zero at 14 April to possibly seventeen at the end of May. Some camps were shown as projected in reports, but never reported as containing prisoners. On 31 May sixteen are shown, of which fourteen were occupied. They were all in the ASCZ, on and near the Rhine (HQ Adsec Com Z, Office of the Surgeon, Report).

26 Status of Med Service PWTE Report, HQ, Adsec, Office of the Surgeon, April–June 1945, RG 332 Box 15, NARS College Park. Also Robert Hughson's official ration book for Bretzenheim, in Dokumentationsstelle, Bretzenheim, which lists hospital occupancy as well as rations and number of POWs in camp. Copy in the author's possession.

27 See p. 17 of the 106th Medical Report. The records for American patients are remarkably complete, showing for instance that the ambulance services of the 106th made 2,434 trips covering 193,949 miles, evacuating 21,551 prisoners to 'evacuation hospitals' in May to 10 July. The Hospital Unit

statistics of the 106th Division Medical Report covered all the American Rhine camps including Bretzenheim from the end of April to 10 July 1945.

28   Interview with the author, November 1987.

29   Dr Joseph Kirsch, cited in Gerard Östreicher, 'Ces prisonniers allemands "Morts pour raisons diverses"' in Le Républicain Lorrain, 3 June 1990.

30   It is possible that some of the 'evacuation hospitals' indeed treated their patients well. The prisoner Werner Borrmann of Quebec reported that he was sent to a small hospital near Idstein, then Bad Schwalbach, where German doctors and nurses treated him well. Borrmann believes that these hospitals were under American supervision; however, the French were taking control of the region in early July, so the responsibility may have lain with them.

31   Experience of many prisoners, including Wolf von Richthofen, Paul Kaps and Heinz Thaufelder.

32   In so-called 'hospitals supporting PWTEs', 16,229 beds were unoccupied in June 1945.

33   Letter from Marshal of the French Army Alphonse Juin to US Army General John T. Lewis, 11 October 1945 (NARS).

34   Lauben to Paul, 7 July 1945 (SHAEF Papers, Modern Military Records, NARS, Washington).

35   The patient load was admissions to hospital units of 44,646 less the evacuations to evacuation hospitals 'further to the rear' of 21,551, equals load of 23,095. But because there were 26,000 to 31,860 people not accounted for and not found at French takeover, it is clear that there were either more deaths in the hospital units than the figures show, and/or more men were evacuated to the evacuation hospitals than the figures show. The most conservative estimate is that 26,000 died in the evacuation hospitals, leaving around 5,860 as the patient load among whom 1,392 deaths were actually recorded. Or it may be that the 1,392 dead formed only the recorded part of the total of 26,000 otherwise unrecorded deaths in the evacuation hospitals and hospital units. In any case, to the hospital unit deaths must be added not only the evacuation hospital deaths as above, but also the deaths in the camp itself, apart

from the hospitals. Reports, HQ 106th Infantry Division, Office of the Surgeon, various dates in 1945. Most are in RG 112, entry 31 ETO, in or near Box 313 (NARS).

36   Report of Jennings B. Marshall, Major, Medical Corps Commanding, 50th Field Hospital, Detachment A, Bad Kreuznach, 29 May 1945. Records of 50th Field Hospital Unit, RG 112 and 407, Boxes 411–14 (NARS).

37   Dokumentationsstelle, Kreigsgefangenenlager Bretzenheim. The lowest death rate so far discovered in an American field hospital unit is reported by the 62nd Field Hospital, where some 4 per cent of the patients died in eighty days (approximately 18 per cent per year). This does not include the deaths in the camp itself (Kripp) nor in the evacuation hospital to which the moribund were sent.

38   See the report of Dr Siegfried Enke of Wuppertal on p. 48 of Bacque, *Other Losses* (Note 21).

39   The calculation is as follows: the Dellmann observations of 3,000 to 4,000, taken with the average population of Bretzenheim – about 73,800 for the ten weeks – show the death rate was around 21 to 28 per cent per year. It is not clear whether Dellmann's figures include both the two hospital unit cages and the twenty non-medical cages, so it is assumed here that they do, leading to a lower estimate for the death rate. Bretzenheim was about 13 per cent of the total 106th population, so it probably accounted for about 3,380 to 4,142 of the 26,000 to 31,860 missing (French source) and not accounted for (American source) in the 106th cages on 10 July. The death total therefore is somewhere between a minimum of 6,380 and a maximum of 8,142. The death rate is therefore somewhere between 45 and 57.5 per cent per year.

40   Sources: Pastor Dellmann, Rudy Buchal, and Captain Lee Berwick plus extrapolations by the author from 50th and 106th records.

41   Bretzenheim's 13 per cent *pro rata* share of total shown as evacuated in 106th records.

42   The total of prisoners disposed of in the breakdowns of returns, deaths, evacuations to the rear and admissions of communicable diseases in the hospital units is slightly more than the

total shown as evacuated from the main part of the camp to the hospital units. The excess may be due to double counting of some prisoners returning alive from the evacuation units, but this is unlikely since none is recorded. Or it may be due to double counting of men with two communicable diseases. The total of these extra people is 2,418. If indeed they were all living prisoners returning from the evacuation units, and are therefore to be subtracted from the 31,860 men for whom the Americans could not directly account, then the total of those for whom the Americans could not account on turnover shrinks from 31,860 to 29,442. The number not there according to Lauben was 22,000; the number missing according to the French was 26,000.

43   The details are as follows:

TOTAL EVACUATIONS FROM ENCLOSURES THEMSELVES	44,646
RETURNED TO ENCLOSURES AFTER TREATMENT	12,786
MISSING/NOT ACCOUNTED FOR (including 1,392 actually reported dead in hospital units)	31,860
DEATHS REPORTED INSIDE ENCLOSURES (apart from evacuations to hospital units)	1,697
	33,557

All 106th Division figures from Reports of the Surgeon, 106th Division, 18 September 1945, signed Lt. Col. M. S. Belzer. Camp populations from HQ AdSec Medical Status of PWTE Reports, NARS, and from original US Army ration book of Camp Bretzenheim, Dokumentationsstelle, Bretzenheim, Germany.

44   The population of the camps in the period was as shown above for 1 May–15 June, plus the figure for 7 July given by Colonel Lauben of 170,000.

45   See Bacque, *Other Losses*, Appendix 2.

46   It was Colonel Lauben who told me in 1988 the true meaning of the term 'other losses', a category of prisoners in the US

Army records. He said that it was almost entirely deaths. Since Lauben was Chief of the German Affairs Branch of SHAEF in 1945, in charge of repatriating prisoners, his word was authoritative. While the BBC was preparing in 1990 a TV documentary on these camps, Col. Lauben received a call from a US Army historian in Washington. The 'Pentagon official', as Lauben called him, said that I had misinformed Lauben about my research and about the state of the prisoners. The army historian, who had not been in Germany, also informed Lauben that he had misunderstood his own experiences. He said that the prisoners had not been maltreated, and any who were shown in the column headed 'Other Losses' had simply been transferred to another US Army command in Europe. There was no other US Army command in Europe. And, of course, it is an absurd notion that a foreign writer could walk into the home of a US Army officer and make him admit against his will that he had been part of a vast atrocity and cover-up. Clearly, great pressure was brought to bear on Lauben by the Army following his voluntary statements to me. Following this, Lauben issued a statement saying that he had made a mistake when talking to me.

47 An honorable exception: Paul Carell and Günther Bödekker in *Die Gefangenen* press this point hard, without, however, being able to advance anything more than well-founded suspicion of the French and American death figures.

48 See Bacque, *Other Losses*, Chapter 9.

49 Ex-prisoner Hans Goertz of Bonn, in interview with author, Bonn, April, 1986.

50 Senator Langer, speech in the US Senate, CRS (microfilm), Vol. 92, Pts 3–4 (29 March 1946), p. 2806. See also *Le Figaro*, 22 and 29 September 1945.

51 Langer, op. cit., pp. 2806–7.

52 Werner Waldemar of Toronto, interview. Also from camps in Norway, Paul Herman Bastian of Bad Kreuznach and Rudi Sauer of Laubenheim/Nahe.

53 Bacque, *Other Losses*, p. 266.

54 Armando Boscolo, *Fame in America* ('Hunger in America'), Chapter XV. Dr Cabito, the doctor in the camp for Italian

POWs in Hereford, Texas, wrote a strong letter of protest in August 1945 about continued inadequate rations, which had often descended to 1,500–1,600 calories per day. During an inspection by an American colonel two days before, the mess of the company was reduced to fried skins of potatoes and officers were eating crickets and locusts which had been fried in mineral oil, sold in the 'Stores' as hair tonic. His letter was forwarded to the Italian ambassador and the Red Cross representative who finally visited the camp on 28 October 1945.

55   The Patterson Papers, Library of Congress.
56   See Bacque, *Other Losses*.
57   Memo dictated 'for files' by General Clark, 30 August 1945. Courtesy of Jane Yates, Archivist, Citadel Archives, Charleston, SC.
58   Interview with the author, Clarksville, Tennessee, March 1988.
59   Memorandum 'Handling of Prisoners of War in the Communications Zone' by Lt. Col. Henry W. Allard, June 1946, Archives, Fort Leavenworth, Kansas.
60   Interview by the author and Elisabeth Bacque with Mr and Mrs Jean-Pierre Pradervand, Switzerland, 1990. From records published in Erich Maschke, *Die deutschen Kriegsgefangenen des Zweiten Weltkrieges*, it appears that in 1945 the ICRC did make a few visits to US Army labour camps where German prisoners worked.
61   This story was brought to my attention by Professor Richard Müller of Aachen. It is given in detail in the report of Plemper to the author, November 1991. Heising adds: 'I am not sure whether I repressed that cruel fact out of my mind or see it in a shadowy way or see it with the eyes of my friend . . . we tried not to see suffering *in extenso* and dying comrades.' Letter to the author, November 1991.

Chapter IV: A Holiday in Hell (pages 64 to 88)

1   Alexander Solzhenitsyn, *The Gulag Archipelago*, p. 525.

2 Captain V. P. Galitski, *German POWs and the NKVD*. The administration for the camps for POWs and internees, the 'Gupwi', was separate from the Gulag. Very little has been written about this administration compared to the Gulag. For excellent first-hand accounts of German prisoners in Soviet hands see Ernst H. Segschneider (ed.), *Jahre im Abseits. Erinnerungen an die Kriegsgefangenschaft*, and Dietmar Sauermann and Renate Brockpähler, *'Eigentlich wollte ich ja alles vergessen . . .'. Erinnerungen an die Kriegsgefangenschaft, 1942–1955*.

3 Interview with Galitski, Moscow, 16 May 1993, translator Martin Reesink.

4 Article by Galitski in *Military Historical Journal* for 1993, issue No. 2.

5 From the article by Galitski in *VIZh* (*Voenno-Istoricheski Zhurnal*), 1993, No. 2, p. 18, quoting an interview between G. Kurtz and Karl-Heinz Friser.

6 *TskhDIK*, F. 47p, op. 22, d. 1, 1. 97, Moscow. See also Galitski in *VIZh*, op. cit. p. 22.

7 Author's estimate. Galitski believes that the number of dead between 1941 and 1944 was somewhat higher, perhaps as high as 250,000, which would mean that the post-war death rate would be reduced.

8 Document E, NKVD order of 18 October 1944, 'To Improve Production', CSSA. The order specifies more rations for the weak and sick, less for criminals and automatic arrest categories.

9 Konrad Adenauer, *Erinnerungen, 1953–1955*, p. 451.

10 It may be objected that these reports cannot be trusted because experience shows that Western Allied reports of adequate rations for post-war prisoners were seldom true. Both the French and the Americans have officially reported that adequate rations were fed to prisoners who were in fact starving. However, these French and American reports have been widely publicized and deposited in, for example, national archives such as the Bundesarchiv in Koblenz. The difference is that the Soviet reports were kept secret for forty years in the KGB archives because they formed part of a series of

documents that, taken all together, reveal a grotesque atrocity. This information was never revealed by the Soviets while they were in power. In general the Soviet documents can be trusted.

11 Anton Chekhov, *The Island: A Journey to Sakhalin*, p. 108.

12 Interview with Galitski, Moscow, May 1993.

13 Interview with Alex Adourian, Toronto, January 1993.

14 Letter from Hans J. Mürbe, a former prisoner in Canada. With the author. See also Henry Faulk, *Die deutschen Kriegs-gefangenen in Großbritannien – Re-education* (Munich, 1970).

15 Edward Norbeck, 'Eddoko: A Narrative of Japanese Prisoners of War in Russia' in *Rice University Studies* (Houston, TX), Vol. 57, No. 1 (Winter 1971), p. 19.

16 Dmitri Volkogonov, *Lenin* (New York: Free Press), p. 29. Volkogonov also told me similar things during an interview at Staraya Ploshschad in Moscow on 17 May 1993.

17 W. Anders, *An Army in Exile* (London: Macmillan).

18 Louis Fitzgibbon, *Katyn: A Crime Without a Parallel*, p. 183.

19 Politburo Minutes, 5 March 1940, File No. P.13/144, Archive of the President of the Russian Federation, Moscow. With thanks to Dmitri Volkogonov.

20 F-2, Op. I, D.259, in the Archive of the President of the Russian Federation, Moscow. With thanks to Dmitri Volkogonov.

21 See Nikolai Tolstoy, *The Minister and the Massacres*; also Tolstoy, *Victims of Yalta*; also Elfrieda and Peter Dyck, *Up from the Rubble*.

22 In conversation with the author, 1993 and 1994. Tolstoy's book *The Minister and the Massacres* gives details of the story.

23 G. F. Krivosheyev (ed.), *Without the Seal of Secrecy*, p. 390.

24 V. P. Galitski presented these figures in a paper given at a conference at Massey College, University of Toronto, on 19 May 1996. Galitski has written his Master's thesis on the topic. An NKVD report signed by Colonel Bulanov reports 356,687 Germans died (Report of the Chief of the Prison Department, NKVD, 28 April 1956, CSSA).

25 Kashirin, *Spravka*, op. cit. Galitski points out that the Soviets counted Austrians separately from Germans, although the

Germans regarded the two as one. Since 1945, the nations have been separate, and therefore have counted their dead separately. The difference of some 27,000 prisoners dead is probably accounted for by different criteria for deciding who was a German. For instance, were ethnic Germans from Alsace-Lorraine regarded as Germans? The difference of 27,000 is approximately 1 per cent of the total take, or 6 per cent of the deaths.

26   See William F. Nimmo, *Behind a Curtain of Silence*.

27   UN *Yearbook* 1951, p. 564. The figure is lower than the missing figure used elsewhere in this book (1.4 million) partly because the continuing investigation revealed more prisoners missing than thought when the UN submission was made, and mainly because the German government calculated the almost 300,000 captive civilians separately from the soldiers. The true total of missing Germans was therefore above 1.4 million.

28   For full details, see Appendices 2 and 7.

29   Interview with the author, Munich, June 1991.

30   See Kurt W. Böhme, *Gesucht Wird* (Munich: Suddeutscher-Verlag, 1970).

31   Dr Bitter was founder of the Ausschuß für Kriegsgefangenenfrage, which under the authority of three German *Länder* (provinces) investigated the fate of missing German prisoners. Dr Bitter began this investigation in 1947. When the Federal government took over in 1950, Dr Bitter continued her contributions. A copy of the eventual Federal government report was deposited by the German government with the United Nations in New York (see UN Library). The version in the author's possession was given him by Dr Bitter. It is entitled *German Prisoners of War and Missing Members of the Wehrmacht (Second World War), Part 1, Volume 1, Third Revised and Completed Edition*, 30 June 1953.

32   Interviews with Dr Bitter in 1991, by telephone and in person. Tapes and transcripts with the author. Dr Bitter went on to say: 'We didn't know exactly where they were, they could have been in any camp. They could have been dead. These were more or less theoretical calculations . . . the time when a

missing person had been last seen could have been many
months before the end of the war. Yes, oh yes. In Russia, they
could have been . . . and they could have been also among
those who had been especially captured by the Americans,
for whom there were no camps, you see . . . they put them in
fields and let them [hesitation] . . . in very bad conditions for
a few months and so and many died and so on . . .' And in
another conversation with the author she said, 'C'est pas certain que les prisonniers disparus étaient en mains Russes' ('It is not
certain that the vanished prisoners were in Russian hands').
For another example, see Arthur L. Smith, one of the major
proponents of the 'dead in the east' theory, in Die 'vermisste
Million'. Zum Schicksal deutscher Kriegsgefangener nach dem
Zweiten Weltkrieg (Munich, 1992). According to one member
of the Volksbund der Kriegsgräberfürsorge, the German agency
in charge of finding and maintaining German war graves in
Russia, this book makes 'no relevant research contribution'.
Letter to Lotte Börgmann of Rheinberg, July 1994.

33   Professor Stefan Karner of the University of Graz, Austria, has
said that perhaps 800,000 of the missing Germans are accounted
for by 'disappearance' between capture at the front and arrival at
the base prison camp. He refers to this himself as a 'Schaetzung',
or estimate: 'Die Schaetzung von mindestens 800,000 vor der
Registrierung verstorbener deutscher Kriegsgefangener basiert
auf Erfahrungen mit der von mir durchgeführten Erhebung
österreicher, luxemburgischer, Sudtiroler und französischer
Kriegsgefangener' in Vierteljahrshefte für Zeitgeschichte, 3 July
1994, p. 449. See also Appendix 2.

34   Bischof and Ambrose, Eisenhower and the German POWs, p.
144.

35   See Note 1, Chapter III.

36   Overmans also says that at the beginning of 1945, the US
army held 300,000 German prisoners, but he does not give any
US Army source for this. The top US Army source, the Theater
Provost Marshal General, reported that, as of 27 December
1944, the 12th Army Group and the 6th Army Group had
together taken over 400,000 German prisoners in the
European campaign since 6 June 1944, plus 229,000 more in

Tunisia. The official American total is therefore more than double the number reported by Overmans.

37 Erich Maschke, *Die deutschen Kriegsgefangenen in amerikanischer Hand* (Munich, Verlag Ernst and Werner Gieseking, 1973), especially the volume by Kurt W. Böhme.

38 At the end of the war, Germans constituted around 68 per cent of the total Soviet catch of Axis prisoners (Bulanov Report, CSSA, Moscow). *Without the Seal of Secrecy* (colloquially in Moscow, 'The Red Book') reports that the total fascist catch at the end of 1944 was 1,836,996. Allowing for 32 per cent of the catch as non-German, Germans in Soviet captivity numbered about 1,248,000 at the end of 1944. See also Maschke, Vol. XV, pp. 194, 224.

39 From Martin K. Sorge, *The Other Price of Hitler's War* (Westport, CT: Greenwood Press, 1986), p. 63. For the missing at 31 March 1945 (1,281,285), see also *Kriegstagebuch des Oberkommandos der Wehrmacht*, Vol. IV, edited by Percy Ernst Schramm (Frankfurt: Bernard Graefe Verlag, 1961), p. 1515.

40 How can we account for the fact that the Soviets reported more captures than the OKW thought they had lost among the army? The difference can be accounted for in part by the losses among the navy and air force. These amounted to 256,000 for the whole war 1939–January 1945, on all fronts (Sorge, op. cit., p. 63). Since most air force and navy losses were in the west, the eastern component was probably under 50,000. The remainder were probably men estimated as dead by the OKW who were actually alive and captured.

41 For a full description of the massive errors in accounting for prisoners in the west, see Bacque, *Other Losses*, with special reference to Col. Philip A. Lauben, Milton A. Reckord and French Army Captain Julien.

42 Hans von Luck, *Panzer Commander*, with an Introduction by Stephen E. Ambrose (New York: Praeger), p. 214.

43 Captain Harry G. Braun, *Of Islands and Ships* (Alameda, CA, 1991), p. 101.

44 Professor Stefan Karner in *Vierteljahrshefte für Zeitgeschichte* (July 1994).

45 See p. 65. The original title is *Dokumentation der Vertreibung der Deutschen aus Ost-Mittel Europa*.

46 Galitski, *German POWs and the NKVD*, op. cit.; and Kashirin, *Spravka*, op. cit.

47 Interviews with two German researchers in the CSSA in Moscow, 1992, and with Mme V. Fatiukhina of the Russian Red Cross.

48 Nimmo, op. cit., p. 96.

49 Ibid., p. 95.

50 Letter from William Nimmo to the author, January 1993.

51 MVD report dated 1950 in Archive of the October Revolution, Moscow. Publicly quoted by Boris Yeltsin and Mikhail Gorbachev following research supplied to them by Alexei Kirichenko, Sector Head, USSR Academy of Sciences, Institute of World Economics and International Relations, Moscow.

52 When questioned as to the possibility that the NKVD records were falsified at some point, the chief prisoner specialist in the CSSA, Ludmilla Nosyreva, said that she did not believe they had been falsified. Anatoly S. Prokopenko, Deputy Head of the Archives Committee of Russia and policy adviser on archival law to Russian president Boris Yeltsin, has said that he does not think that the NKVD records were falsified, although it is likely that one part – the entry for the cause of death on the certificates – was sometimes altered to make it appear more 'natural', or less shameful to the Soviets.

53 According to Eddy Reese, one of the senior archivists of the Modern Military Records of the US NARS in Washington, soon after the war, and while the Germans under Dr Bitter were investigating the fate of their missing prisoners, 'all non-record camp documents were destroyed'. Conversation with the author, Washington, 1987.

54 Years after the publication of *Other Losses*, the Public Records Office has said that the Report is at last available.

55 Report of T. de Faye, Major, Acting Commander, 4th Regiment, Winnipeg Rifles, to HQ 2/7 Canadian Infantry Brigade, 23 November 1945. In RG 24, Vol. 10,976, File 260C7009 D19, NAC.

56 Approximately 1.4 million were determined missing in the incomplete survey instituted by Dr Bitter. Most Germans living west of the Soviet zone were covered, but fewer than 50 per cent in the Soviet zone were covered. *Pro rata* to population, probably another 300,000 or so were missing without Dr Bitter's researchers being notified. In addition, nearly 300,000 civilian and paramilitary prisoners were taken. See Appendix 2.

Chapter V: And the Churches Flew Black Flags (pages 89 to 111)

1 Diplogerma Multex, Berlin to Moscow, 27 February 1941, FYI. Found in Murphy Papers, Box 69, HIA. There is a typo in the original German, which reads in translation that 'there will be no neutral commission'. It is clear from the context, which is all predicated on the existence of such a commission, that this is an error, here corrected.
2 See Dwight Eisenhower, *Crusade in Europe*.
3 Victor Gollancz, *In Darkest Germany*, p. 92.
4 Captain Albert R. Behnke, USN MC, 'Physiologic and Psychologic Factors in Individual and Group Survival', June 1958 (Behnke Papers, Box 1, HIA).
5 See Herbert Hoover, *An American Epic*, Vol. IV, and *Addresses Upon the American Road*, 1945–48.
6 Gustav Stolper, *German Realities*, p. 67.
7 The worst famine in Holland occurred for some people in the winter and spring of 1945, 'when the calorie value of the official rations fell to 400 per day in the larger western cities'. All the preceding quotes about Holland are from Behnke, op. cit.
8 Montgomery to the British Foreign Office, 27 February 1946, PRO FO 943/452. Quoted in John E. Farquharson, *The Western Allies and the Politics of Food*, p. 110.
9 Hoover, *The President's Economic Mission to Germany and Austria*, Human Events Associates, Chicago, 1947, p. 6. Copy at Presidential Library, West Branch, Iowa.
10 John D. Unruh, *In the Name of Christ*, p. 146.

11   A. O. Tittmann, letter to Hoover, 30 January 1947, in FEC Papers, Box 3, HIA.

12   From various sources, including the Patterson Papers, Library of Congress; Henry C. Morgenthau, *Germany is Our Problem*; Report on Agricultural Production – Germany, Behnke, op. cit.; OMGUS, Economic Policies, submitted by Members of the Select Committee on Foreign Affairs, House of Representatives, September 1947, p. 19; and Stolper, op. cit.

13   Letter to the author from Ernst Kraemer, Bonn, 30 July 1994. Kraemer was at two camps, Büderich and Rheinberg.

14   Grasett to Smith, June 1945. Box 37, Smith Papers, Carlisle Barracks, PA.

15   Letters from ex-prisoners on file with author.

16   F. Roy Willis, *The French in Germany*, p. 115.

17   The estimates for the total of Germans subject to expulsion varies, but De Zayas has settled on 16.6 million in all categories, including stay-at-homes, dead during flight, and living arrivals. See De Zayas, *Nemesis at Potsdam*. It is highly likely that the death rate among the stay-at-homes during 1945–50 was far above normal. For example, the figure accepted in 1947 by the (Allied) Council of Foreign Ministers meeting was 400,000 Germans still living in ex-German territory held by Poland. In fact, the Canadian Chargé d'Affaires in Warsaw, K. P. Kirkwood, reported to Ottawa on 28 January 1949 that only 289,000 Germans remained. That is 28 per cent fewer people than formerly believed. RG 25, Vol. 57A, File 7-CA-14, NAC.

18   Emigration was forbidden for most of the period 1945–50. By 1950, around 600,000 had been permitted to emigrate, according to estimates of the Statistisches Bundesamt, Wiesbaden. The USA and Canada were the top destinations for Germans once emigration was permitted after 1950, but a cursory check of US and Canadian immigration figures for the period shows that this 600,000 estimate is far too high. One effect of an excessive estimate is to reduce the number of Germans missing/not accounted for in the 1950 Census. See Note 28, Chapter VI.

19   Stolper, op. cit.

20 See John Gimbel, *Science, Technology and Reparations*; also Michael Balfour and John Mair, *Four-power Control in Germany and Austria*; also Tomberg, *Report on Economic Conditions in Germany for 1948*, RG 25, Vol. 3807, NAC.

21 Economic Directorate of Allied Control Authority, Food and Agricultural Co-ordinating Committee paper, 24 July 1946, PRO FO 943/147. Quoted in Farquharson, op. cit., p. 257.

22 De Zayas, op. cit., p. 8.

23 Ibid., p. 10.

24 Robert Greer, 'Letter from Berlin' in *Reading*, February 1946, pp. 27–8. Robert Greer is the pseudonym for Robert Greer Allen, then a lieutenant in the Canadian Army seconded to the Canadian Broadcasting Corporation in Germany in 1945. He became a distinguished producer and administrator for CBC TV, Toronto. His article was adapted from a letter to his wife.

25 Johannes Kaps (ed.), *The Tragedy of Silesia, 1945–1946*, p. 189.

26 Theodor Schieder (ed.), 'The Expulsion of the German Population from Czechoslovakia' in *Documents on the Expulsions of the Germans from Eastern Central Europe*, Vol. IV, p. 459.

27 Ibid., pp. 453 et seq.

28 Ibid., pp. 399–409.

29 Ibid., p. 431.

30 Ibid., p. 449.

31 Ibid., p. 449.

32 Kaps, op. cit., p. 189.

33 Ibid., p. 195.

34 Ibid., p. 223.

35 Ibid., p. 228.

36 Hugo Rasmus, *Schattenjahre in Potulitz*, p. 55.

37 Interview with Dr Martha Kent, Phoenix, 1997.

38 Letter from Dr Kent; see also Rasmus, op. cit.

39 Rasmus, op. cit., p. 151.

40 Ibid., p. 189.

41 Kaps, op. cit., p. 324.

42 Ibid., pp. 526 et seq.

43 Solzhenitsyn, *Prussian Nights*, translated by Robert Conquest, p. 39.

Chapter VI: Death and Transfiguration (pages 112 to 141)

1   Konrad Adenauer, *Memoirs, 1945–1953*, translated by Beate Ruhm von Oppen, p. 148.

2   Health and Medical Affairs, MG Report, December 1947. In Behnke Papers, HIA.

3   Census and mortality reports of Statistisches Bundesamt, Wiesbaden.

4   Health and Medical Affairs, Military Governor's Report, p. 10, December 1947. In Behnke Papers, op. cit.

5   Brian R. Mitchell, *International Historical Statistics*. Mitchell has reported his German sources to be either the UN *Yearbook* or the Statistisches Bundesamt.

6   See Bacque, *Other Losses*, Epilogue One.

7   Lucius Clay, *The Papers of General Lucius D. Clay*, p. 97.

8   Resolution by the German Physicians, Brüggen, in Behnke Papers, op. cit.

9   Gustav Stolper, *German Realities*, p. 31.

10   If the predicted 2.5 million did die in the Soviet zone in the six months to spring 1946, the death rate for the period would be 135%%. This is more than ten times the pre-war rate for Germany.

11   Statistiches Bundesamt, *Bevölkerung und Kultur*, Reihe 2: *Natürliche Bevölkerungsbewegung*, p. 33. Also Statistisches Bundesamt, *Bevölkerung und Wirtschaft, 1872–1972*, p. 90.

12   When asked in October 1994 for his published source for the death rate, Mitchell replied that he was unable to say whether it was the UN *Yearbook* or the Statistisches Bundesamt. He agreed that the primary source was probably the Allied Control Council. It was in this correspondence that he expressed his reservations about the 'official death rate'.

13   Statistisches Bundesamt, *Bevölkerung und Wirtschaft, 1872–1972*, p. 90, gives 12.2 per thousand per year, and *Natürliche Bevölkerungsbewegung*, p. 33, gives 12.1.

14   Alfred de Zayas saw this letter in the ICRC archives in Geneva when he was doing research for a book. He asked for permission to photocopy the letter, which was refused. The

ICRC has several times refused entry to the present author to their archives, on the grounds that they never open their archives to writers. Not only has De Zayas been given permission, but also two other writers.

15   Council of Foreign Ministers Meeting, Moscow, April 1947. In Murphy Papers, HIA.
16   Johannes Kaps (ed.), *The Tragedy of Silesia, 1945–1946*, p. 224.
17   Ibid., p. 237.
18   Ibid., p. 252.
19   Ibid., p. 276.
20   Ibid., pp. 403–12.
21   Ibid., p. 443.
22   Konrad Adenauer, *Memoirs, 1945–1953*, p. 48. Adenauer gives a lower figure for expellee arrivals than appears elsewhere in the present work because he was speaking in March 1949, whereas the cut-off date used for expellees in this work is September 1950. In the years 1949–50, at least 600,000 more expellees arrived.
23   The prisoners returned in the period numbered as follows:
     1.4 million from the Americans (Report on Estimated Strength of DEF/POWs, October 1945–June 1946), inclusive, in HQ, USFET, G1, Weekly PW and DEF reports and inserted at 2 November 1945, Modern Military Records, NARS Washington, plus 375,000 in camps in USA;
     0.2 million from small eastern countries (Maschke, *Die deutschen Kriegsgefangenen des Zweiten Weltkrieges*, op. cit.);
     0.8 million from the British (Maschke, op. cit);
     0.9 million from the French (Buisson, *Historique du service des prisonniers de guerre de l'Axe*, Appendix IV. He says the French had about 0.85 million at the end of 1945, but as has been demonstrated in Bacque, *Other Losses*, Buisson under-reported the intake of prisoners by at least 100,000 and over-reported the number the French returned to the Americans);
     1.5 million from the Soviets (Kashirin, *Spravka*, op. cit.; and Galitski, *German POWs and the NKVD*, op. cit.), as follows: 2.7 million total capture, 800,000 released in 1945, 400,000 dead to 1 Jan 1946.

24 Monthly Report of the Control Commission (British Element), June 1947. In RG 25, Volume 3809, Dossier 8380-c-40 seq, NAC.
25 Ambassador Murphy, CFM Prep. papers, 1947, HIA.
26 The source for this is the Murphy Papers, including the Council of Foreign Ministers papers at Stanford. Many authorities in Germany and elsewhere have written about the expellees, but there is no record at the HIA of any scholar having published these figures of Murphy's before. This lack of a publication record may mean little, because a scholar may in fact have used some of these figures without notifying Hoover. Courtesy of Ron Bulatoff, HIA, October 1994. These papers were declassified in several bunches, beginning in 1988. Others were declassified in 1991 by the State Department.

These papers include documents prepared for and presented at the Council of Foreign Ministers meetings in Moscow and elsewhere, from 1947 to 1949. They are based on statistics gathered by the ruling interzonal agency operating in Germany at the time, the Allied Control Council, under the aegis of the several Military Governments. Murphy states in April 1947 (CFM Papers, 9 April 1947, Statement by US Delegate, Box 61, Murphy Papers, HIA) that 5–6 million refugees had arrived. Since all other population figures in these papers are based on the census of October 1946, we can be sure that this figure is also for that date. The French delegate in the Moscow meeting said on 17 March 1947 that only 4.5 million had arrived. Murphy's assistant Brad Patterson stated on 18 May 1949 that 12 million had arrived (Murphy Papers, Box 67, file 67–6). The figure usually accepted by all authorities for the total arrivals in 1950 is 12 million. (The effect on the death estimates in this book of accepting the 12 million figure for May 1949 as valid for the final total of deaths in 1950 is nil.) This means that according to the Americans, between 6 and 7 million expellees arrived between October 1946 and May 1949. Since arrivals of 6 million are conservative in the sense of implying the fewest deaths, this is the figure I use in this book. If the French start figure is accepted, then some 500,000 to 1,500,000 *more* Germans arrived in the period October 1946–September 1950. This would increase deaths by the amounts shown. The American figure is largely confirmed by figures obtained from the Polish government by the Canadian Chargé d'Affaires in Warsaw in January 1949, showing that only 289,000 Germans remained in the new Polish territories, of the original 7,400,000. I have accepted only the most authoritative papers, the US State Department CFM collection, and from them, the number of arrivals demonstrating the fewest possible deaths. Therefore for the purposes of this book, the expellee arrivals in 1946–50 totalled 6 million. The British author Malcolm Proudfoot said that at July 1946, some 7.4 million expellees had arrived, leaving some 5 million still to come of the 12.4 million which he says arrived by 1950. Allowing arrivals of 1 million from July to October 1946, we see that Proudfoot was estimating in this (census) 1946–50 period an influx of some 4 million expellees. Proudfoot was writing long before the authoritative CFM papers were available to authors, so the sources on which he depended were not the best. For instance, in presenting population figures for 1946 in Table 40, Proudfoot does not refer to the census of October 1946. It appears that the figures in this census were not known to him, although the 1950 census was. For the crucial figure of expellee arrivals in January 1946 in his Table 40, he relies on an estimate made by a German author, Kornrumpf, without so specifying. This figure first appears on p. 371, properly identified as an estimate, then re-appears in the Table without being identified as an estimate. In the Table, it is cited beside the census figures of 1950, as if they are of equal authority. This implied equality of authority is clearly in error. The effect of accepting Proudfoot's estimates would be to reduce the estimated deaths of residents by 2 million, viz from 5.9 million to 3.9 million.

27   Total 2,643,525 rounded to 2,600,000 as follows:

For the Americans, 333,525, as follows: Disarmament and Disbandment of the German Armed Forces, Office of the Chief Historian, European Command, Frankfurt, 1947, in Center for Military History, US Army, Washington. Courtesy of Dr Ernest F. Fisher. (The figure of 250 prisoners held in the

USA that appears in this document has been augmented by
the author to 50,000 from information in the Patterson Papers,
LC, showing that President Truman ordered that this number
be held in the USA to help with the 1946 harvest. This harvest
was still in progress in September, when the prisoners would
have had to have been on board ship home to have been
included in the October census. Should further research reveal
that some or all of these 50,000 had been liberated before
October 1956, their number should be subtracted from the
eventual death total of German civilians shown in this book.)

For the Soviets, Statement of Soviet Delegate to CFM
Conference that in March 1947 there were 890,000 Germans
still imprisoned in the USSR. CFM Papers. The present
author estimates that there were 1,100,000 on hand in
October 1946, less author's estimate of deaths before release
1946–50, based on Kashirin, *Spravka*, op. cit., and the Kruglov
Report, 1 July 1945, in CSSA; and Bulanov Report, op. cit.

For the French, 657,000 (November 1946), less 57,000
estimated deaths 1946–50: in Buisson, op. cit.

For the British, 510,000: from UK Delegate to the CFM
meeting, March 1947, plus Griffith to McCahon, September
1946 et seq., US State Department Central Decimal File
F11.62114/12–145 to 3146. The total on hand at March 1947
was 435,000, to which must be added those repatriated from
October 1946 to March 1947. This total was 75,000, because
repatriations had been running at the rate of 15,000 per
month for five months. See also *The Times*, 22 August 1946,
and *Hansard*, 16 July 1946, p. 180, for total of prisoners on
hand at 30 June 1946 (518,000).

Plus 200,000 prisoners on hand in Yugoslavia, Poland, and
the Benelux countries, being 235,000 on hand less estimated
35,000 deaths. From Maschke, op. cit. It has been disputed
that all the arriving prisoners should be added to the potential
population as of the 1950 census. See Appendix 8.

28　Deaths and emigrants from Statistisches Bundesamt, Wiesbaden. The emigration figures (c. 600,000) given by the West
German government are incredibly high. For nearly all the relevant period, emigration was forbidden. When it did begin,

the destination countries put Germans at the bottom of the list of acceptables. There are strong conflicts between the figures given out by Wiesbaden and the figures for two of the most popular destinations for German émigrés, Canada and the US. For 1946–50, the arrivals in Canada according to the West German government were 86,900, but according to the authoritative book *The German–Canadian Mosaic Today and Yesterday* by Gerhard Bassler, only some 24,000 Germans arrived in Canada. Similarly American government figures show arrivals of 219,742 (Historical Statistics of the US, Washington, 1975) whereas the German government says émigrés totalled 401,700. This is still another example of the fact that statistics issued by the German government on subjects connected to Allied atrocities usually err, and the error usually masks the atrocity.

If it is true that the West German government figures are far too high, to reduce them to the correct level would increase the number of deaths in 1946–50. In order to err on the side of caution, I have used but do not believe the figure of 600,000 emigrants given by the German government.

29 Murphy Papers, op. cit. The American authority making most decisions affecting interpretation of these statistics was the US State Department, which in effect meant Robert Murphy. Murphy's major concern, as it was for all the Allies, was to analyze the effect of the population changes in Germany. He was especially interested in the ratio of agricultural land to numbers of people. However, Murphy appears to give two slightly different population figures for Germany at October 1946 which differ by 200,000, or 0.3 per cent. They are 65,200,000 and 65,000,000. The ACC census itself, as reproduced in the Military Governor's Reports for March 1947 (OMGUS Papers, NARS), shows that the total population was 65,911,180. There were two sub-totals: the German civil authorities reported a total of 64,778,202 German civilians, and the Allies reported a further 1,132,978 people under their direct control including three categories – Prisoners of War in camps in Germany; non-German Displaced Persons in UNRRA camps (non-German but provisioned there) and

German civilian internees. The non-German DPs numbered about 700,000 (UNRRA Situation Report, 31 October 1946, cited in Murphy). These he subtracted from the 65,900,000 (rounded) saying there were then left '65,200,000 inhabitants'. But when he took a base figure for population in order to calculate future changes including additions of returning POWs, he assumed there were 65,000,000. Why did Murphy subtract an additional 200,000 unspecified people? It is reasonable to assume that these 200,000 people were the German POWs and civil internees known to be present in Germany in Allied hands (and therefore in the Allied part of the census total), who were destined to return to the population in the next three years. Since Murphy was already including them in his calculations as new additions soon to come to the population, he did not include them as part of the original population. He was being careful to avoid double counting. This accounts for 900,000 of the 1,132,978 people shown under the category 'Population Registered by Occupation Authorities'. Neither the census nor Murphy says who those 232,978 people were. However, Murphy did not regard them as German, so they may have been Allied soldiers and civilians in the Military Government, who were counted alongside Germans, because they were being provisioned from German sources.

30 Statistisches Bundesamt, op. cit., p. 33. With thanks to Annette Roser. Also Mitchell, *International Historical Statistics*, op. cit., pp. 102, 109.

31 Statistisches Bundesamt, op. cit., and Mitchell, op. cit. The UN *Yearbook* 1956 reports that for the period of the four calendar years 1947 through to 1950, total deaths recorded in all zones were c. 3,297,194.

32 See *Bundesamt für Auswanderung, Tätigkeitsbericht der Bundesstelle für das Auswanderungswesen*, Bremen, 1951.

33 UN *Yearbook* 1956. The census for the eastern zone was taken under Soviet supervision at 31 August 1950 and the census for the west under British, French and American supervision at 13 September 1950. Both 1946 and 1950 totals exclude the Saar. Proudfoot says 68,794,000, but may include some non-German DPs.

34   The delegates to the various CFM meetings sometimes dis-
     agree with each other as to the number of arrivals at various
     dates between 1946 and 1950, but they all agree with each
     other that the total of arrivals was around 12 million in
     August–September 1950, which has become the figure
     accepted by the West German government. See De Zayas,
     Proudfoot and others.
35   Report of Town of Brilon, 24 April 1946. In MG 31 B 51,
     Friesen, GA-1945/46, NAC.
36   See Appendix 5 for details of Marktoberdorf.
37   Press release by HQ US Forces in Austria, 15 April 1946, re:
     Clark's interview with Hoover. General Clark believed that in
     the US zone, health standards remained above the standard in
     Vienna. But he also warned that 'the supplies turned over to
     UNRRA are estimated to maintain the existing 1,200 calorie
     ration scale throughout all of Austria until about 1 June 1946',
     when it would be necessary for the Austrians to feed them-
     selves, except for what UNRRA could bring in. He estimated
     the indigenous sources at 450 calories per day. In FEC Papers,
     Box 16, HIA.
38   Report on Economic Conditions in Germany especially the
     Bizone, for 1948, by Dr W. Tomberg. In RG 25, Vol 3807,
     NAC.
39   Gabriele Stüber, *Der Kampf gegen den Hunger, 1945–1950*,
     p. 810.
40   Chief Medical Officer of the Allied Expeditionary Force/Chief
     Surgeon of the ETO: Report, entitled 'The Disease Potential
     in Germany', p. 21. FEC Papers, Box 4, HIA.
41   See Hoover, *The President's Economic Mission to Germany and
     Austria*.
42   Murphy to State, 20 February 1947, Memorandum No. 90,
     re: Polish Administered German Area, in Council of Foreign
     Ministers preparatory papers for CFM meeting, April 1947,
     Box 61, Murphy Papers.
43   See Appendix 1.
44   De Zayas, *Nemesis at Potsdam*, p. xxv.
45   Figures published by the Polish government, reported in the
     Minutes of the CFM, April 9 1947. In Murphy Papers,

September 1947.

46 Theodor Schieder (ed.), *Documents on the Expulsions of the Germans from Eastern Central Europe*, Vol IV, p. 128.

47 See population trees in Stolper, op. cit., pp. 26–30. About 56 per cent of the German population in 1946 were females. In populations undamaged by war, females slightly outnumber males. The number of men between 20 and 50 was 9.6 million in 1950, or about 20 per cent of the population. Since young men normally die at a very low rate in peacetime, it is reasonable to conclude that over 80 per cent of the deaths occurred among women, children and old men.

48 The figure was actually far higher. See Appendix 2.

49 The highest estimates for the three wartime causes is given in Martin Sorge, *The Other Price of Hitler's War*, around 4,600,000. Other authorities place the figure much lower, e.g. around 2.3 million in John Ellis, *World War Two: A Statistical Survey*. The death rate for Germans including prisoners and expellees during this period was around 29 per thousand per year, while in other areas ravaged by the German attacks, such as Hungary and Poland, the rate was less than half that.

50 See Appendix 2.

51 Patterson to Marshall, 13 June 1947, Patterson Papers, Library of Congress.

52 Heinrich von Treitschke, *History of Germany in the Nineteenth Century*, Vol. I, quoted in Stolper, op. cit., p. 231.

53 See Hoover, *An American Epic*, Vol IV.

54 During the war approximately 3.8 million Germans died in the armed forces, another 500,000 in air raids and about 300,000 in Hitler's concentration camps. Sorge, op. cit., p. 67.

55 Peter Hoffmann, *The History of the German Resistance*, p. 16. These are overall figures including imprisonment based only on suspicion, and imprisonments based on judicial process. Some police arrest figures that probably include some imprisonments in the latter category appear in Detlev J. K. Peukert, *Inside Nazi Germany*.

56 James Taylor and Warren Shaw, *A Dictionary of the Third Reich*, p. 78.

57   The Dulles and Roosevelt quotes are from Peter Grose, *Gentleman Spy: The Life of Allen Dulles* (Boston: Houghton Mifflin, 1994), pp. 202–3.

58   Niemoller was later used by the British to propagandize or re-educate German prisoners in the UK.

59   Patricia Meehan, *The Unnecessary War*, p. 376.

60   *Hansard*, Series 5, Vol. 402, 2 August 1944, col. 1487. Quoted in Peter Hoffmann, 'The Question of Western Allied Co-operation with the German Anti-Nazi Conspiracy, 1938–1944' in *The Historical Journal*, No. 34, 1991, pp. 463–4.

61   Foreign Office Papers 371/39062, C 9896. Quoted in Martin Gilbert, *The Road to Victory*, p. 868.

62   I am indebted to Professor Pierre van den Berghe of Seattle for this passage about the German communist and socialist resistance.

63   Interview with Dr Raabe, March 1992.

64   Interview with Robert Kreider, in North Newton, Kansas, September 1994. Kreider was the MCC representative on CRALOG (Council of Relief Agencies Licensed to Operate in Germany).

65   Hoover, *An American Epic*, op. cit., pp. 101, 116; and *The Columbia Encyclopedia*.

66   The quotation is from a speech by Senator Capehart, 5 February 1946, in the CRS, p. 876.

67   The author has encountered several cases of such suppression. The farmer Otto Tullius of Bretzenheim, Germany, has dug on his own land to find traces of prisoners formerly held there when the land was used for an American and then a French prison camp. He was ordered to stop by the police under threat of a fine of 250,000 Deutschmarks. Interview with Otto Tullius, Bretzenheim, June 1991.

In Rheinberg, a young farmer, Martin Adams, together with his father worked the land of the former US prison camp, discovering human bones 'probably from the prison camp era'. According to Lotte Börgmann of Rheinberg and the town archivist H. Janssen, the police said that the bones had been buried in 'the old Jewish cemetery' at that location. Both Mrs Börgmann and Herr Janssen have said that the 'old Jewish cemetery' was nowhere near the camp. Martin Adams and his father ended up reburying the bones. In this and other instances, the news of the discovery of the bones was sent to the official German tracing agency WASt (a.k.a. Die Deutsche Dienstelle) in Berlin. The author has been unable to discover from the agency evidence of any further investigations. Apparently the news was reburied. At Lambach in Austria, recent discoveries of bones have provoked a controversy over their origins which may be a cover-up of POW deaths in US camps nearby.

An exception was the case of Hechtsheim near Mainz, where bones uncovered during highway building were identified as Hungarian.

From the Tullius case, it is clear that the police threat of an enormous fine is enough to deter most if not all investigators.

Chapter VII: The Victory of the Merciful (pages 142 to 182)

1   Attorney General William D. Mitchell to Herbert Hoover, at page F-12 of typeset manuscript by Hoover reporting on relief activities 1939–40 and after, in FEC Papers, HIA.
2   Hoover, *An American Epic*, Vol. IV, p. 84.
3   Ibid., p. 106.
4   Ibid., p. 87.
5   Ibid., p. 116.
6   Calculation is based on world population estimate of around two billion in 1939 (this is deliberately estimated low, which means that given a higher 1939 population total, there would be more food available per capita post-war than is shown here). One per cent of production sufficient for 2 billion people equals sufficiency for 20 million. This sufficient consumption pre-war is estimated by the author to be 2,000cpd, and shortfall for Germans at 800cpd (1,200 vs 2,000). Thus 2,000 x 20 million cpd translates to 800cpd for 50 million.
7   Hoover, op. cit., p. 177.
8   Patterson Papers, LC, Washington. For a succinct summary of

the situation showing that others agreed with Patterson, see Office of Foreign Agricultural Relations, Report, October 1946, quoted in John C. Campbell, *The United States in World Affairs, 1945–1947*, p. 323.

9 See Hoover, *Addresses Upon the American Road*.

10 Notes made by Secretary of War Robert Patterson after Cabinet meeting 29 March 1946. Patterson Papers, LC.

11 Patterson to Truman, 20 November 1946, Patterson Papers, LC.

12 Patterson to Marshall, 13 June 1947, Patterson Papers, LC.

13 Mackenzie King, *Diaries*, p. 878 (14 September 1945). NAC, MG 26 J 13.

14 The Canadian price was 30 per cent below current market price in 1946. By 1947, it was predicted, the world price would go to $2.25 per bushel, 50 per cent more than Canada was charging the UK. From J. E. Farquharson, *The Western Allies and the Politics of Food*, pp. 103–4.

15 Norman Robertson to Mackenzie King, 17 February 1946, C188701-3, King Papers, NAC.

16 Patterson to Truman, FEC Papers, Box 26, HIA.

17 Patterson to Truman, 8 July 1946, FEC Papers, Box 26, HIA.

18 In 1946, Hon. Thomas Jenkins reported in the US Congress that Hoover had already reduced the food shortfall from an estimated 11,000,000 tons to about 3,000,000 tons, which Hoover believed would fall by a further possible 1,500,000 tons. CRS, Vol. 92, Pt 4, pp. 5051–5.

19 Richard Norton Smith, *An Uncommon Man*, p. 359.

20 Hoover, from a speech in Ottawa quoted in *An American Epic*, Vol. IV, pp. 219–220. See also Gabriele Stüber, *Der Kampf gegen den Hunger*, for figures in the British zone, pp. 285–7. For figures on TB, see Stüber, p. 297.

21 King, *Diaries*, 28 June 1946, p. 599, NAC, MG 26 J13.

22 Gabriele Stüber, quoting from NAC External; 8376 K-40, C Cypher No. 55, 9 May 1946, NAC. In *Zeitschrift der Gesellschaft für Kanada-Studien*, p. 41.

23 Memorandum for files, 22 December 1946, Patterson Papers, LC.

24 See Bacque, *Other Losses*, Chapters 3–4.

25 Morgenthau Diary (China), Vol. 2, pp. 1529ff. For a fuller account, see Bacque, *Other Losses*, p. 83.

26 Patterson to Marshall, 13 June 1947, Patterson Papers, LC.

27 Stüber, *Der Kampf gegen den Hunger*, pp. 55ff.

28 Dr Frank D. Graham and Lt. Col. J. J. Scanlon, 'Economic Preparation and Conduct of War Under the Nazi Regime', 10 April 1946, Box 20, Patterson Papers, LC.

29 F. S. V. Donnison, *Civil Affairs and Military Government*, p. 340.

30 A. E. Grasett to Chief of Staff, W. B. Smith, 8 June 1945. Smith Papers, Army War College, Carlisle Barracks, PA.

31 John C. Campbell, *The United States in World Affairs*, p. 323.

32 The National Food Situation, pamphlet of the Bureau of Agricultural Economics, US Department of Agriculture, January 1946, FEC Papers, Box 9, HIA. Also résumé of meeting chaired by Dr FitzGerald, a Director, US Department of Agriculture, in his office, to give details to reporters of world food situation, 20 February 1946. Résumé in FEC Papers, HIA.

33 World Food Situation 1946, US Department of Agriculture, Washington DC. In FEC Papers, Box 25, HIA.

34 UN Report, Washington, 26 December 1946. Copy in FEC Papers, HIA.

35 USDA pamphlet and résumé.

36 Patterson to Byrnes, 27 December 1944. Also part-manuscript and notes of proposed book by Patterson, never published. These documents were declassified for this book in 1992.

37 Hoover, Introduction to *Food, Relief, Famine and the Economic Front in World War Two*, FEC Papers, HIA.

38 Foreign Office Paper, 9 July 1947, microfilmed in NAC, Ottawa at 8376-K-40C, PRO, London. Murphy estimated 'about 1,700cpd'.

39 Grasett to Chief of Staff (General W. B. Smith), 8 June 1945. Box 37, W. B. Smith Collection, Army War College, Carlisle Barracks, PA.

40 Foreign Office Paper, 9 July 1947, File 8376-K-40C, Vol. XXX; also M. S. Szymczak, *Our Stake in German Economic Recovery*, Federal Reserve Bulletin, July 1947, p. 681. Copy found by author in FEC Papers, Box 2, HIA; also Hoover, *The President's*

Economic Mission to Germany and Austria, op. cit. General
Clay said (*Decision in Germany,* p. 265, quoted in Balfour, op.
cit., p. 14) that the pre-war production in the western zones
would have provided only 1,100 cpd. If he meant 1,100cpd for
the pre-war population, this figure was not correct. This is
shown by the production actually achieved under much worse
circumstances in 1945, according to Hoover.

41 Foreign Office Paper, 9 July 1947, File 8376-K-40C, Vol. XXX.
42 CFM Papers, 61-62 File, Box 61, HIA.
43 See Michael Balfour and John Mair, *Four-power Control in Germany and Austria.*
44 See Balfour and Mair, op. cit., and Donnison, op. cit.
45 Szymczak, op. cit, p. 684, and Donnison, op. cit., among others.
46 Balfour and Mair, op. cit., pp. 12ff.
47 Szymczak, op. cit., p. 685.
48 Hoover, *An American Epic,* Vol. IV, p. 241.
49 F. Roy Willis, *The French in Germany,* p. 124. John Gimbel
points out that General Marshall misled, or lied to, Molotov
when he stated that the US reparations amounted to only
about $275 million of which most was external assets. Direct
'removals' from within Germany were only about $10,000,000,
Marshall said. Gimbel comments: 'Any evaluation approaching the truth would undoubedly have been embarrassing to
Marshall . . . for it would have revealed how distorted, misleading and propagandistic the statement released in Moscow
had been.' According to Gimbel the US took about $5 billion
and the British the same. The sum of $10 billion in today's
terms, allowing for inflation and the growth of the economies
involved, would be far above $200 billion. John Gimbel,
Science, Technology and Reparations, Chapter 8.
50 Interview with Peter and Elfrieda Dyck, September 1994.
51 ICRC President (Interim) Max Huber, to State, 30 August
1945. In 800.142/9-2745, State Department Archives,
Washington.
52 Huber, op. cit. Thousands of train-car loads were returned.
See also letter of E. L. Maag, ICRC Delegate to Canada, to
Minister for External Affairs, Ottawa, 17 April 1945, in RG 25
Vol. 3400 621MZ40C, NAC.

53 Stüber, *Der Kampf gegen den Hunger*, p. 442.
54 Malcolm Proudfoot, *European Refugees*, Table 40. There is a conflict between Proudfoot and official British army reports of refugees at that date, for which see Chapter V. The difference between the British report and Proudfoot is 400,000, but it is not clear how much of the difference can be attributed to the year 1946, which is the year in question here.
55 Donnison, op. cit., p. 335; civilians in Westphalia had 1,040cpd in 1945; see *Report on Economic Conditions in Germany*, especially the Bizone, for 1948, by Dr. W. Tomberg; in RG 25, Vol. 3807, NAC. Also Stüber, op. cit., p. 810.
56 Stüber, op. cit., p. 463.
57 Relief dates from Robert Kreider, Mennonite Member of the CRALOG, interview, September 1994.
58 It officially began on 19 February 1946, with at first eleven and later sixteen member organizations (*Mitgliedsverbände*) of American welfare agencies (*Wohlfahrtspflege*). But it was not really until autumn 1946 that the necessary aid was sent to Germany.
59 Stüber, *Die Zeitschrift der Gesellschaft für Kanada Studien*, p. 42.
60 Hoover, *An American Epic*, Vol. IV, pp. 162–3.
61 Patterson to Anderson, 5 May 1947, Patterson Papers, LC.
62 Patterson to Marshall, 13 June 1947, Patterson Papers, LC.
63 This was in the spring of 1946. Hoover, op. cit., p. 164.
64 Quoted by Stüber in *Der Kampf gegen den Hunger*, pp. 523–4, from the files of the Kieler Stadtmission.
65 Col. G. W. McPherson in Berlin, 19 March 1946, to Norman Robertson, Ottawa. In RG 24, Vol. 5717, NAC.
66 United Nations, *World Food Appraisal for 1946–1947*, Washington, 26 December 1946.
67 King, *Diaries*, 4 August 1946, p. 700, NAC.
68 Notes of Cabinet Meeting, 29 March 1946, by Robert Patterson. Patterson Papers, LC.
69 Stüber, op. cit., p. 763.
70 Quoted in John Unruh, *In the Name of Christ*, p. 146.
71 Quoted in Stüber article in *Zeitschrift der Gesellschaft für Kanada-Studien*, p. 48.
72 Unruh, op. cit., p. 147.

73   Ibid., p. 149. This number was later increased to 5,400: see
     Stüber *Der Kampf gegen den Hunger*, p. 537.
74   Stüber, op. cit., p. 400.
75   Unruh, op. cit., p. 151.
76   In June 1947 the Danish Red Cross co-ordinated with the
     'Hoover-Spende' in a feeding program for 66,500 schoolchildren
     in Schleswig-Holstein, which included approximately seven-
     teen areas (*Gebiete*) and cities (*Staedte*). Stüber, op. cit., p. 502.
77   Proudfoot, *European Refugees*, pp. 186–8.
78   See Bacque, *Other Losses*, Chapter 6.
79   See *Twenty-five Silver Years, 1939–1964*, pamphlet published
     by the Irish Red Cross Society, pp. 11, 12. Archives of the Irish
     Red Cross, Dublin.
80   Stüber, op. cit., p. 571.
81   Herr Körschner's note in the Stadtarchiv Bonn 'Schul-
     kinderspeisung', kindly supplied by Annaliese Barbara Baum
     of Bonn.
82   Stüber, op. cit., p. 576.
83   Interview with Stephen Cary, European Commissioner of the
     American Friends Service Committee, November 1986.
84   See Bacque, *Other Losses*, Chapter 6. Trainloads were refused
     at Augsburg and elsewhere. See also ICRC, *Report of the
     International Committee of the Red Cross on its Activities During
     the Second World War*, p. 388.
85   ICRC, op. cit., p. 426.
86   Farquharson, *The Western Allies and the Politics of Food*, p. 92.
87   Unruh, op. cit., p. 152.
88   Paul Nitze, quoted in Gregory A. Fossedal, *Our Finest Hour*,
     p. 227.
89   Bevin is quoted in Fossedal, op. cit., p. 240.
90   Ibid., p. 231.
91   Acheson here paraphrases Joseph Jones and Francis Russell,
     who were informed by Will Clayton. In Fossedal, op. cit.,
     p. 221.
92   Hoover, *An American Epic*, Vol. IV, pp. 165–6.
93   Ibid., p. 163.
94   King Papers, C255123, NAC.
95   FEC Papers, Box 23, HIA.

96 Aloys Algen to Hoover, 5 February 1948, FEC Papers, Box 23, HIA.
97 Elfrieda and Peter Dyck, op. cit., pp. 141–3.
98 Quoted in De Zayas, *Nemesis at Potsdam*, p. 139.
99 Maurice A. Pope, *Memoirs* (University of Toronto Press, 1962), p. 309.
100 De Zayas, op. cit., p. 140.
101 Ibid., p. 139.
102 Gary Dean Best, *Herbert Hoover: The Post-Presidential Years*, Vol. II, p. 324. See also Gimbel, op. cit.
103 Report of conversation with A. H. Graubart, Captain US Navy Intelligence, Berlin, Lochner Reports, FEC Papers.
104 Gimbel, op. cit., p. 134.
105 Ibid., p. 135.
106 Gimbel, 'The American Exploitation of German Technical Know-how After World War Two' in *Political Science Quarterly*, Vol. 105, No. 2, 1990, p. 300.
107 Gimbel, *Science, Technology and Reparations*, p. 160.
108 Gimbel, *The Origins of the Marshall Plan*, p. 273. Emphasis in original.
109 According to the curator David Wigdor in the manuscript division of the Library of Congress, only one scholar has ever worked on these papers, a graduate student from Stanford, whose work has not been published.
110 Recipients' copies of the letters to such figures as Marshall, Anderson and Truman may have been consulted by scholars in other archives. However, there is no evidence that the important memos, which do not exist elsewhere, have ever been used by scholars until now. Finally, the general tenor of the sections on food – that the difficulties for Patterson lay in getting 'priority' or 'fiscal' resources to ship available food – has to the best of my knowledge never appeared in print before now.
111 Gimbel, *The Origins of the Marshall Plan*, p. 174.
112 Ibid., p. 174.
113 The dollar figures for the 1945–50 period must be multiplied by six to seven times for the equivalent in 1997. Felix Rohatyn in the *New York Review of Books*, 14 July 1994, p. 49.
114 Martin Gilbert, *The Road to Victory*, p. 1181.

115   Gimbel, *Science, Technology and Reparations*, p. 152. He bases this on a manuscript giving the history of FIAT (Field Information Agency, Technical) which he discovered in the archive of the OMGUS historical office, RG 319 CMH, NARS.
116   Gimbel, 'The American Exploitation of German Technical Know-how After World War Two', p. 305.
117   Gimbel, *A German Community Under American Occupation*, pp. 126–7.
118   See Voltaire, *The Calas Affair: A Treatise on Tolerance*.
119   Gimbel, op. cit., pp. 1ff.
120   Mark Roseman, 'The Uncontrolled Economy' in *Reconstruction in Post-war Germany: British Occupation Policy and the Western Zones 1945–1955*, edited by Ian D. Turner (New York: Berg, 1989), pp. 102ff.
121   Gimbel, op. cit., p. 81.
122   The Tsarist regime, once regarded as the most tyrannous in Europe, had on average 94,769 prisoners both political and criminal in its notorious jails in 1881. The population then was around 104 million. This was a particularly bad year for the Russians, because Tsar Alexander II had just been assassinated, and the country was swarming with revolutionary movements.

The United States in the latest year reported, 1992, when there were no international or internal revolutionary threats, had slightly over 1,225,000 people behind bars, i.e. *four times as many per capita as Tsarist Russia* in one of its most violent years. The United States has today more people per capita behind bars than Nazi Germany had in 1939, when there were approximately 125,000 criminals on average in German conventional jails. This was also a particularly dangerous year for the Germans: one of their senior officials abroad had recently been assassinated, there were plots against the life of the Chancellor, war was anticipated. The Gestapo had in 1936 around 6,000 prisoners in three camps; in April 1939, they had 162,739 persons in six concentration camps including Buchenwald and Dachau, in 'protective custody', who were mainly political prisoners. Whether the German figure is from

1936 or 1939, the Americans today still have more prisoners per capita than Nazi Germany in peacetime.

Statistics are blind to the horrors of Nazi racial policies, which have no counterpart in the US. But it must also be remembered that the American prison population has a disproportionate number of blacks, hispanics and native/aborigines whose leaders have been saying for many years that they are the victims of systemic discrimination, leading to increased death rates in their *barrios*, ghettoes and reservations, and also to higher rates of incarceration and longer sentences for crimes than whites receive for similar offences.

For Russia: *The Ministry of Internal Affairs: A Historical Review, 1802–1902* (St Petersburg: Printer of the Ministry of the Interior, 1902), p. 135.

Russian population estimate of 104 million is pro-rated from 1858 census of 74 million compared with 1897 census of 125 million. Russian population figures from (1858) *Encyclopedic Dictionary* of F. A. Brockhaus and I. A. Efron, St Petersburg, 1899, Volume 27A, p. 75. And 1897 from T. Shanin, *Russia as a Developing Society* (New Haven: Yale, 1986). With thanks to Martin Reesink.

The German figures are from Professor Peter Hoffmann and from a professor who has asked not to be named, who says there were approximately 6,500 political prisoners in KZL (concentration camps) in 1936, apart from the criminals in conventional jails. The Gestapo policy varied considerably, becoming much more repressive through denunciations from 1936 on, so an average from 1936–39 would be appropriate.

Re autumn 1939: Professors J. Noakes and G. Pridham in their book *Nazism, 1919–1945* (New York: Schocken, 1988), have estimated that there were only 25,000 people imprisoned in September 1939, in the same six concentration camps (p. 520, Vol. II). The Report by the Chief of the SS Economic and Administrative Main Office of 30 April 1942 showed that there were 21,400 prisoners in the same six camps at September 1939. *Trial of the Major War Criminals*, p. 363.

Re spring 1939 figures from Günther Wiesenborn: *Der Lautlose Aufstand. Bericht über die Widerstandsbewegung des deutschen Volkes, 1933–1945*, p. 30. Quoted in Peter Hoffmann, *The History of the German Resistance*, pp. 15–16. On p. 16, line 10, of Hoffmann, please note that 'sentence' should read 'indictment'.

The average influx into political imprisonment was 37,500 persons per year from 1933 to 1939.

Chapter VIII: History and Forgetting (pages 183 to 198)

1 Klaus Schwabe, *Woodrow Wilson, Revolutionary Germany and Peacemaking, 1918–1919* (Chapel Hill, NC: University of North Carolina Press), p. 89.
2 Joseph Tumulty to Wilson: Arthur Walworth, *Woodrow Wilson* (Boston: Houghton Mifflin), Vol. II, p. 187.
3 See Bischof and Ambrose, *Eisenhower and the German POWs*.
4 The book making the charge was *Hitler's Willing Executioners: Ordinary Germans and the Holocaust* (London: Little, Brown, 1996) by Daniel Jonah Goldhagen, which in its first year of publication had sold 20,000 copies in Britain.
5 Klemens von Kemperer, *German Resistance Against Hitler* (Oxford: Clarendon Press, 1992), p. 386.
6 Conor Cruise O'Brien, quoting an earlier essay, in his book *On the Eve of the Millennium*, p. 141.
7 Murphy to State, 12 October 1945, Foreign Relations of the United States, 1945, Vol. 2, pp. 1290–2. Quoted in De Zayas, *Nemesis at Potsdam*, p. 115. Bertrand Russell in England wrote strong letters of protest to *The Times* and the *New Leader*. De Zayas, op. cit., pp. 108–9.
8 De Zayas to the author, January 1995.
9 *Times Literary Supplement*, 14–20 September 1990.
10 *New York Times Book Review*, 25 February 1991, p. 1.
11 See Ramsey Clark, *The Fire This Time: US War Crimes in the Gulf*.
12 Stanley Kutler, Professor of History and Law, University of Wisconsin, in the *New Yorker*, 14 December 1992, p. 91.
13 David Irving, *Goebbels*, p. 418.
14 Konrad Adenauer, *Memoirs, 1945–1953*, p. 148.

15   See Philip Hallie, *Lest Innocent Blood Be Shed*; Peter Hellman, *Avenue of the Righteous*; and Bacque, *Just Raoul*.

Appendices (pages 199 to 224)

1   Brian R. Mitchell, *International Historical Statistics*, pp. 102, 109.
2   See Note 27, Chapter VI. The UK figure is also derived from Murphy Papers, Box 62, HIA, plus Griffith to McCahom, September 1946 et seq., State Central Decimal File F11.62114/12-145 to 3146. State Department Archives, Washington. Total equals 435,000 at March 1947 and repatriations were at the rate of 15,000 per month since October meaning that the original October total must have been 510,000. Also see *The Times*, 22 August 1946.
3   The West German government has estimated a death total of 710,000 for the whole year of 1945. The proportion who died from the beginning of August to the end of December 1945 is about 296,000. For all of 1946, they officially reported 588,331, of which some 490,000 occurred in January to October 1946. So in the whole period August 1945 to October 1946, the official figure is about 786,000.
4   The 1946 figure is an estimate, according to the Statistisches Bundesamt.
5   CFM Papers, HIA.
6   Senator Capehart, CRS, 5 February 1946, p. 878.
7   'Protokoll Zusammenkunft mit President a.D. Hoover', 13 April 1946, Geiler Papers, Staatsarchiv, Wiesbaden, in Gimbel, *The American Occupation of Germany*, p. 55.
8   CAME, *The Land of the Dead*, p. 31.
9   Ibid., p. 32.
10   K. P. Kirkwood, Chargé d'Affaires, Warsaw. In RG 25, Vol. 5719, File 7-CA-14, NAC.
11   All from CFM Papers, Murphy Boxes, HIA.
12   It might be thought that Königsberg, because it was taken over by the Soviets, is outside our range of investigation, but

it must be remembered that the statistics of deaths among the refugees who did arrive in the Soviet zone of Germany are mainly estimates, which depend largely on assessing from outside the Soviet zone, how many refugees remained behind and alive in the seized territories. And, of course, the statistics from Murphy and the census comparison all include the statistics for the Soviet zone.

13 Gabriele Stüber, *Der Kampf gegen den Hunger*, p. 285. Minutes of the meeting are in the Bundesarchiv Bonn 1/253.

14 Vital Statistics, Hansestadt Hamburg, 1938, undated British Army Report. In FEC Papers, at or near Box 14, HIA.

15 Pope to External, 4 July 1947. External Affairs Records, File 8376-K, NAC.

16 Address by Surgeon-General, Navy Day, 27 October 1947, Bethesda. In Behnke Papers, Box 1, HIA.

17 Lucius Clay, *The Papers of General Lucius D. Clay*, p. 96.

18 Red Cross report reproduced in Kurt W. Böhme, *Zur Geschichte der deutschen Kriegsgefangene des Zweiten Weltkrieges* (Munich: Verlag Ernst und Walter Gieseking, 1973), p. 282.

19 The population figures on which the percentages are based come from the Allied Census in October 1946, quoted in Gustav Stolper, *German Realities*, pp. 22ff.

20 Smith in *Deutschland zwischen Krieg und Frieden* (Bonn: Bundeszentrale für politische Bildung), p. 110.

21 Archivist Edward Reese, NARS, Washington, to the author in conversation, 1987.

22 Taped interview in front of a witness with the author, Munich, June 1991.

23 See Böhme, *Gesucht wird*.

24 Ernest F. Fisher Jr., *Monte Cassino to the Alps* (Washington: Center for Military History, Department of the Army), p. 485. Also Charles B. MacDonald, *The Last Offensive* (same publisher), p. 464.

25 See *Statistisches Jahrbuch für die Bundesrepublik Deutschland* (Stuttgart: W. Kohlhammer, 1952).

SELECT BIBLIOGRAPHY

Adenauer, Konrad, *Erinnerungen, 1945–1953* (Stuttgart: Deutsche Verlags-Anstalt, 1965)
——, *Erinnerungen, 1953–1955* (Stuttgart: Deutsche Verlags-Anstalt, 1966)
——, *Memoirs, 1945–1953* (translated by Beate Ruhm von Oppen – Chicago: Regnery, 1966)
Anders, Wladyslaw, *An Army in Exile: The Story of the Second Polish Corps* (London: Macmillan; Nashville: Battery Press, 1981)
Bacque, James, *Other Losses: An Investigation into the Mass Deaths of German Prisoners of War at the Hands of the French and Americans After World War Two* (Toronto: Stoddart, 1989)
——, *Just Raoul* (Toronto: Stoddart, 1990)
Balfour, Michael, and Mair, John, *Four-power Control in Germany and Austria, 1945–1946* (Oxford: OUP, 1956)
Baum, Anneliese Barbara, *Bonn zwischen Kriegsende und Währungsreform. Erinnerungsberichte von Zeitzeugen* (Bonn: Bouvier-Verlag, 1991)
Benz, Wolfgang, and Schardt, Angelika (eds), *Kriegsgefangenschaft. Berichte über das Leben in Gefangenenlagern der Alliierten von Otto Engelbert, Kurt Glaser, Hans Jonitz und Heinz Pust* (Munich: Oldenbourg, 1991)
Best, Gary Dean, *Herbert Hoover: The Post-Presidential Years*, Vol. I,

1933–1945 and Vol. II, *1946–1964* (Stanford, CA: Hoover Institution Press, c. 1983)

Bischof, Günther, and Ambrose, Stephen E., *Eisenhower and the German POWs* (Baton Rouge, LA: Louisiana State University Press, 1992)

Blum, John Morton, *Roosevelt and Morgenthau* (Boston: Houghton Mifflin, 1970)

Boscolo, Armando, *Fame in America* (two editions – Milano: Edizione La Motonautica, 1959 and 1965)

Buisson, Louis, *Historique du service des prisonniers de guerre de l'Axe, 1943–1948* (typescript – Paris: Ministère de la Défense Nationale, 1948)

Byrnes, James F., *Speaking Frankly* (New York: Harper, 1947)

Campbell, John C., *The United States in World Affairs, 1945–1947* (New York: The Council on Foreign Relations, in association with Harper, 1947)

Carell, Paul, and Böddeker, Günter, *Die Gefangenen. Leben und Überleben deutscher Soldaten hinter Stacheldraht* (Berlin and Frankfurt: Ullstein, 1980)

Charmley, John, *Churchill: The End of Glory* (Toronto: McFarlane, Walter & Ross, 1993)

Chekhov, Anton, *The Island: A Journey to Sakhalin* (London: Century; also published as *Journey to Sakhalin* by CUP, Cambridge, 1993)

Churchill, Winston, *The Grand Alliance* (London: Cassell, 1950)

Clark, Ramsey, *The Fire This Time: US War Crimes in the Gulf* (New York: Thunder's Mouth Press; 1992)

Clay, Lucius, *The Papers of General Lucius D. Clay: Germany 1945–1949* (edited by Jean Edward Smith – Bloomington, IN: Indiana University Press, 1974)

de Zayas, Alfred M., *Die Anglo-Amerikaner und die Vertreibung der Deutschen* (Munich: Beck, 1977)

——, *Nemesis at Potsdam: The Expulsion of the Germans from the East* (third revised edition – Lincoln, NE: University of Nebraska Press, 1988)

——, *The Wehrmacht War Crimes Bureau, 1939-1945* (Lincoln, NE: University of Nebraska Press, 1990; also in German, *Die Wehrmacht-Untersuchungstelle*, Berlin: Ullstein, 1987) de Zayas, Alfred M., *Anmerkungen zur Vertreibung der Deutschen aus dem Osten* (third edition – Stuttgart: W. Kohlhammer, 1993)

——, *The German Expellees: Victims in War and Peace* (London, Macmillan, 1993)

——, *A Terrible Revenge: The Ethnic Cleansing of the East European Germans, 1944–50* (New York: St Martin's Press, 1994)

Donnison, F. S. V., *Civil Affairs and Military Government: North-west Europe, 1944–1946* (London: HMSO, 1961)

Dyck, Elfrieda, and Dyck, Peter, *Up from the Rubble* (Scottdale, PA: Herald Press, 1991)

Einsiedel, Heinrich Graf von, *Tagebuch der Versuchung, 1942–1950* (Berlin: Ullstein, 1985)

Eisenhower, Dwight D., *Crusade in Europe* (Garden City, NY: Doubleday, 1948)

Ellis, John, *World War Two: A Statistical Survey* (New York: Facts on File, 1993)

Farquharson, John E., *The Western Allies and the Politics of Food: Agrarian Management in Post-war Germany* (Dover, NH: Berg Publishers, 1985)

Fitzgibbon, Louis, *Katyn: A Crime Without a Parallel* (London: Tom Stacey, 1971)

Fossedal, Gregory A., *Our Finest Hour: Will Clayton, the Marshall Plan and the Triumph of Democracy* (Stanford, CA: Hoover Institution Press, 1993)

Galitski, V. P., *German POWs and the NKVD* (Master's thesis – on deposit: Russian Academy of Military Science)

Gilbert, Martin, *The Road to Victory: Winston S. Churchill, 1941–1945* (Toronto: Stoddart, 1986)

——, *'Never Despair': Winston S. Churchill, 1945–1965* (Toronto: Stoddart, 1988)

Gimbel, John, *A German Community Under American Occupation: Marburg, 1945–1952* (Stanford, CA: Stanford University Press, 1961)

——, *The American Occupation of Germany: Politics and the Military, 1945–1949* (Stanford, CA: Stanford University Press, 1968)

——, *The Origins of the Marshall Plan* (Stanford, CA: Stanford University Press, 1976)

——, *Science, Technology and Reparations: Exploitation and Plunder in*

Post-war Germany (Stanford, CA: Stanford University Press, 1990)
——, 'The American Exploitation of German Technical Know-how After World War II' in *Political Science Quarterly*, Vol. 105, No. 2, 1990, pp. 295–309
Gollancz, Victor, *Leaving Them to Their Fate; the Ethics of Starvation* (London: Gollancz, 1946)
——, *Our Threatened Values* (London: Gollancz, 1946)
——, *In Darkest Germany* (London: Gollancz, 1947)
Harriman, W. Averell, *Special Envoy to Churchill and Stalin, 1941–1946* (New York: Random House, 1975)
Hoffmann, Peter, *Widerstand, Staatsstreich, Attentat: der Kampf der Opposition gegen Hitler* (Munich: R. Piper, 1969)
——, *The History of the German Resistance 1933–1945* (London: McDonald & Jane's, 1977)
Hoover, Herbert, *The President's Economic Mission to Germany and Austria: Report on Agriculture and Food Requirements. Report on the Revival of German Exports and the Economic Recovery of Europe* (Chicago: Human Events Associates, 1947)
——, *The President's Economic Mission to Germany and Austria: No Reconstruction Without Food. A Remedy for Near Starvation in Germany* (New York: Common Cause, 1948)
——, *Memoirs*, Vol. 1: *Years of Adventure* (New York: Macmillan, 1951–52)
——, *An American Epic*, Vols. I–IV (Chicago: Regnery, 1959–64)
Hoover Institution on War, Revolution and Peace, *Herbert Hoover: A Register of His Papers in the Hoover Institution Archives* (compiled by Elena S. Danielson – Stanford, CA: Hoover Institution Press, c. 1983
Horn, Christa, *Die Internierungs- und Arbeitslager in Bayern, 1945–1952* (Frankfurt and New York: Peter Lang, 1992)
Hull, Cordell, *The Memoirs of Cordell Hull* (New York: Macmillan, 1948)
Hunger in Bizonia (New York: published by the American Association for a Democratic Germany, 1948)
International Committee of the Red Cross, *Report of the International Committee of the Red Cross on its Activities during the Second World War (1 September 1939– 30 June 1947)*, Vol. 3: Relief Activities (Geneva: ICRC, 1948)

International Wheat Council, *World Wheat Statistics* (London: The International Wheat Council, 1955–87)

Irving, David, *Goebbels* (London: Focal Point, 1996)

Jelenski, K. A. (ed.), *History and Hope: Progress in Freedom* (London: Routledge & Kegan Paul, 1962)

Kaps, Johannes (ed), *The Tragedy of Silesia, 1945–1946: A Documentary Account With a Special Survey of the Archdiocese of Breslau* (Munich: 'Christ Unterwegs', 1952–53)

Karner, Stefan, 'Die Sowjetische Hauptverwaltung für Kriegsgefangene und Internierte. Ein Zwischenbericht' in *Vierteljahrshefte für Zeitgesichte*, Vol. 42, No. 3 (July 1994), pp. 447–71

——, *Im Archipel GUPVI* (Munich: Oldenbourg, 1995)

Kennan, George F., *Memoirs, 1925–1950* (Boston: Little, Brown, 1967)

Kennedy, Paul, *The Rise and Fall of the Great Powers* (New York: Random House, 1988)

Kimminich, Otto, *Der völkerrechtliche Hintergrund der Aufnahme und Integration der Heimatvertriebenen und Flüchtlinge in Bayern* (Munich: Iudicium, 1993)

Krivosheyev, G. F. (ed.), *Without the Seal of Secrecy: The Losses of the Soviet Armed Forces in Wars, Military Campaigns and Conflicts. A Statistical Research Study* (Moscow: Voennoe, 1993)

Langer, Senator William, 'Investigation of Starvation Conditions in Europe' in the Congressional Record of the Senate (microfilm), Vol. 92, Pts. 3–4 (29 March 1946), pp. 2798–811

Lerski, George J., *Herbert Hoover and Poland: A Documentary History of a Friendship* (Stanford, CA: Hoover Institution Press, 1977)

Maschke, Erich, *Die deutschen Kriegsgefangenen des Zweiten Weltkrieges. Eine Zusammenfassung* (Munich: Verlag Ernst und Werner Gieseking, 1974)

McCullough, David, *Truman* (New York: Simon & Schuster, 1992)

Meehan, Patricia, *The Unnecessary War: Whitehall and the German Resistance to Hitler* (London: Sinclair-Stevenson, 1992)

Mitchell, Brian R. (ed.), *International Historical Statistics: Europe, 1750–1988* (third edition – New York: Stockton Press, 1992)

Morgenthau, Henry C., *Germany is Our Problem* (New York: Harper, 1945)

Murphy, Robert, *Diplomat Among Warriors* (Garden City, NY: Doubleday, 1964)

Nash, George H., *The Life of Herbert Hoover*, Vol. 2: *The Humanitarian, 1914–1917* (New York: W. W. Norton & Co., 1988)

Nicolson, Nigel, *Portrait of a Marriage* (London: Weidenfeld & Nicolson, 1973)

Nimmo, William F., *Behind a Curtain of Silence: Japanese in Soviet Custody, 1945–1956* (New York: Greenwood, 1988)

Norbeck, Edward, 'Eddoko: A Narrative of Japanese Prisoners of War in Russia' in *Rice University Studies* (Houston, TX), Vol. 57, No. 1 (Winter 1971), pp. 19–67

O'Brien, Conor Cruise, *On the Eve of the Millennium* (Concord, Ont.: Anansi, 1994)

O'Brien, Francis William (ed.), *The Hoover–Wilson Wartime Correspondence, 24 September 1914 to 11 November 1918* (Ames, IA: Iowa State University Press, 1974)

—— (ed.), *Two Peacemakers in Paris: The Hoover–Wilson Post-Armistice Letters, 1918–1920* (College Station, TX: Texas A&M University Press, 1978)

Overy, Richard, *The Road to War* (London: Macmillan, 1989)

Proudfoot, Malcolm, *European Refugees, 1939–1952: A Study in Forced Population Movement* (London: Faber & Faber, 1957)

Rasmus, Hugo, *Schattenjahre in Potulitz, 1945* (Münster: Nicolaus-Copernicus-Verlag, 1995)

Roseman, Mark, 'The Uncontrolled Economy' in *Reconstruction in Post-war Germany: British Occupation Policy and the Western Zones, 1945–1955*, edited by Ian D. Turner (Munich: Berg, 1989)

Sauermann, Dietmar, and Brockpähler, Renate, *'Eigentlich wollte ich ja alles vergessen . . .'. Erinnerungen an die Kriegsgefangenschaft, 1942–1955* (Münster: Coppenrath, 1992)

Schenck, Ernst-Günther, *Das Menschliche Elend im 20. Jahrhundert. Eine Pathograhie der Kriegs-, Hunger- und politischen Katastrophen Europas* (Herford: Nicolai, 1965)

Schieder, Theodor (ed.), *Documents on the Expulsions of the Germans from Eastern Central Europe*, Vols. I–IV (Bonn: Ministry for Expellees, Refugees and War Victims, 1960–61)

Segschneider, Ernst Helmut (ed.), *Jahre im Abseits. Erinnerungen an die Kriegsgefangenschaft* (Bramsche: Rasch, 1991)

Smith, Richard Norton, *An Uncommon Man: The Triumph of Herbert Hoover* (New York: Simon & Schuster, 1984)

Solzhenitsyn, Alexander, *The Gulag Archipelago, 1918–1956* (translated by Thomas P. Whitney – New York: Harper and Row, 1974–76)

——, *Prussian Nights* (translated by Robert Conquest – New York: Farrar, Straus & Giroux, 1977)

Sorge, Martin, *The Other Price of Hitler's War* (New York: Greenwood Press, 1986)

Statistisches Bundesamt (Wiesbaden), *Bevölkerung und Kultur*, Reihe 2: *Natürliche Bevölkerungsbewegung* (Stuttgart: W. Kohlhammer, 1966)

——, *Bevölkerung und Wirtschaft, 1872–1972* (Stuttgart: W. Kohlhammer, 1972)

Stimson, Henry L., and Bundy, McGeorge., *On Active Service in Peace and War* (New York: Harper, 1948)

Stolper, Gustav, *German Realities* (New York: Reynal & Hitchcock, 1948)

Stüber, Gabriele, *Der Kampf gegen den Hunger, 1945–1950. Die Ernährungslage in der britischen Zone Deutschlands, insbesondere in Schleswig-Holstein und Hamburg* (Neumünster: Karl Wachholtz, 1984)

——, 'Kanadische Deutschlandhilfe in den ersten Jahren nach dem Zweiten Weltkrieg' in *Zeitschrift der Gesellschaft für Kanada-Studien*, Vol. 11, No. 2 (Neumünster: Karl Wachholtz Verlag, 1986), pp. 39–62

Tolstoy, Nikolai, *Victims of Yalta* (London: Hodder & Stoughton, 1977)

——, *The Minister and the Massacres* (London: Century, 1986)

Unruh, John D., *In the Name of Christ: A History of the Mennonite Central Committee and Its Service, 1920–1951* (Scottdale, PA: Herald Press, 1952)

Vogel, Karl, *M-AA 509. Elf Monate Kommandant eines Internierungslagers* (Memmingen: Selbstverlag, 1951)

Voltaire (François Marie Arouet), *The Calas Affair: A Treatise on Tolerance* (translated and edited by Brian Masters – London: Folio Society, 1994)

Walch, Timothy, and Miller, Dwight M., *Herbert Hoover and Harry S. Truman: A Documentary History* (Worland, WY: High Plains, 1992)

Wherry, Kenneth Spicer, 'Investigation of Starvation Conditions in Europe' in the Congressional Record of the Senate (microfilm), Vol. 92, Pts. 1–2 (29 January 1946), pp. 509–20

——, 'Investigation of Starvation Conditions in Europe' and 'The Report of the Economic Committee for Europe': speeches of Kenneth S. Wherry in the Senate of the United States, 29 January, 1 and 7 February 1946 (Washington: US Government Printing Office, 1946)

Willis, Edward F., *Herbert Hoover and the Russian Prisoners of World War I: A Study in Diplomacy and Relief* (Stanford, CA: Stanford University Press, 1951)

Wolfe, Robert, *Americans as Proconsuls: United States Military Government in Germany and Japan, 1944–1952* (Carbondale, IL: Southern Illinois University Press, 1984)

Willis, F. Roy, *The French in Germany, 1945–1949* (Stanford, CA: Stanford University Press, 1962)

Ziemke, Earl F., *The US Army in the Occupation of Germany, 1944–1946* (Washington: Center of Military History, US Army, 1975)

277

INDEX

accounting, false, 36, 157, 176
Acheson, Dean, 168
Adenauer, Konrad, 113, 188; on
  Berlin death rate, 212; condemns
  expulsions, 194–5; government's
  surveys of missing persons, 77, 80,
  130, 203, 221; as Lord Mayor of
  Cologne, 177; moderate statistics
  of, 112, 118–19
Adourian, Alex, 68
agriculture, German: loss of
  farmlands, 94, 100; production,
  156–7, 158–9, 167, 216
Albrecht, Hans, 34–5
Aldington, Lord (Toby Low), 75, 76,
  191–2
Algen, Aloyus, 170
Allard, Henry W., 29, 62
Allensworth, John, 47–8
Allied Control Council, 116, 120,
  121, 123
Alt-Wette, 118
Ambrose, Stephen E., 81, 83, 186,
  191
American Relief Administration
  (ARA), 9, 13–14, 145
anarchy, 184–5

Andernach, 44–5
Anders, Wladyslaw, 74
Anderson, Clinton, 147, 149, 160,
  161
Anglo-Saxon militarism, 20, 40
anti-Semitism, 10–11, 109
ARA, *see* American Relief
  Administration
Arbeiterwohlfahrt, 159
archives, Soviet, *see* CSSA
archives, Western, 87–8, 192–3
Argentina, 142, 147, 150, 180
Asquith, Herbert, 4
Atlantic Charter, 140, 184
atomic secrets, 180
Augsburg, 212
Aurich camp, 88
Ausschuß für Kriegsgefangenenfragen,
  79–80, 203, 220–2
Aussig, 104–5
Australia, 142, 147
Austria: complaint against Canadian
  troops, 88; death rate, 125, 211;
  food rations, 151, 160; and
  Hoover's food relief, 169–70; mass
  graves, 46, 107; 'transfer' of
  prisoners to, 59

Düsseldorf, 32–4
Dyck, Cornelius, 163
Dyck, Peter and Elfrieda, 171
dysentery, 49

Earle, Ambassador, 74
Early, Steve, 143
Ebensee camp, 62
economy, European, 177
economy, German, 157, 172–4
Eden, Anthony, 27, 97
Einsiedel, Heinrich von, 69
Eisenhower, Dwight D., 62, 183, 186;
    death penalty order, 41–4, 45, 47,
    95; and destruction of food, 94–5;
    forbids Quaker aid, 164; and
    missing prisoners, 59, 80, 81, 115;
    and Morgenthau Plan, 25, 28–9
emigration: forbidden to Germans,
    112–13; from Germany (1946–50
    statistics), 122
Enke, Siegfried, 55
European Court of Human Rights,
    191
exports, German, 157, 176
*Expulsion of the German Population
    from the Territories East of the
    Oder–Neisse Line*, 84
expulsions, 29–30, 96, 97–111, 119,
    128, 129, 158, 178, 188–90;
    atrocities, 102, 103, 104–5;
    condemned by Adenauer, 194–5;
    death rates, 113, 114, 117–19, 129,
    130–1, 203–5; difficulties of
    feeding children, 165; evidence for
    fate of expellees, 203–5; numbers
    taken to the Gulag, 84; opponents
    of, 133; West's cover-up of, 194

factories, destruction of, 95–6, 157,
    173, 178
fertilizer production: reduced by
    Allies, 91, 96, 156, 157

First World War, 3–10; aftermath,
    10–15, 134–5
fishing fleet, 91, 157
food rations, 34, 93, 95, 115–16, 125,
    145, 151, 158, 160; in Britain, 168;
    in Canada, 148
food relief programmes, 142–52,
    159–66; blocked by Allies, 91–2,
    158, 166–7; for children, 159, 163,
    164, 165–6; First World War, 3–6;
    see also Hoover, Herbert
food supplies, 161–2; Germans
    deprived of, 94–5, 155–9;
    hoarding by farmers, 167; imports,
    96–7; myth of world shortage, 30,
    32, 130, 145–6, 153, 154–5, 168;
    problem of getting surpluses to the
    starving, 147, 150–1; production
    drop in France and UK, 152;
    urban shortages in 1947, 167–8; in
    wartime Germany, 153, 157;
    world production, 30, 153, 154–5;
    see also Morgenthau Plan;
    starvation
Foreign Office (UK), 156
France, 161; conditions in camps, 29,
    48–50, 60–3; conditions in Vosges
    area, 50, 62; food production, 152;
    government statistics, 114, 117–19;
    prisoner death statistics, 59–60;
    refugees saved in, 110, 196
freedom of discussion, 191–5
French zone of Germany: death rates
    in, 35–6, 216; starvation in, 35–6,
    94, 177
Freud, Sigmund, 2
Frings, Joseph, 137, 141
Fürstbischofliche Knabenseminar,
    Graz, 169–70

Galbraith, John Kenneth, 146
Galitski, V. P., 84, 218
Garmisch-Partenkirchen camp, 95

Geneva Convention, 48, 60, 62, 76, 151, 184

Germany: agrees to food relief in Belgium, 90; agricultural capacity, 156–7, 158–9, 167, 216; anti-American feeling, 178, 179; food shortages and starvation, 32–6, 93–7, 150–179; government statistics, 113, 116, 121–2, 123–4, 125–6, 210, 223; history of anger against, 133–5; industry, 95–6, 152, 156–7, 167, 173, 178–9; land confiscations, 94, 100, 155, 187–8; and Marshall Plan, 172–3; post-1918 blockade of, 12, 14–15; post-1945 collapse, 92–3; pre-war food consumption and production, 153; refugee numbers, 158; relinquishes land claims (1990), 189–91; and reparations, 95, 173–7, 190; resistance movements, 135–41; surveys of missing persons, 77–8, 79–80, 220–2; Weimar Republic, 10, 17; *see also* death rates; food relief programmes; Morgenthau Plan; starvation

Gilbert, Martin, 30

Gimbel, John, 174, 175, 176, 177, 178

Glogau, 118

Goebbels, Joseph, 28, 193

Goldhagen, Daniel Jonah, 186

Gollancz, Victor, 33–4, 36

Gorbachev, Mikhail, 76, 87

Gouzenko, Igor, 180

Grasett, A. E., 154, 156

Graudenz camp, 108

Greece, 92

Greer, Robert, 100–2

Grey, Lord (Edward), 4

Grüber, Probst, 35

Grünwald, Bürgermeister, 51

Guderian, Heinz, 17, 112, 114, 118

Gulag, 64–73; economic viability of, 67–9; and re-education, 69–70, 137–8

Gulf War, 192

Gummersbach, 48

Hamburg, 32, 34, 214, 215

Havel, Václav, 188

Heising, Johannes, 63

Henrys, General, 10

Hess, Rudolf, 136

Hilfs-Ausschuß, 164

Hilfswerk der Evangelischen Kirchen in Deutschland, 159, 162, 163

Hilldring, J. H., 34

Hitler, Adolf, 17–18, 60, 72, 100, 134, 135, 153, 186; Hoover on, 168; number of books on, 197; persecution of churches, 171; resistance to, 136, 137, 138

Holland, 161; famine in, 89–91, 93

Homma, Masaharu, 29

Hoover, Herbert, 91, 194, 195; ability and character, 12–13; advises Truman, 37, 117, 144; and anti-Semitism, 10–11; and bolshevism, 8–9, 10–11; condemns Allies' policy, 20, 93; and First World War relief programmes, 3–10, 12, 13–15, 146; on Hitler, 168; not remembered, 196–7; post-1945 food-relief programmes, 38, 143–7, 149–52, 155, 156, 159, 160–1, 167, 169–70; and relief of Dutch famine, 89–90, 91; on reparations, 173; reports on conditions in Germany, 125; on role of USA, 11–12

Hoover Aid (*Hoover-Spende*), 165–6

Hoover Famine Emergency Commission, 126, 173–4

Hoover Institution, 152

CRIMES AND MERCIES

Ludwigshafen, 164
Lutheran Church, 164

MacArthur, Douglas, 86, 133
Mackenzie, William Lyon, 21
Magadan Gulag, 65
Maifritzdorf, 110
Maisky, Ivan, 176
Malik, Jakob, 86
Marburg, 178
Marburger Presse, 177–8
Marktoberdorf, 124, 211, 212
Marshall, George C., 132, 147, 160, 174
Marshall, Jennings B., 57
Marshall Plan, 170, 171–3, 175, 177, 185
Marxism, 2
Maschke, Erich, 82
media, 191
Medical History of the European Theater of Operations, 53, 58
Meehan, Patricia, 137
Mennonites, 94, 139–40, 158, 162–3, 164, 170–1
Middleton, Drew, 183–4
missing persons, 77–8, 79–80, 131, 203, 220–2; Japanese, 86–7
Mission Militaire de Liaison Administrative, 164
Mitchell, Brian R., 116, 124
Molotov, V. M., 75, 174
Molotov–Ribbentrop pact, 17
Moltke, Helmut von, 141
Monde, Le, 191, 210
Montgomery, Bernard Law, 36, 93
Morgenthau, Henry C., 11, 25, 30, 37, 152
Morgenthau Plan, 25–32, 96, 126, 174, 179–80, 186; US senators' opposition to, 30–2, 37–9
Mückusch, Hermine, 102–3
Müller, Max, 51

Murphy, Robert, 123, 133, 156, 168; estimate of number of expellees, 205; estimates of German death rate, 115, 126–8, 199–201, 202–3; on omission of prisoners from censuses, 223–4; protests against conditions caused by expulsions, 189

Nazis, 186–7; local resistance to, 136–41; scientists, 139
Neisse, 105–6
New York Times, 19, 183–4, 191, 210
Niederhermsdorf, 118
Niedersachsen, 166
Niemöller, Pastor, 137, 141
nineteenth century, 1–2
Nitti, Francesco, 15
NKVD (People's Commissariat for Internal Affairs, USSR), 65, 66–7, 69, 73–4, 76, 219–20
North Rhine province, 214
Nuremberg trials, 74–5, 90–1, 135, 204

O'Brien, Conor Cruise, 188–9
O'Grady, Gerald B., 174–5
oil, 22, 152, 157
OKW war diaries, 82–3
OMGUS (Office of the Military Governor, US), 174, 179, 221; statistics, 113, 114–17, 123, 125–6
'Other Losses', 58–9
Other Losses (Bacque), 53, 57, 78, 205, 207
Overmans, Rüdiger, 80, 81, 82, 203

Paris Peace Conference, 13
Patterson, Brad, 123
Patterson, Robert, 175; efforts to prevent famine, 132, 145–6, 147, 148–9, 151, 160, 167; on US food surpluses, 147, 148–9, 155; wish to release POWs from USA, 61

284

123, 125–6; omission of prisoners from censuses, 222–4; post-war surveys, 220–2; reasons for secrecy, 132–5; sources, 201, 214, 217–20; Soviet, 72–7, 78, 83–7, 88, 123, 218–20; surveys of missing persons, 77–8, 79–80, 220–2; *see also* death rates
Statistisches Bundesamt, 113, 116, 121–2, 123–4, 125–6, 210, 223
Stauffenberg, Claus von, 141
Stettinius, Edward, 37
Stimson, Henry L., 12, 27–8, 144
Stolper, Gustav, 112, 114, 116, 118, 119, 224
Strahov stadium, 103–4
Sudetenland, 97, 102–3; *see also* Czechoslovakia
Sweden, aid from, 158, 164, 166
Switzerland, aid from, 163, 164, 166

TB, *see* tuberculosis
theft of goods, 157
Thirty Years' War, 134
Thomaswaldau, 118
Thompson, Dorothy, 19–20, 204
Tolstoy, Nikolai, 76, 191
totalitarianism, 3, 19–20, 181
Treaty of Brest-Litovsk, 7
Treaty of Versailles, 10, 17, 135
Treitschke, Heinrich von, 134
Truman, Harry S., 137, 148–9; arranges investigation into camps, 117; enlists Hoover's help, 37, 38, 117, 143, 144–5, 151–2; keeps German prisoners in USA, 61; lifts US price controls, 147; and Marshall Plan, 172; and reparations, 173; response to protests about famine, 31–2, 36–8
tuberculosis, 33, 34, 150, 215
Tullius, Otto, 46
typhus, 118

Ukraine, 23
unconditional surrender, principle of, 185–6
United Kingdom, *see* Britain
United Nations, 24, 140, 187, 190; and Human Rights, 184, 189; statistics, 122; Third Committee, 79; World Food Appraisal report (1946), 154
United Nations Relief and Rehabilitation Administration, 32, 38, 140, 144–5, 157, 169
United States of America, *see* USA
UNRRA, *see* United Nations Relief and Rehabilitation Administration
US Army: Adsec (Advance Section), 58; destruction of records, 221–2; 50th Field Hospital Detachment, 57; 560th Ambulance Company, 52; handover of camps to French, 56–7, 58, 60; Medical Officer, 125; obstructs relief efforts, 166–7; 106th Division, 53, 54–5, 56, 57–8; PW and DEF reports, 58; starvation of prisoners policy, 41–53
US Office of Foreign Agricultural Relations, 154
US Public Health officers, 35
US Senate: ignorance of US camps, 62–3; opposition to Morgenthau Plan, 30–2, 37–9, 62
US State Department: opposition to Hoover, 144, 151–2; 'Outline of Factors Determining Russia's Interest in American Credits', 23; and reparations, 174
US zone of Germany: death rates, 113, 114–17, 124, 125, 222–4; food relief in, 162–3, 165; starvation in, 93–4; *see also* OMGUS